Practising development

In recent years development organizations have frequently called for social science perspectives to be incorporated into the design and management of development programmes. *Practising Development* is a thorough assessment of the successes and failures of practical responses to such calls.

The contributors combine academic expertise and practical aid experience to examine, from a social science and anthropological perspective, the processes of intervention and the methods by which this intervention can be assessed. They discuss the ways in which development 'problems' and 'needs' are identified and explain the socio-economic and political worlds within which intervention and development evolve. They clarify specific contexts and present perspectives not usually covered by policy makers and they stress the importance of understanding local diversity in order to be able to turn broad, universal policies into effective local practice.

Based on first-hand experiences and reflections on the successes and failures in using social science perspectives in the practice of development programmes, the papers in *Practising Development* are cautiously optimistic about the future of planned intervention. The book will be welcomed by development practitioners and by students and teachers of anthropology and sociology.

Johan Pottier is Senior Lecturer in Anthropology at the School of Oriental and African Studies, London.

Practising development

Social science perspectives

Edited by Johan Pottier

London and New York

First published in 1993
by Routledge
11 New Fetter Lane, London EC4P 4EE

Simultaneously published in the USA and Canada
by Routledge
a division of Routledge, Chapman and Hall Inc.
29 West 35th Street, New York, NY 10001

Typeset by J&L Composition Ltd, Filey, North Yorkshire
Printed and bound in Great Britain by
Biddles Ltd, Guildford and King's Lynn

British Library Cataloguing in Publication Data
A catalogue record for this book is available from the British Library.

Library of Congress Cataloging in Publication Data
Practising development: social science perspectives/edited by Johan
  Pottier.
  p.   cm.
  1. Applied anthropology. 2. Social sciences—Methodology.
  3. Community development—Case studies. 4. Economic development
  programs—Case studies. I. Pottier, Johan.
  GN397.5.P74   1992
  307.1′4—dc20   92-13084
                                                          CIP

ISBN 0–415–08910–7
     0–415–08911–5 (pbk)

Contents

Contributors

Margaret Casey, Ph.D., Opportunities for Women, Centre Two, Ossian Mews, London N4 4DX

James Fairhead, Ph.D., Natural Resources Institute, Chatham, Kent

Bill Garber, Band Aid, c/o The London Institute, The London College of Fashion, Golden Lane Annex, Baltic Street, London EC1Y 0TB

Philip Gatter, Ph.D., Department of Social Sciences, South Bank Polytechnic, London SE1A 0AA

Geoff Griffith, Ph.D., Independent Consultant based in Brighton, specializes in South Asia

Susan Hutson, Ph.D., Department of Sociology and Anthropology, University College, Swansea SA2 8PP

Penny Jenden, Band Aid, c/o The London Institute, The London College of Fashion, Golden Lane Annex, Baltic Street, London EC1Y 0TB

Mark Liddiard, Department of Sociology and Anthropology, University College, Swansea SA2 8PP

Tim Morris, Ph.D., Independent Consultant, author of *The Despairing Developer*

Johan Pottier, Ph.D., School of Oriental and African Studies, University of London, London WC1H 0XG

David Seddon, Ph.D., School of Development Studies, University of East Anglia, Norwich NR4 7TJ

Preface

EIDOS (European Inter-University Development Opportunities Study-Group) was founded in 1985 and brought together British, Dutch and German anthropologists studying development discourse. Currently, the main participating institutions are the Department of Anthropology and Sociology, School of Oriental and African Studies, University of London; the Institute of Cultural Anthropology/Non-Western Sociology, the Free University, Amsterdam; the Department of Rural Sociology, the Agricultural University, Wageningen; and the Sociology of Development Research Centre, University of Bielefeld, Germany. EIDOS also has a wide network of participating social anthropologists and sociologists from other European institutions.

EIDOS's aim is to assess critically the dissemination and specialization of anthropological and sociological knowledge and development studies in different European centres by arranging student exchanges and by providing support for a series of workshops. The purpose of EIDOS workshops is to further understanding of how anthropological and sociological research and arguments are relevant to theories and debates on development, development priorities, patterns and projects, and the socio-cultural implications and consequences of new development programmes. The workshops examine new approaches to a number of the more specific and intractable problems of social and economic development, including practice and policy transformation in development; indigenous knowledge and the generation of ignorance; the analysis of power relations and resource distribution between interest groups, actors and institutions; and organizational linkages and the 'translation' of meaning and policy. Arising from these European workshops and common themes, a number of seminar series have also been held at the host institutions, producing several volumes. Volumes include *Bush Base,*

Forest Farm – Culture, Environment and Development; *The Growth of Ignorance*; *Policy and Practice*; *The Traders' Dilemma*; *African Languages, Development and the State*.

The current volume originates in a London University Intercollegiate Seminar at SOAS during spring 1989. The volume addresses the broad theme of how social science perspectives can be built into the design and management of sustainable development programmes. The papers are first-hand experiences and reflections on the successes and failures in using social science perspectives in the practice of development programmes. They focus on two key phases of the project cycles: appraisal and mid-term assessment. More specifically, they cover discussion of the status of ethnography in development work (Pottier); appraisal in IFAD pastoral projects in Niger and Mali (Seddon); methodology and appraisal, with reference to the Republic of Maldives (Griffith); the Band Aid perspective (Garber and Jenden); research carried out for a British children's charity (Hutson and Liddiard); primary health care in North Yemen (Morris); farming systems research in Zambia (Gatter); representations of knowledge in a CIAT programme for Zaïre (Fairhead); gender and decision making in a tubewell irrigation project in Indonesia (Casey).

I wish to thank the School of Oriental and African Studies for financing the follow-up workshop on which this volume is based and Sharon Lewis for tireless assistance in the organizational preparations.

Johan Pottier

Introduction: development in practice
Assessing social science perspectives

Johan Pottier

QUALITATIVE RESEARCH

An important aspect of the drive towards community-based, sustainable programmes has been the emphasis on research informed by ethnography. This new emphasis, now prominent within many institutions, including the CGIAR group, UNRISD, IFAD, Band Aid and others, stems from a client-focused, participative philosophy which has displaced the previously popular but misconceived view that Western models of technology and management can be transferred wholesale. The participative philosophy upholds an empirically founded belief in the managerial capabilities of vulnerable groups: what the poor lack is access to and control over resources; what they need is assistance with the removal of constraints.

The participative approach to development has in recent years provided several openings for qualitative, contextual research which aims to gauge the impact and acceptability of programmes already implemented and to gather information relevant for the design and management of future interventions. It is time now to go beyond the buzzwords generated by this approach (such as 'sustainability', 'farmer-orientated research') and to start assessing the difference which the new philosophy has made. Moreover, the concepts of 'participatory' research and 'participatory' development, which exist in a wide variety of culture-specific versions, must themselves be examined critically (see my chapter on the role of ethnography in project appraisal).

Contributors here spell out how the global shift in development discourse translates into concrete practices, as experienced both by target communities and by field-based development personnel. Our detailed analyses reveal that the transition from a top-down to a participative orientation is not unilinear but influenced by local circumstances. Actual programmes disclose a diversity of participative styles, occasional controversy and, sometimes, reluctance on the part of interest groups or office holders to let go of past models of development or antiquated methods for measuring impact. Sometimes too, participative efforts are constrained because of unresolvable dilemmas.

From an ethnographic viewpoint, the reality of development planning and implementation is marked simultaneously by the recurrence of broad, seemingly universal patterns and by a diversity of local contexts. However, while the broad patterns receive ample attention in the work of economists, statisticians and agronomists, the importance of diversity remains largely underreported and insufficiently understood. Today there is growing concern about the use of hold-all categories that describe what appear to be universalistic phenomena: labels such as 'capitalist' economy or 'totalitarian' regime or 'advanced' technology, and so on. These broad categories, it is increasingly realized, do nothing to reveal the vast heterogeneity of location-specific conditions, but a lot to generate bland analysis and nonsensical prescription. Diversity, we show, is just as meaningful as the more familiar, broad categories that seem to be omnipresent. The rationale for this position lies in the fact that any attempt at designing or implementing a programme must ultimately be situated within a local and potentially complex setting.

Our intention is not to criticize intervention as such – sometimes, rather, the contrary is true – but to examine critically processes of intervention in order better to understand the socio-economic and political worlds within which they evolve. The unifying objective of this volume is the *contextualization* of a particular set of recurring global issues. These include the identification of problem areas, the selection of development targets, the social categories with which agencies operate, the use of research techniques, and the assessment of results. As social scientists we aim first and foremost to clarify specific contexts and to present perspectives not usually considered by policy makers. Our findings therefore complement the insights arrived at by development staff trained in other disciplines.

Organizations committed to client-focused, participative programmes, including research, tend to engage social scientists as consultants on development teams, intermittently or full-time. In recent years, however, a new generation of social analysts has emerged. This new generation of (mainly) social anthropologists has gained relevant experience by eking out autonomous positions at the interface between local-level agency personnel and targeted beneficiaries. Their research experience, achieved during first-time fieldwork, is characterized by long-term involvement in the field (as opposed to the normally short-term consultancies of the first category), but their findings are still to be incorporated in the literature on development. The present volume is unique in that it considers the results from both long- and short-term consultancies and from the more autonomous style of recent social science research.

It is from fairly autonomous positions, working simultaneously *within and outside* development teams, that Gatter and Fairhead report on the experience of cultural brokerage. Their development brief, given respectively by ARPT (Adaptive Research Planning Team, Zambia) and CIAT (International Center for Tropical Agriculture), was to generate useful ethnography over a sustained timespan. They acquired these positions during doctoral fieldwork, through a combination of circumstances: independent funding, previous training in agricultural science, current training in social anthropology. The chapters written by Gatter and Fairhead exemplify a significant departure from the approach taken in conventional anthropological research, so often criticized for being isolationist and unrelated to community needs (see my chapter on ethnography). Other chapters in the volume have been written by social scientists who analyse development processes mainly *from within* organizations. Their findings are based on employment which was/is either of considerable duration (Griffith; Garber and Jenden; Morris) or short-term (Casey; Hutson and Liddiard; Seddon). Invariably though, the development brief on which each chapter is based was to help prepare and launch new programmes or review existing ones, and to ensure that appropriate social objectives were formulated and put into practice.

As a collection, the papers illustrate a variety of organizational responses to the discourse of participative development, thus providing thoughts of value for any debate on the nature and practice of participative policy making. Somehow, 'putting the last first' is not always as simple as might seem at first sight.

PROGRAMMES INFORMED BY ETHNOGRAPHY

An ethnographic understanding of local conditions reduces the risk that false assumptions creep into the design of development programmes. The risk is high at the stage of 'problem identification', especially given the often limited time which appraisers have at their disposal. Put crudely, not everything is visible. From the open window of a Land Cruiser, for example, an observer may see 'bad' agricultural practice when trees are not planted in the fight against erosion and may deduce that ignorance is the problem. This deduction, as Fairhead shows, may however turn out to be faulty once it is understood that trees relate to people (a point Gatter also argues for crops) and that questions need to be asked about land tenure arrangements and the symbolic meanings attached to planting trees.

Several authors address the thorny but central issue that problem identification results from human judgement, even political pressure. They conclude that problems, needs, priorities and ultimately the definition of social groups, must all be understood as *social constructs*. The myth of a value-free identification of problem areas is well exposed by Hutson and Liddiard in their analysis of how UK agencies working with young homeless people define 'who is to benefit' as a result of 'what kind of problem'. Hutson and Liddiard found that the definition of problems and clients depended less on the objective characteristics of the homeless (that is, on observable reality) and more on the history, the political and social objectives, the skills, resources and funding base of the agencies under consideration. Similarly, using research material from the Republic of Maldives, Griffith illustrates that the identification of problem areas can reflect political pressure and decisions taken beforehand rather than real need. Following his inquiry into the procedure through which some large NGOs had identified agricultural loans as a general need, Griffith concludes that the appraisers had failed to differentiate empirically observable need from an imagined one cultivated by outsiders.

The emergence of a conflict of interests, typically between researchers fulfilling investigative roles and government officials aiming to secure advantageous deals, may be acute in settings where strong patron–client ties prevail. Under such conditions it may be common, as Morris shows for a primary health-care project in North Yemen, to find that implementing agencies adopt mystifying methodologies when evaluating their own performance; a trick which enables them to turn a blind eye to numerous malpractices. Casey, however, also worked in an area where significant patron–client ties exist, but she has a happier story to tell, at least from a methodological point of view. She was able to convince those authorities who first favoured 'stratified samples' and 'structured interviewing' to drop this approach and to go for a more qualitative 'informal survey', with semi-structured interviews, which was better suited for reviewing the project.

Although our critiques of 'problem identification' aim, generally speaking, not to cast doubt on existing projects but to instil *greater awareness* of the complex construction of definitions, it emerges from other articles (Gatter; Fairhead; Garber and Jenden; Seddon) that this awareness is already being valued and put into practice by some agencies. For instance, as one of its major criteria in selecting programmes for funding, Band Aid (Garber and Jenden) is interested to know 'how' and 'by whom' priorities are identified. The identification of problems and priorities is influenced by local political processes, and the latter must be understood if resources and efforts are to be used to good effect. Garber and Jenden argue in this respect that the lack of adequate ethnographic or historical analysis of the problems to be tackled is perhaps the most serious difficulty that development projects have to face. Seddon shares that opinion, and locates the cause of the difficulty in the short period normally devoted to preparatory phases, but, as his account of IFAD policy and practice shows, there are ways in which this particular difficulty can be overcome.

What then is to be done? In the Band Aid experience of African projects, it is rare for a proposed programme to be accompanied by a sociological analysis of the different groups involved, of their interests *vis-à-vis* one another, and *vis-à-vis* the planned activities of the project. Such information, none the less, is vital, especially where projects relate to environmental recovery. To overcome the problem and meet the need for ethnographic information, data must be gathered *as programmes develop*; a point Garber and Jenden make specifically with reference to the study of rights in resources, the rationales of farming systems, the perspectives of different groups and the value of indigenous technical knowledge (ITK).

The Band Aid strategy has some affinity with the approach taken in Farming Systems Research (FSR), where the need for continual data collection is also stressed (Gatter; Pottier), yet it constitutes a new challenge through proposing that the production of data for social analysis should be carried out in a joint effort involving local project staff and beneficiaries, both of whom must develop their own ethnographic understanding. The challenge has implications for the recruitment of professional (usually expatriate) anthropologists. Garber and Jenden argue that the answer to inadequate background knowledge, expertise and local staffing is not to recruit professional anthropologists on short-term consultancies but to provide special training for all categories of project staff so that they can begin to adopt 'the anthropological approach' themselves.

This viewpoint, which merits further reflection, is also taken up by Griffith, who maintains that anthropologists have a duty to inform appraisers of methodologies that may help reduce the frequency with which mistakes are made. After examining several errors made during an appraisal which allegedly 'established' the need for agricultural loans in the Maldives, Griffith provides a simple check list of basic questions which could have been used to obtain a more accurate reading of local problems and needs. He does not deny the restrictive influence which political climates may exert (appraisers can be 'pawns in political wheeling and dealing'), nor does he underrate the skill of professional anthropologists adept at combining set procedures with intuition. His point is that anthropologists must invest in the production of essential methodological guidelines for use by appraisers whose basic training is outside the social sciences. One may doubt that the production of such guidelines will help appraisers overcome the political pressures they are up against, as some political milieus are certain to want to continue with rigid, wholly inappropriate methods – a conclusion one must draw from Morris's account of primary health care in North Yemen. On the other hand, consideration of Griffith's proposal would at least indicate that anthropologists are serious about providing the special training called for by Garber and Jenden.

IFAD's answer to the need for detailed analysis of local level structures and their operation is to give full weight to 'the anthropological approach' when new programmes are prepared. The focus implies recruitment of mission personnel, foreign and indigenous, predisposed to adopting such an approach and committed to involving beneficiaries throughout the project cycle. Combining an anthropological and a participative approach does not in itself guarantee a successful programme, a point Seddon stresses, but it heightens the chances of greater effectiveness and sustainability. Interestingly though, IFAD and Band Aid report contrasting experiences regarding the availability and usefulness of published ethnography. Unlike the projects reviewed by Garber and Jenden, all of which had to start the data collection process, the pastoral rehabilitation projects in Mali and Niger were able to build upon extensive, diachronic information about the constitution, general functioning and dynamics of the targeted groups (namely, herders' associations). Moreover, members serving on the IFAD appraisal teams had acquired long-term familiarity of the societies with whom they sought to cooperate.

Notwithstanding this contrast, both Band Aid and IFAD recognize the need for *continual data collection*. While pre-knowledge of local conditions certainly enabled IFAD's appraisal missions to plan and execute with some speed, team members remained aware that success through optimum participation would still demand a continuous monitoring of activities and, where necessary, modification as the projects evolved.

PROGRAMMES SUSTAINED THROUGH CONTINUAL ETHNOGRAPHY

Continual ethnography, we argue, is the key to successful, cost-effective project management, *because the social worlds within which development efforts take shape are essentially fluid*. Production patterns, access to or control over resources, the make-up of residential units, the allocation of responsibility within units, patterns of social stratification, and so on, are all liable to some form of ongoing change. An understanding of these fluid worlds, which implies data collection over a sustained period, is essential if programmes are to be regularly reviewed, adjusted and turned into success stories. Several development agencies are already aware of the need for continual ethnography, often following mid-term setbacks in their programmes, and have started to recruit social scientists for this purpose. Four chapters in the volume (Casey; Fairhead; Gatter; Hutson and Liddiard) are the direct product of this growing awareness and positive response within development organizations.

A social science perspective on the internal dynamics of evolving worlds will take account of the fact that planned interventions contribute to change. Whether initiatives introduce new power relations and ideologies or support existing ones, every intervention remains a political statement the significance of which must be grasped before programmes can be monitored correctly. This then is the reason why social scientists, as we show, must go beyond the debate on 'ethnography in development' and highlight aspects of the 'ethnography of development'.

If new power relations emerge within a project, their content, scope and impact on realizing the programme will need to be studied as part of the ethnography (or anthropology) of that project. This is aptly documented in Casey's analysis of the irrigation scheme she reviewed in Madura, Indonesia. In addition, project ethnography must focus on the internal functioning of the development organizations themselves; in particular on their ideologies, the modes adopted for decision making, and the practice of personnel recruitment. Although our contributions touch on all three domains, relatively more emphasis has been given to understanding ideologies, especially through an appreciation of the values and assumptions that underpin the new experience of collaborative research with beneficiaries.

The idea of continual collaborative research at ground level is certainly to be welcomed from a pragmatic, project-effectiveness point of view. On the other hand, the concept is very novel and strongly influenced by Western development rhetoric, which implies that it should be scrutinized carefully. (Nor should academics forget, as Hutson and Liddiard remind us, that their ideas too unfold within a context of custom and expectation!) The recent origin of the concept of participative research demands from social scientists that they apply a generous dose of self-criticism and avoid getting carried away by naïve enthusiasm for assumedly unproblematic programme building. While 'optimism' may be essential for the implementation of sustainable programmes (Seddon), it is nevertheless crucial that social scientists continue to ask critical questions about the new paradigms to which they, and the development community at large, subscribe. For instance, the notion that 'the poor' are potentially the most effective and efficient investors – certainly a very worthy view – must itself be put on the agenda for continual ethnographic research. The idea has its empirical foundations, as Seddon shows, yet the endless variety of possible social configurations is such that local factors will always necessitate the introduction of some nuance. Because of this variety, social scientists must continually and constructively query the value of maintaining the assumptions, institutions, imagery, and the methods of inquiry to which development workers are, or become, attached.

This volume does not have a chapter which looks critically at 'the poor' as investors, but it has in the contributions of Gatter and Fairhead two in-depth critiques of a comparable image, which is that of the 'rational farmer'. Fairhead argues that although this notion has done much to create a favourable image of local practices, it has also driven optimistic academics and scientists to choose to present only the 'respectable' side of local agricultural knowledge whilst ignoring other explanatory forms. Development thinkers thus inclined are redefining ITK by assuming that every farming activity is systematically related by the farmers themselves to a static body of local knowledge. Also damaging in this respect are the failure to appreciate the *provisional* nature of much local farming knowledge, and the scientists' assumption that their paradigms are universal. With reference to plant pathology, Fairhead argues that the adoption of such narrow perspectives impedes full dialogue between the presumed beneficiaries and those whose actions aim to stimulate community self-help.

Gatter is equally critical of the high level of systematicity which development workers tend to read into farming practices. He shows how questions related to 'the traditional village way' are devoid of meaning, in the same way that the standard interest in household categories (based on production figures – a *single* variable) stifles the understanding of social processes. Gatter has special criticism for the regularly made association between the categories 'vulnerable group' and 'female-headed household'. Mostly assumed to be straightforward, this association really misconstructs the social universe. Instead of assuming the link, social analysts should investigate the complementarity of gender-based production activities as well as the quality of the exchange networks through which products are channelled. The implication is that development experts must abandon the idea that replicable, uniform methodologies exist for every kind of investigation. Rather, they must come to appreciate that in order to be understood, social realities demand a qualitative approach which takes people to be involved in meaningful choices. This perspective, requiring time and continual data collection, promises to be a major improvement over the purely economistic approach to understanding social worlds.

The need to grasp the complementary roles of male and female household members, as a prerequisite for project design, is also demonstrated in Casey's review of the tubewell irrigation project in Madura. The project was originally designed to increase rice production and based on the assumption that most Madurese farmers would be male. After some ten years, during which village-based water management associations were formed, it became apparent to project staff that women were involved in making decisions about agriculture, yet these women were not integrated in the project. Because of her previous research experience in another part of Indonesia, Casey was briefed to conduct a study of Madurese women in agriculture, focusing on female roles in decision making and production, and to make recommendations as to how the extension programme might become more effective in conveying advice to women.

The Madura project also adds a further dimension to the debate on appraisal and ethnography: it does not suffice to ask whether ethnographic accounts exist (in this case what little information existed was available only in Dutch), the social scientist must proceed to ask *whether and how* this ethnography is being used. The 'how' aspect is equally illustrated by Gatter, who points out that several ethnographic facts which he was asked to investigate and record were already known. In full agreement with the Band Aid perspective (Garber and Jenden), Gatter demonstrates that what was needed was not 'more facts' but a new approach to the training of local project staff, focusing on how to interrelate the facts that were available.

The above concerns show the debate on useful ethnography to be more complex than is usually imagined. Existing ethnography may be relevant or irrelevant to project design and management; it may be available but ignored, or available and misinterpreted. In the latter case, a really difficult conceptual puzzle is often set: how do appraisers (who may well belong to an educated local or national elite) assess the quality and practical value of data generated by others (who may have been outsiders)? Even when development organizations attempt to narrow the gap between staff/researchers and beneficiaries through the simultaneous involvement of external and indigenous social scientists, it is still necessary to ask further questions and to ascertain how far one will need to go in 'narrowing the gap' before participative initiatives become genuinely successful.

Perhaps such success will depend on the promotion of very small-scale projects; programmes of the kind Band Aid has now begun to fund, in which 'the artificial distinction between project staff and beneficiaries has disappeared and technicians are working directly for the community rather than an external employer'. What makes the idea attractive is that the disappearance of the noted distinction may help solve the problem of *who controls* (for example, who decides not to use) relevant ethnographic data. This latest idea from Band Aid, another example of how social scientists can help put into operation perspectives hitherto not considered, does not diminish the need for a continual updating of the ethnographic record, but it could reduce the likelihood that local initiatives are misinterpreted or 'hijacked' by external interest groups.

Research into the nature of the dialogue between 'beneficiaries' and 'experts', no matter how time-consuming this may be, will become very significant in the debate on continual ethnography. Such research is the logical outcome of that growing interest in the politics of team-work, a topic marked by cross-disciplinary as well as cross-cultural interaction. Social scientists are just beginning to pay attention to the politics of team-work, an important aspect of which is the partnership between indigenous and external sociologists or anthropologists. Four contributors (Casey; Gatter; Pottier; Seddon) discuss such partnerships on the basis of first-hand experience, and with an openness which is still rare in the published literature.

CAUTION AND OPTIMISM

Essays in this book reveal that the enthusiasm for participative development is not just rhetorical: conscious efforts are being made and lessons are being learned. On the other hand, social scientists still need to become more aware that their participation in the day-to-day running of development programmes or projects remains to be negotiated. There is no time for complacency.

The direction in which development-orientated social science research may be expected to move during the 1990s is here presented in terms of a focused response to the problems that recur each time the development worker is confronted with 'real lives'. At the rhetorical level, the development community is aware that rigid projects fail, and it is mostly agreed that the remedy is a flexible approach which tunes into the ethnographic reality. But theoretical consensus is not enough. The ethnographic reality is so varied in its social, political and economic facets that problems invariably surface whenever aid workers move from rhetoric to practice. In our view, these variations assume such importance for successful programme management that the primary task (and hence major role) of the social scientist is to become sensitive to this complexity and to persuade others to follow suit. We show that sensitivity is particularly needed in relation to the use of definitions (for example, the identification of problems, social categories, targets) and with regard to the methodology used when assessing impact and progress.

The consequences for working out an appropriate methodology may seem obvious – the development worker must 'listen and learn' – yet exactly how this listening and learning is to be achieved is as much a matter of informed guesswork, experience and intuition as it is a question of analytic rigour. While the need for systematic recording and representativeness of data is beyond dispute, our findings caution that inflexible methods are deceptive tools; political instruments that restrict the in-depth understanding required for successful intervention. Social science perspectives on development are sometimes dismissed because of their negative messages, their uncertainties and controversies. Not shying away from either controversy or 'grey areas', contributors here also feel that now is the time to supply evidence that a good deal of positive thinking, rethinking, adjustment and success, has been achieved since the term 'participative development' first entered the vocabulary. Gone are the days when anthropology could be labelled 'long and lost' (Chambers 1983: 59); gone too the time when policy-relevant research was invariably 'short and shelved'.

REFERENCE

Chambers, R. (1983) *Rural Development: Putting the Last First*, London: Longman.

1 The role of ethnography in project appraisal

Johan Pottier

PARADIGMS, OLD AND NEW

The dominant development paradigms of the 1950s, 1960s and even the 1970s were mostly based on the evolutionary belief that 'economic growth' was the antidote to 'backwardness'. The overall approach was outward-looking, technocratic and generally contemptuous of local resources and know-how. In the mental picture we retain of those decades, the 1970s will also be remembered for the many global negotiations that attempted but failed to bring about significant development – that is, development for large numbers of people.

The 1980s, in contrast, may be remembered as a soul-searching decade during which it became clear that imitations of the so-called developed world were neither possible nor necessarily desirable. *May* be remembered, because even if impressed, future critics will not fail to spot the strong traces of neo-colonialism and international nepotism that remained visible in those many instances where top-down development was still practised. Nevertheless, the 1980s were marked by a search for alternative strategies; a search led 'by a number of Third World governments, by social movements of various kinds, by small groups of researchers and planners, as well as by people in different international organizations' (Stavenhagen 1986). The search implied rejection of externally imposed models, more emphasis on the needs of the poor (the very poor, especially), greater respect for the physical environment, a better appreciation of social forces, more awareness that development efforts must be sustainable and based on policies that are participatory rather than technocratic.

The buzzwords of the 1980s – 'sustainability', 'grassroots development', 'participatory research' – still have to prove that they have something significant to offer. They may make an impact where other approaches have failed; they may also end up in the graveyard where so many buzzwords have already gone to rest. What matters at the beginning of the 1990s is not that development specialists have coined new buzzwords, but that their concepts stem from a thorough questioning of former paradigms.

Theoretical specialists and planners alike are now indicating that they are better aware of the processes involved in development and of the role therein played by people, poor people, whose needs are only rarely satisfied through pure monetary incentives or tightly centralized state planning. This awareness has been given expression in a shift of emphasis, away from investments in programmes and projects that ignored the presumed beneficiaries and 'towards investment in poverty-oriented projects' (Cernea 1982). This is a true departure, since classic development theory never gave any thought to critical social factors: socio-economic differentiation, the importance of decision making within household economies, long-term survival strategies, the cultural construction of ideas and practices, gender, divisions of labour, patterns of responsibility, and so on.

The late discovery of 'the human factor' has had consequences for the employment of anthropologists and sociologists. Until recently, development agencies typically restricted the recruitment of anthropologists (*if* they employed them) to two specific, disjointed tasks. First, anthropologists were asked to carry out 'appraisal' in the narrow, conventional sense; they carried out social feasibility studies prior to project implementation. Second, anthropologists conducted *ex post facto* evaluations once projects had been implemented. Today the scene has changed. Although their involvement often remains restricted, anthropologists are now increasingly incorporated in project work from beginning to end, whilst they are also being called upon to contribute to policy making. This continuous employment has already been put to good use, particularly within those international agricultural programmes where anthropologists have become drawn into a fuller and more satisfying research effort. Reviewing the work of anthropologists at the International Potato Center (CIP), Rhoades states the Center's view that piecemeal anthropological input in isolation of the full research process, as happened in the past, contributes directly to project failure (Rhoades 1986).

Interestingly, though, the anthropologists themselves have sometimes been blamed for their former restricted participation in development-related research. The complaints are well known: anthropologists take too long to conduct their fieldwork; they are too slow when writing up results or too elaborate on cultural issues; and

they are at times unable or unwilling to communicate their knowledge (Chambers 1983: 47; Conlin 1985: 84). Looking back to the late
1970s and early 1980s, I would suggest as a counter-argument that
the problem of partial participation (or intellectual isolation) must
be seen in context. It is not just the anthropologist who, a decade
ago, was troubled by an all too narrow participation; other key
participants too were routinely isolated. Moreover, it is equally
erroneous to assume that only anthropologists needed time in order
to collect and digest useful, accurate information – a point to which
I shall return.

Instances of routine isolation beyond that of the social scientist are
identified in a 1981 critique by the Pan-African Institute for Development (PAID). The Institute is particularly concerned about the often
reported absence of links between projects and other development
activities in the same environment (PAID 1981). This type of
isolation or lack of coordination can lead to bizarre scenarios, as in
the case of Chad, where 'a private Swiss project gave out free
fertilizer and insecticides in a zone where the Chadian National
Agency for Rural Development (ONRD) was demanding 7500
FCFA/hectare for the same products' (PAID 1981: 62). This is only
one of several examples the PAID critique lists of projects 'doing
their own thing' irrespective of other initiatives in the area.

Whether it addresses the isolation of the social scientist or isolated
activities within a given region, PAID stresses that the problem of
isolation is really the by-product of what it calls 'project rigidity',
which is the common occurrence of inflexible design and management. PAID claims that project rigidity is responsible for the
widespread failure to ensure 'constant monitoring and evaluation',
and ultimately success, in project management (PAID 1981: 17).

The above complaints call for a closer look at the project approach.
What is it? Why is it favoured by so many agencies? How does it fit
in with national and international programmes?

THE PROJECT APPROACH

For an account of the wider setting in which projects take place it is
necessary to turn to international politics, especially to the time when
many developing countries were gaining independence.

The typical scene within newly independent states is aptly
portrayed by the French political scientist B. Lecomte. With independence, the majority of Third World states expressed a desire for
making 'rational use of available resources' (Lecomte 1978), through

which they hoped, first, to limit the chance factor when spending their budgets, and secondly, to guide development towards specific, measurable objectives. The dual emphasis on control and measurement resulted in the drafting of national development plans in which activities became clearly specified with reference to time and space. Activities were meant to be planned closely, that is, interconnected through a well-defined set of common objectives: employment, health, agriculture, water, infrastructure.

The core idea in the project approach to development was that one could be clear about all the aspects involved: goals, resources, means, results. In addition, because of their small scale, projects could be subjected to detailed, continuous study with a view to better performance and improved cost effectiveness. Another hoped-for advantage was that projects would facilitate the demarcation of every partner's role and powers.

In spite of the emphasis on clear specifications *vis-à-vis* time and space, project results were often disappointing. For the 1960s and 1970s, the PAID report points out that project evaluations, including assessments at the grassroots level, generally showed (1) that objectives were rarely achieved and (2) that project performance was regularly hampered by the absence of *detailed analyses of initial conditions* – for instance, of agro-ecological, economic and sociological relations (PAID 1981: 14). The report was also critical of the poor understanding of *local views on needs and priorities*, an oversight which had caused many projects to fail. To obtain better results in the future, the Pan-African Institute for Development pleaded for the inclusion of a more broad-based ethnography.

But why were initial conditions not fully grasped? The answer can be found in the political climate of the immediate post-independence era. Lacking the necessary expertise and unable to control the financial resources required, newly independent states usually feared that foreign aid would be refused if they prioritized truly national initiatives. They had little choice but to clasp the lending hand of more powerful nations. (The same lack of choice often exists today, as Crehan and Von Oppen (1988) have documented for Zambia.) Seeking assistance, however, meant learning 'the rules of the game' and accepting the imposition or continuation of economic ties. Trying to plan closely and having to accept external involvement, most development planners allowed their plans to shape up as collections of 'investment projects based on national priorities but influenced by foreign agencies' (PAID 1981: 10). The earlier example of the distribution of fertilizer and pesticides in Chad is just one illustration of how national programmes may lose out as a result of international involvement elsewhere in the country.

Despite the poor results that came with top-down approaches to development, the trend overall has not been to scrap the project approach but to learn from past experiences. In this context, 'small' remained potentially beautiful because it remained potentially controllable.

The pervasiveness of the notion that projects occur in a controlled, stage-by-stage, rational context is made clear in the following extract, taken from Curtis's contribution to the 1983 ASA conference on 'Anthropology and Development' (Grillo and Rew 1985).

> Project management is usually discussed in terms either of a linear programme or of a cycle of activities that include identification, appraisal, planning, implementation, operation and maintenance, and evaluation. In the cyclical model, evaluation leads once again into the preparation of new projects.
>
> (Curtis 1985: 103)

The questions that need to be asked in project management often appear very straightforward, and the answers, it is then implied, will be just as clear. The 'appraisal' phase, for instance, seeks to establish

> *what* will happen if a particular option is taken up, *where* antici-pated effects will occur, *who* will gain and lose, *when* those effects will occur, and the *efficiency* of the investment in relation to the resources used and the benefits derived.
>
> (Conyers and Hills 1984: 132)

This point-for-point agenda appears clear-cut and logical, as are the agendas for each of the other stages within the lifespan of a project, yet the questions asked are ethnographic; that is to say, they refer to real-life situations that are unlikely to lend themselves to neat analysis or accurate prediction.

In the next section I will look at texts that illustrate or discuss the role of ethnography in the so-called life-cycle of projects, focusing on the need for accurate predictions.

PREDICT OR PERISH: 'THE' CHALLENGE FOR ANTHROPOLOGY?

The above-mentioned paper by Curtis has the virtue that it discusses not only what is expected from development anthropologists but also what kind of ethnography is useful to planners. Curtis makes the point that anthropologists could be usefully employed at every phase of the project cycle, but that they are most often called upon at the early stage of appraisal 'to provide background information on the people involved or to identify the nature of social problems' (Curtis 1985: 103). This, Curtis adds, is perhaps the role in which anthropologists have been happiest, because the basic instruction has been to go out and observe, with few restrictions upon their liberty. In possession of a *carte blanche*, the anthropologist can then search for linkages and indulge in that favoured discovery 'that all is not as it seems' (1985: 103). On the other hand, Curtis warns that, although the anthropologist's involvement in appraisal may be professionally stimulating and useful, there is no necessary correlation between more data and better or more humane administration. There is no guarantee that ethnographic background information and feasibility studies will 'encourage authorities to conceive projects that are closer to the values and interests of their client population' (1985: 103). In fact, quite the opposite may happen, in that background studies can at times encourage administrators 'to be more sure-footed in [the] imposition of their prejudices' (1985: 103).

In their *Introduction to Development Planning in the Third World*, Conyers and Hills make a similar point. 'Appraisal', they write, 'is not the same as decision-making, [but] decision-makers can use the information presented in appraisal to help them make what are, essentially, political decisions' (Conyers and Hills 1984: 132). Much here depends on the planner, who stands between the person carrying out the appraisal and the decision maker. The planner will draw the attention of the decision maker to 'variations in the "pay offs" generated by different courses of action', but, in the end, being a politician, the decision maker will apply 'his own value judgement to the results of the appraisal and will make his final choice accordingly' (1984: 133). Advice and action are thus separated by a political filter and a personal judgement.

Unlike Conyers and Hills, Curtis is more cautious when considering who to blame when appraisal does not translate into action. He suggests a compromise, asking for the blame to be shared: 'to be fair to the administrator, it is also true that anthropological studies have scarcely ever been conceived within a framework that would *enable authorities to predict*' (Curtis 1985: 103; emphasis added). The problem, Curtis believes, is that anthropologists with field experience are reluctant to generalize. There is a contrast to be made 'between the [approach in] typical anthropological field studies and the requirements of project management information' (1985: 105).

The typical anthropological approach is 'aggressively empirical' – a term borrowed from Adam Kuper (1970) – to the extent that it 'militates against the kind of generalization that carries over easily from one study to another' (1985: 105). It would help if anthropologists restrained the tendency 'of finding unique social configurations in [even] the most ordinary places', to concentrate more on grasping the 'structural regularities' shared by development projects (1985: 105). Curtis illustrates this search for structural regularities by referring to the design and operation of rural water supplies in Botswana. Here he concludes that to be able to influence project planning at the design stage, the practising anthropologist needs to be able to advise, for instance, on which forms of local organization, including new ones, can be used to facilitate the introduction and acceptance of technically sound interventions (1985: 113). As viewed in the early 1980s, the anthropologist's special challenge in development situations lay in the art of prediction. This implied an ability to transcend the particularities of any data collected in specific social settings.

The concern that anthropologists must transcend the characteristics of particular field situations is most certainly justified, and shared by many if not most practitioners, as is the view that useful ethnography must meet the requirements of project management information. These two concerns stand absolutely central to any discussion of the relationship between anthropology and appraisal (see, for example, Rhoades 1986, on CIP).

The importance of these concerns must not, however, detract from the relevance of political context; for instance, from the importance of understanding *how* definitions are arrived at and sustained (see the chapters by Gatter; Hutson and Liddiard). As already shown, clear evidence exists to suggest that social science background information is not sought routinely or (when available and useful) necessarily incorporated in project design. It is imperative, therefore, that social scientists should assess critically whether this underutilization reflects their own inability to transcend ethnographic situations or whether it results from the noted 'rigidity' that exists within many realms of the development industry (also Garber and Jenden, this volume); the result perhaps of that hierarchical power relationship involving designers, planners and appraisal personnel.

I have some sympathy with Curtis's claim that administrators and anthropologists should share the blame when appraisal efforts come to nothing, yet I am also aware that the experiences he recalls occurred in a setting seemingly free of technology-transfer trauma.

Curtis is confident, no doubt with good reason, that the technological choices made with regard to his water supply project were sound and that they would not cause the kinds of frustration so often reported for other technological interventions, as with many Green Revolution transfers. However, where confidence makes way for frustration and failure, one becomes more aware of the wider political economy within which decisions are made and thus less inclined to accept that anthropologists must always share the blame for failed interventions. An article by Moris and Hatfield (1982), on Western technology and Maasai pastoralism, is of interest here. Not only is the article a rare, *published* example of detailed project ethnography, but it also illustrates the sore point that anthropologists are too often called in when it is already too late to contribute constructively. They are then expected, at best, to sort out the mess; at the very worst, to cover up irreversible mistakes.

Since few anthropologists have ever reported, publicly and in detail, how they view the relationship between ethnographic knowledge and project management, it is fitting to draw attention to the experience of Moris and Hatfield, and to reflect further on the technological and political challenges which all practising anthropologists must face.

THE POLITICS OF TECHNOLOGY TRANSFER

The dearth of ethnographic data on the political and economic contexts of policy making and implementation has two sources. First, the anthropological 'field' was originally defined as remote; that is, located as far away as possible from direct exposure to colonial administrators. Secondly, development anthropologists who rely on the development industry for their daily bread and butter are not so eager to publish.

The narrow perception of anthropological field research may be traced back to Malinowski's pioneering work in anthropological methods, but it is a legacy which is hard to erase. A little over a decade ago, Margaret Mead complained:

> there is presently no preparation for anthropologists to understand their own cultures or the versions of an emerging planetary bureaucratic culture, represented by the specialized UN agencies, the multinationals, the World Bank, or a new coalition like the Organization of Petroleum Exporting Countries.
>
> (Mead 1977: 7)

Although a few ethnographic accounts of 'bureaucratic cultures' have since been written, the sad truth is that such accounts are still, by and large, contained in unpublished reports (E. Chambers 1987: 310). This is the second reason why 'project ethnographies' are virtually unavailable to the public. I call this a sad truth, since the availability of such complete ethnographies would permit us to re-examine Curtis's argument that the main reason for anthropology's failure to direct project management lies in the difference between the presentation of anthropological knowledge and the knowledge requirements of project management (Curtis 1985: 102). I do not dispute the existence of a problem related to 'presentation', since it has already received much attention in Farming Systems Research (but see Gatter, this volume, for a balanced critique), yet I am reluctant to accept, given the political context in which practising anthropologists work, that this particular problem would be the chief reason for anthropology's low profile in development during the 1970s and early 1980s.

The political context of project management is well portrayed by Moris and Hatfield. Launched in 1964, the Maasai project they evaluated had originally aimed 'to develop and integrate a package of structures and skills [with a view to] improving livestock production and range preservation within the framework of Tanzania's 1964 Range Development and Management Act'. By 1967 the project was struggling, and it continued to do so throughout the 1970s. When called upon, Moris and Hatfield understood that 'many of the problems in the Maasai Project derived from the inappropriateness of its various tools, which, for the most part, [had been] exempted from interference by the social scientist' (1982: 45). The exemption – a political act – was due not to 'presentation' failure on the part of the social scientists involved, but attributable to the conviction held by the technical staff that their major challenge was the successful transfer of a tried-and-true, American-style technology.

As defined by American specialists, range management 'was unknown to the Maasai and in some instances directly violated their traditions of open range and flexible adjustment to the weather' (1982: 45). The obstacle to project success was not some form of local cultural conservatism but the *rigid* imposition of premises 'appropriate only to the US cultural setting' (1982: 46). One such alien premise was the idea that all Maasai livestock producers were orientated towards production for profit rather than for subsistence.

Not surprisingly, the Maasai livestock producers found the project's range technician 'grossly uninformed about details vital to herd management' and chose to evade his proposals. Their reaction, however, was interpreted by project personnel as confirming the foreign technician's view that

> pastoralists shared an underlying conservatism about livestock management [which] placed them beyond the reach of rational (modern) practices. It did not occur to the technician that there might have been local constraints or that his theory was defective when applied to non-Western field situations.
>
> (Moris and Hatfield 1982: 50)

This raises an interesting problem. Although the development anthropologist may be employed to identify corporate groups that can be used as bases for action (a legitimate request) or asked to persuade a target group of the value of certain technical measures (which may be legitimate), the practitioner is rarely asked to probe the concepts and underlying premises imported by foreign technical experts. And yet, as the Maasai Project so clearly shows, a given development package may turn out to be inappropriate for the setting in which it is introduced, thus constituting a major barrier to local participation.

It is counterproductive to regard the anthropological focus on the articulation of systems of thought as tardy or unwanted. The analysis of conceptual confrontations of the kind just described, the exposure of conceptual error, I suggest, must be considered respectable ethnography if beneficial adjustments are to be made in due course.

Although the account by Moris and Hatfield is instructive for what it says about the position of the anthropologist as team member (who could improve his or her performance), it also makes clear that the project formulation stage, in this case, had been preceded by a detailed survey report which had drawn attention to several Maasai practices that later emerged as reasons for non-participation. Among these were the importance of sheep and goats to the Maasai economy and the orientation towards dairying with cattle, as opposed to beef production. Although available from the start, in a language understood by all team members, these and other ethnographic insights were ignored at the project formulation stage. If no subsequent action was taken to accommodate that information during the design stage, surely this time one could not have blamed the providers of sociological data. (For more positive accounts of design informed by ethnography, see Almås 1988; Derricourt 1988.)

The lesson to draw is that project management is a complex political field – something to be investigated – and that it will not do to point an accusing finger at the team member who is drafted in late to 'fine tune' the package to on-site reality.

CHALLENGES IN THE 1980s

By the early 1980s, *post mortem* stories like that of the Maasai Project were heard so frequently that remedial action had to be considered. The anthropologist's divorce from the whole chain of research activities, it had become clear, was not only frustrating for the individual practitioners concerned but also counterproductive in terms of achieving results.

One remedy, characteristic of the CGIAR group, IFAD (International Fund for Agricultural Development) and other international donor agencies, was to tackle the problem by bringing in anthropologists early and for the entire duration of projects (see especially Rhoades on research at CIP – the International Potato Centre; Plucknett *et al.* 1986; and Seddon's chapter in this volume). At the World Bank too, there was a similar reaction, a trend whereby

> sociologists and anthropologists [were now used] . . . not only at the [early] appraisal [stage] or at the end – evaluation – of a project, but also in supervising the actual implementation process of these development projects and for analyzing on an ongoing basis the reactions of the project-affected population.
>
> (Cernea 1982: 127)

Within the context of this greater involvement by anthropologists and sociologists, some managers advocated a strict division of labour. The view at CIP was that both the social and the agricultural sciences had clear foci and refined methods; there was no need to mix them up. Rhoades expresses the CIP position on field methodology: 'the agronomist's methodological tool kit is well equipped for calculating yields, as is [that of] the economist for dealing with profit projections' (Rhoades 1986). There was no need for anthropologists to be involved in those kinds of activity. CIP managers argued that yields and profits, whilst important, represented only two parts of the farmer's world. Anthropologists at CIP, therefore, would be involved in research in a different dimension and within their own field of competence. Anthropologists thus became involved in research on the dynamics of technology choice and the impact at household and village levels (Ruttan 1982). Highly complementary to both agronomic and economic research, these latter issues were regarded important enough to constitute full-time investigations. They also demanded a methodological approach quite different from that taken by agronomists or economists. At CIP, and at other institutions within the CGIAR, anthropologists were asked not to copy what other scientists did better; their task as ethnographers was formidable enough.

A second (potential) remedy against project failure was to promote the training of national/local evaluators, sometimes called 'participant evaluators' (Feuerstein 1988; Tripp 1985). Here the underlying idea was that those presumed to be beneficiaries should become 'valid partners with [their] own goals and objectives', and be included at every stage in the life of a project (PAID 1981: 58–9). The emphasis on local participation as a condition for success made 'participatory development' one of the stronger buzzwords of the 1980s. The notion that certain individuals within target groups could become 'professional partners for outsiders' (R. Chambers 1987) quickly warmed many hearts, yet, as social analysts found out subsequently, a 'condition' for success is not the same as a 'guarantee' for that success.

A major obstacle to participatory development is that the individuals selected to become 'participant evaluators' do not necessarily constitute a homogeneous group. The issue, a very anthropological one, has been aptly described by Feuerstein in her review of four programmes in the Far East and North Pacific. Writing about situations in which trainee evaluators were asked to suggest solutions to particular problems, Feuerstein admits that

> it was not always easy to find effective solutions which were fully appreciated by those with primary education only and which did not at the same time slightly frustrate those with postgraduate levels of education and technical training.
>
> (Feuerstein 1988: 16)

The problem showed up in relation to the use of quantitative evaluation methods. Here Feuerstein noted how higher-educated trainee evaluators demonstrated

> an uncritical subservience to the mystiques of conventional evaluation approaches, an unswerving bias towards complex, costly and highly quantitative evaluation methods, [an] inability to perceive the need for a broader range of evaluation approaches and skills, and a general reluctance to extend participatory principles to evaluation.
>
> (1988: 16)

Feuerstein wets the ethnographer's appetite by exposing problematic areas of relevance which local people either forgot to look at or did not want to look at. Arguing that it would be beneficial to explore such areas, Feuerstein recommends the presence of experienced, sensitive outsiders (who could be anthropologists, 'home' and/or 'foreign'), so that trainee evaluators could be encouraged to formulate their own thinking more systematically within a global context. These outsiders could assist by helping to ensure that the wider and deeper issues relating to project impact are not being passed over too rapidly. (The theme is also explored in this volume, especially in the chapters by Casey; Garber and Jenden; and Gatter.)

Where decision makers and planners are able to overcome the political constraints inherent in project work, they may develop some commitment to the adoption of participatory methods for assessing activities. Once again, though, what is called for is an ethnographic approach: first of all, an understanding of broad-but-relevant local ethnography, and secondly, an understanding of the participatory process itself.

I am hopeful that anthropologists, provided they speak the relevant technical and cultural languages, will become involved as facilitators in this new venture. My hopes rest to some extent upon Chambers's powerful assertion that 'putting the priorities of poor people first can achieve not only [the local] objectives but also those of professionals and policy makers' (R. Chambers 1987). Hope also rests on the fact that most contributors to the present book became involved in the kind of work they write about precisely because of the growing appreciation that ethnographic insights can be fruitfully incorporated into, and generated during policy design and implementation (see Garber and Jenden). If development planners are serious about testing and demonstrating Chambers's hypothesis, then we may expect that the commitment to *continuous* 'participatory evaluations' will increase and that, in future, sociologists and anthropologists will be called upon more regularly to assist in that process.

The challenge for anthropology, then, is not just to predict at an early stage and to come up with answers; it is also, in typical anthropological fashion, a matter of broadening the range of concerns – for example, through documenting and scrutinizing the 'participatory process' itself (see Casey; Gatter; Fairhead), while searching for questions that are useful to those involved in management.

Some of these new questions, raised by anthropologists and

appreciated by managers, will be discussed later on. First, though, it seems appropriate to comment on how the term 'appraisal' is currently used.

APPRAISAL: TOWARDS A BROADER CONCEPT

Earlier on I used the term 'appraisal' in the conventional sense, in which it denotes that phase of a project when a range of proposals is described together with their respective merits. The term, nowadays, is also used in a wider sense, which goes beyond the mere comparison of options, to include study of the actual implementation process and its social and environmental consequences (Cernea 1982: 127; Conyers and Hills 1984). In this broader sense, the term includes '*ex ante* evaluations' and 'impact assessments' – labels usually reserved for the activity of monitoring social and environmental effects when there is still time to make adjustments.

Conyers and Hills provide a useful summary of the full range of issues to be covered by 'appraisal' in the wider sense. These include studying:

1 the nature and scale of the resources deployed;
2 the nature and scale of the effects produced, both beneficial and adverse;
3 the incidence of these effects – where they occur and who is affected by them;
4 the time period over which they occur;
5 the relationship between resources deployed and effects produced and the extent to which goals and objectives of planning are achieved.

One important aspect of 'appraisal' in this broad sense has been its tendency to turn into an ever-growing checklist of special issues for investigation. In 'Sustainable livelihoods' (R. Chambers 1987), Chambers criticizes the add-on approach to appraisal, and writes: 'With project appraisal, in succession, we have had [studies of] impact on the poor, impact on women, and now impact on the environment' (R. Chambers 1987). Viewing the history of project appraisal as a history of arbitrary add-ons, Chambers proposes to start afresh by focusing on sustainable livelihoods. The underlying idea is that policy makers and planners – if they want results – must appreciate how much sustainable development 'depends upon reversals', upon breaking that long tradition of a top-down, centre-outward approach, 'upon starting with the poorer and putting their priorities first' (R. Chambers 1987).

From a 'reversals' perspective, the task of the appraiser is to establish whether poor people are on course to overcome the conditions that force them to live from day to day, rather than plan ahead. The agenda is overtly political. The conditions to be monitored (and ultimately overcome) relate to access and control. Fundamentally, the 'reversals' agenda stipulates that appraisal must address two questions: first, are the priorities of the poor built into the objectives and running of the project? Secondly, are the poor securing long-term stakes in the resources deployed?

As the next section will show, answering these questions requires a long and hard look at the political scene surrounding intervention. The challenge is a familiar one for anthropologists.

APPRAISAL THROUGH PROJECT ETHNOGRAPHY

The paradigms of intervention that dominated the 1960s and 1970s conceptualized development as a neat progression bounded by time and space. Distinguishing between 'policy design', 'implementation' and 'results', and using clinical terms such as 'diagnosis' and 'prescription', the paradigms oversimplified what many practitioners knew to be a much more complex reality. The world familiar to them was marked not by neatness or linearity but by a 'complicated set of processes which involve[d] the reinterpretation or transformation of policy during the implementation [phase]. . . . There [was] in fact no straight line from policy to outcomes' (Long and Van Der Ploeg 1989: 227). The paradigms needed to be 'unpacked' or 'deconstructed'.

Throughout the 1980s, development anthropologists endeavoured to deconstruct the world of planning and intervention. They stressed that 'target populations' were made up of heterogeneous groups, households and individuals, and highlighted the varied ways in which units and individuals could organize themselves to appropriate, reject, and modify the strategies and resources introduced by intervention. Anthropological research suggested a new perspective on the relationship between policy, implementation and outcomes; a model which portrayed development as a negotiated, socially constructed, never-ending interaction between many social actors. These actors included beneficiaries and non-beneficiaries, the development institutions themselves, a range of civil interest groups, and the state. Interventions ceased to be thought of as discrete activities that culminated in 'the execution of . . . already-specified plan[s] of action with expected outcomes' (Long and Van Der Ploeg 1989: 228), but instead, came to be regarded as foci for ideological and inter-institutional struggles. Attempts at planned intervention, it was increasingly acknowledged, created competitive worlds marked *not* by unilear progress and value-free diagnostic concerns and remedies, but by 'messy business'. Reflecting on fieldwork in Zambia, Crehan and Von Oppen remarked:

> A project is never realized as a linear process, proceeding in an orderly fashion from 'correct' initial analysis through 'correct' decisions towards 'good' goals. It is often a messy business of decisions that have to be taken in difficult circumstances on the basis of inadequate knowledge, reactions, counter-reactions and it always constitutes *a learning process* for all involved.
>
> (Crehan and Von Oppen 1988: 114; emphasis added)

Despite the growing evidence that interventions in practice have neither a clear beginning nor a clear end, many development specialists still cling to images of linearity – images which they see reinforced by the idea of the 'project cycle'. The notion that such a cycle exists also 'encourages the view that project preparation and implementation take the form of a "rational" problem-solving process' for which experts are needed (Long and Van Der Ploeg 1989: 229).

Against the mechanistic model of intervention stands the actor-orientated perspective which portrays intervention as a particular learning process which takes place within a particular political arena; a multiple reality 'made up of differing cultural perceptions and social interests, and constituted by the ongoing social and political struggles that take place between the social actors involved' (Long and Van Der Ploeg 1989: 227). Within this broad, dynamic framework, the so-called target groups are not just 'beneficiaries' or 'victims', but rather self-motivating actors capable of exerting their own influences – that is, capable of social engineering.

It is against this 'multiple reality' view of development that Chambers's questions regarding the priorities of the poor must be set and answered. Likewise, it is within that same 'multiple reality' framework that future debates on participatory development and research must unfold.

For anthropologists, the ethics of social engineering are exceedingly complicated. It is still fairly safe, morally speaking, to advise planners on 'which social groups' they should work with; it is much more difficult to confront fellow social scientists who work in their own cultures as 'participant evaluators' with alternative interpretations and courses for action. At issue here is the extent to which dialogue is possible *between* 'participant evaluators', and how far the external adviser (who may well be a 'home' anthropologist) can go in trying to impose her or his views on the nature of participative development. One particular challenge for anthropologists working in the 1990s, and highlighted in the chapters by Casey and Gatter, is *to explore ethnographically the dialogue between participant evaluators*. I view such explorations as relevant for project management and, from an academic standpoint, important for the writing of 'total project ethnographies' (Rew 1985).

An example from my own fieldwork in Rwanda, where in 1986 I became involved in research on an urban vegetable-producing cooperative, may help to illustrate this challenge. Although the cooperative in question received encouraging support from the local administration, it had run into serious problems as members failed to repay their debts. Throughout my involvement I worked closely with a local social scientist, a woman teacher-cum-administrator whose input into the project I valued immensely (Pottier 1989). This colleague's views about the cause of the debts, however, differed from my own. She believed, as did other administrators, that the problem related to the absence of a regular bulk buyer: it was a market problem that needed to be solved. For me, as for the majority of the workforce, consisting of about 80 per cent of women producers, the problem had more to do with an imbalance in the power relations between male and female members; an imbalance upheld by Rwanda's dominant culture.

That our respective readings of the situation differed never soured our relationship. My colleague enjoyed hearing a different opinion; I too was satisfied, because I was given ample opportunity to express my views in the presence of the members of the cooperative. More important for the present argument, I felt privileged to have as colleague a local woman who was both relatively powerful *and interested in agriculture*. Because I valued this preciously rare combination, I, the external evaluator/anthropologist, was careful not to make my impact any greater than was necessary. For me, it was more important that I should live with our differences, which after all were not irreconcilable, than that I should take them out into the open, for instance, during the regular meetings members attended (see Derricourt 1988: 35, for a comparable situation, related to project work in Britain).

Since 'foreign' anthropologists are increasingly asked to work with 'home' social scientists, it will become necessary and valuable to deconstruct the reality of participatory research. The warning that social scientists are not immune to imposing their own assumptions (Curtis 1985: 108) still holds, and gross errors can result from that lack of immunity (Pottier 1985: 41–2), but the situation with project work today has become very complex, particularly where 'home' and 'visiting' social scientists interact or where the 'home' social scientist is up against the sociological assumptions of, say, a biological scientist who believes that she or he can take care of the project's social aspects (the 'anything you can do I can do better' syndrome; Rhoades 1986). In such instances, it cannot suffice to generalize about possible social science assumptions; rather, analysts will need to differentiate between the assumptions made by individual 'outsiders' and those made by individual 'insiders'; they will need to contrast these assumptions and discover areas of overlap as well as discrepancies. If appraisers are to achieve any real understanding of *intervention as process*, they will need to make all participating evaluators (including their own selves) part of the object of appraisal.

PARTICIPATORY RESEARCH: CAN CORNERS BE CUT?

While there may be a basis for the complaint that some anthropologists spend too much time 'in the field', I do not think it too extravagant to have a thorough knowledge of the socio-economic and political scene before possible courses of action are planned. In fact, in-depth knowledge can be essential to have, as shown in the Farming Systems Research literature, especially when several years are to be invested in an agricultural research project – which is, after all, common practice (DeWalt 1985: 108; see also Weiss 1986: 219, on the 'agonizingly slow' pace with which some decision makers turn 'recommendations' into 'practice'). DeWalt stresses in this respect that it may be possible, thanks to previous anthropological knowledge, 'to gather reliable data in a short period of time', yet he is firm that it is 'unrealistic to expect that a sondeo can provide the same quality of data as a longer-term diagnostic study' (1985: 108).

Similar reservations could be voiced against the current popularization of rapid techniques for carrying out rural appraisal, since institutionalized 'rapid appraisal' may well perpetuate the myth that intervention is a process neatly bounded by space and time. Equipped with a tool kit of techniques designed to gain quick access to indigenous worlds (for example, aspects of resource management and political decision making), researchers engaged in rapid appraisal are allowed 'optimum ignorance' (R. Chambers 1985: 38) but promised 'cost-effective ways in for outsiders' (R. Chambers 1983: 199). The Rapid Rural Appraisal (RRA) practitioners' peculiar dilemma is that they are expected to be committed to 'qualitative description' (McCracken *et al.* 1988: 11) in spite of this 'optimum ignorance' which is allowed. The two ideas are virtually impossible to reconcile, except perhaps in the case of very experienced researchers (see Bentley *et al.* 1988). For the not-so-experienced, for the vast majority who try their hand at 'rapid appraisal', there are haunting questions to be asked, such as: how can I live with 'optimum ignorance' and at the same time aspire to produce a qualitative description which responds to the 'multiple realities' of intervention? Above all, the question begs: how can I allow scope for political ignorance if sustainable development depends upon reversals?

Encouragingly, some RRA practitioners are now bracing themselves to think reflexively about their involvement as fieldworkers and to contemplate spending more time 'in the field'. Recent discussion of the role of 'outsiders' and 'insiders' in rapid appraisal (Scheuermeier 1991: 25/*RRA Notes 10*) suggests that some practitioners have already understood the need for a more accurate perception of the context within which appraisal takes place. With questions such as 'What on earth am I doing here?' and 'Why should poor people answer my questions?', Scheuermeier points to the pressing need for a better ethnographic understanding of what constitutes participatory research; that very initiative held to be the cornerstone of all sustainable development. It is questionable, though, that research into the nature of participatory research can ever be rapid. As Mitchell and Slim write in the same RRA volume: 'if the interviewer wants to learn a little, he or she had better stay around – watching and living' (Mitchell and Slim 1991: 21).

CONCLUSION

Back in 1983, at the ASA conference, Alan Rew suggested that would-be practitioners should focus their research on 'the ethnography of the total project rather than the ethnography of an ethnic group or a set of local populations' (Rew 1985: 188). He proposed that the anthropological contribution to project/programme appraisal should take a good look 'at the complete range of actors and ideologies involved in development work and policy making' (1985: 185). In several ways, Rew's proposal is close to the argument developed in this introductory chapter, but there is one very significant difference. Whereas Rew's 'ethnography of the total project' was presented as a contribution to anthropological theory (see also Cernea 1982), the message now is that project ethnography, with a focus on understanding participatory processes, must also be regarded a major contribution to making planned intervention both more humane and more effective.

REFERENCES

Almås, R. (1988) 'Evaluation of a participatory development project in three Norwegian rural communities', *Community Development Journal* 23(1): 26–32.

Bentley, M., Bentley, M. E., Pelto, G. H., Straus, W. L., Schumann, D. A., Adegbola, G., De La Pena, E., Oni, G. A., Brown, K. H. and Huffman, S. L. (1988) 'Rapid ethnographic assessment: application in a diarrhoea management programme', *Social Science Medicine* 27(1): 107–16.

Cernea, M. (1982) 'Indigenous anthropologists and development-oriented research', in Hussein Fahim (ed.) *Indigenous Anthropology in Non-Western Countries*, Durham, NC: Carolina Academic Press, pp. 121–37.

Chambers, E. (1987) 'Applied anthropology in the post-Vietnam era: anticipations and ironies', *Annual Review of Anthropology* 16: 309–37.

Chambers, R. (1983) *Rural Development: Putting the Last First*, London: Longman.

—— (1985) 'Shortcut methods in social information gathering for rural development projects', *Proceedings of the 1985 International Conference on Rapid Rural Appraisal*, Thailand: Khon Kaen University, pp. 33–46.

—— (1987) 'Sustainable livelihoods, environment and development: putting poor rural people first', Sussex: Institute of Development Studies, Discussion Paper 240.

Conlin, S. (1985) 'Anthropological advice in a government context', in R. Grillo and A. Rew (eds) *Social Anthropology and Development Policy*, London: Tavistock, ASA Monograph 23.

Conyers, D. and Hills, P. (1984) *An Introduction to Development Planning in the Third World*, Chichester: John Wiley & Sons.

Crehan, K. and Von Oppen, J. (1988) 'Understandings of "Development": an arena of struggle', *Sociologia Ruralis* XXVIII (2/3): 113–45.

Curtis, D. (1985) 'Anthropology in project management: on being useful to those who must design and operate rural water supplies', in R. Grillo and A. Rew (eds) *Social Anthropology and Development Policy*, London: Tavistock, ASA Monograph 23.

Derricourt, N. (1988) 'Evaluating the process of community work: some issues of accountability and procedure', *Community Development Journal* 23(1): 33–9.

DeWalt, B. (1985) 'Anthropology, sociology, and farming systems research', *Human Organization* 44(2): 106–14.

Feuerstein, M-Th. (1988) 'Finding the methods to fit the people: training for participatory evaluation', *Community Development Journal* 23(1): 16–25.

Grillo, R. and Rew, A. (eds) (1985) *Social Anthropology and Development Policy*, London: Tavistock, ASA Monograph 23.

Kuper, A. (1970) *Kalahari Village Politics*, Cambridge: Cambridge University Press, Studies in Social Anthropology 3.

Lecomte, B. (1978) 'Participation paysanne à l'aménagement et techniques des projets', *Tiers-Monde* XIX(73).

Long, N. and Van Der Ploeg, J. D. (1989) 'Demythologizing planned intervention: an actor perspective', *Sociologia Ruralis* XXIX(3/4): 226–49.

McCracken, J., Pretty, J. and Conway, G. (1988) *An Introduction to Rapid Rural Appraisal for Agricultural Development*, London: IIED.

Mead, M. (1977) 'Anthropology and the climate of opinion', *Annals of the New York Academy of Sciences* 293: 1–11.

Mitchell, J. and Slim, H. (1991) 'The bias of interviews', *RRA Notes* 10: 20–2.

Moris, J. and Hatfield, C. (1982) 'A new reality: western technology faces pastoralism in the Maasai Project', in International Rice Research Institute (ed.) *The Role of Anthropologists and Other Social Scientists in Interdisciplinary Teams Developing Improved Food Production Technology*, Manila: IRRI, pp. 43–61.

Pan-African Institute for Development (PAID) (1981) *The Project Approach to Rural Development: An Internal Critical View*, Douala: PAID.

Plucknett, D. L., Smith, N. J. H. and Herdt, R. W. (1986) 'The role of International Agricultural Research Centers in Africa', in A. Hansen and D. E. McMillan (eds) *Food in Sub-Saharan Africa*, Boulder, CO: Lynne Rienner Publishers.

Pottier, J. (ed.) (1985) *Food Systems in Central and Southern Africa*, London: SOAS.

—— (1989) 'Debating styles in a Rwandan cooperative: reflections on language, policy and gender', in R. Grillo (ed.) *Social Anthropology and the Politics of Language*, London: Routledge, *Sociological Review* 36, pp. 41–60.

Rew, A. (1985) 'The organizational connection: multi-disciplinary practice and anthropological theory', in R. Grillo and A. Rew (eds) *Social Anthropology and Development Policy*, London: Tavistock, ASA Monograph 23.

Rhoades, R. (1986) 'Using anthropology in improving food production: problems and prospects', *Agricultural Administration* 22: 57–78.

Ruttan, V. W. (1982) *Agricultural Research Policy*, Minneapolis: Minnesota University Press.

Scheuermeier, U. (1991) 'The outsider effect', in *RRA Notes* 10: 23–5.

Stavenhagen, R. (1986) 'Ethnodevelopment: a neglected dimension in development thinking', in R. Apthorpe and A. Krahl (eds) *Development Studies: Critique and Renewal*, Leiden: Brill, pp. 71–94.

Tripp, R. (1985) 'Anthropology and on-farm research', *Human Organization* 44(2): 114–24.

Weiss, C. (1986) 'Research and policy-making: a limited partnership', in F. Heller (ed.) *The Use and Abuse of Social Sciences*, London: Sage, pp. 214–35.

2 Agencies and young people

Runaways and young homeless in Wales

Susan Hutson and Mark Liddiard

Homeless young people sleeping on friends' floors, in old cars and night-shelters in the cities and the countryside of Wales, may seem a long way from farmers growing beans and herding cattle in Africa. However, the dynamics of such situations may not be so different. Once these situations are defined as problematic, agencies may intervene and clients may be required to alter their behaviour. In all cases, social scientists can be called in to help this intervention succeed, usually by gathering information about the characteristics and the orientation of the clients.

In this chapter ethnography is used to show the way in which the problems of homelessness and running were defined – principally by agencies but also by clients and by the media. It became clear, quite early in the research, that it was important to look at the definitions of those delivering the services as well as the values of those at the receiving end. We were alerted to this by the way in which certain elements of homelessness and running were being over-played whilst others were being under-played. This interest in definitions is not merely academic. It is obvious that the way in which clients are defined will affect the type of services which are considered appropriate.

In analysing the field material we began to realize that the definitions used were dependent, not wholly on the characteristics of the client, but also on the basic aims of the agency; the services they can supply and, lastly, the legal, economic and political constraints of the country in which they are working. In view of this, we suggest that there is a need for social scientists to shift their attention from the client to the agency (this volume: Garber and Jenden; Morris). The importance, in part, of the social scientist's knowledge depends on the extent to which it influences policy, but little is known about this process of policy making. Anthropologists often have informal information about their own and other agencies. Social scientists, experts in the study of gossip, rumour and scandal in Third World societies, are often employed, generally implicitly, to gain information in places where officials cannot easily pass. Although this information may be used informally, it seldom reaches the report of the academic press. It is often not seen to be relevant and, moreover, could be risky to publish.

This chapter looks at the nature of this ethnographic information or knowledge, which is the main tool of the professional anthropologist. It is felt to require a particular sensitivity for social situations, a certain 'outsider' empathy with the informant. This kind of information is often gathered through fieldwork, which requires time and is often carried out as part of a long professional training. It is not surprising, therefore, that this type of ethnographic knowledge can differ from other kinds of knowledge which are part of a development or a welfare delivery situation. It is also not surprising that the quick questionnaire, the checklist or the self-monitoring data, which can be used by the agency itself or by trained nationals in a situation of 'participatory development', can be seen as a threat to the professional anthropologist.

It should be realized, however, that the social scientist's view represents only one more definition of the situation. Such knowledge is currency in at least two markets – the agency and the university. For example, the researcher may be drawing, from the situation, points which neatly fit into papers to further an academic career. Research students must struggle in the field, not only for the immediate development situation, but also for the higher degree. Data, which may be passed over by the agency, may be of considerable value and worth in teaching undergraduates. Just as the social scientist's data are often required for strategic purposes, so they will be collected strategically, with other agendas also in mind. Thus, in gaining a full picture of a development or welfare delivery situation, it may be necessary for a discerning eye to be turned upon the agencies involved and a sideways glance to be cast on the writer of the advisory report.

This chapter is based on four months' research carried out for a national children's charity. In 1985 the charity had set up a 'safe house' in London catering to young people, under 17, on the run in London. The basic aim was to provide a refuge, a breathing space and a point from which a return to home or care could be negotiated. In the first two years 532 young people moved through the 'safe house', of whom 60 per cent came from outside London.

The West and Wales regional office of the children's charity was anxious to know if there were young people on the run in the towns and cities of Wales. Our official brief was to find out whether there were young people, under 18, living on the street and supporting themselves through stealing, begging, prostitution or casual employment. If there were, we were to establish what kind of problem these young people presented both to themselves and to others.

Our instructions were to concentrate on interviewing statutory agencies (Police, Probation, Social Services, housing departments) and voluntary agencies, particularly those working in the fields of youth and housing such as the Cyrenians, Shelter and the Young Single Homeless Group. Our research covered the major cities of Cardiff, Swansea and Newport and the more rural county of Clwyd in the north. In all, we collected 102 interviews – of which 75 per cent were with agency workers and the rest were with young people.

THE PUBLIC DEFINITION OF THE PROBLEM

Anyone living in London in the 1990s must be familiar with the problem of homeless young people. Documentaries and reports about children, whether the theme be running, homelessness or abuse, have become part of the public consciousness. In this area media images are particularly important, as children are always newsworthy and it is a sensitive area where professionals and policy makers often take note of public opinion. Moreover, many of the agencies in the field depend on the collecting box for their funds. For all these reasons, this is an area in which public definitions are prominent.

The publication of two books (Sereny 1984; Agnelli 1986) created an interest in runaways in America and Europe. There were, at that time in the British press, reports of under-age prostitution and rent boys in London and other British cities.

The 'safe house' of our funding agency was set up in London in the wake of some of this publicity, although the main impetus for its formation came from the practical pressures of other agencies in Central London which were unable, legally, to accommodate the increasing numbers of runaways under 16. The 'safe house' was innovative, and it was well received in the press. At this time the charity was closing down most of its residential children's homes around the country because of a population decline in this age group and because of changing ideas about residential care and doubts about its value. A new focus was thus needed within the agency, and a gap in existing services had been successfully identified.

With regards to young homeless people, the 1960s documentary 'Cathy Come Home' may have shocked the British public, but this concern was not kept up. It was not until the 'Costa del Dole' reports – that young unemployed people were drifting to seaside towns – hit the headlines in 1985 that the British public were reminded again of young people living away from home. In this case, however, they were not viewed as victims but rather as culprits and scroungers in the welfare system. The consequent reaction of the government was the board and lodging 'move on' regulations of 1985.

An acute lack of jobs and accommodation, suitable for young people at the lower end of the labour and housing market, lies behind the continuing problem of young homeless people. In areas where work, albeit casual and low paid, is increasing (as in London), rents are also soaring. Reduction in Income Support to those under 25 and changes in the way Housing Benefit is paid is also increasing the problems of young people who can, no longer, live with their parents. In the face of the resulting demand from homeless young people, agencies dealing with traditional homeless groups, such as the Cyrenians, are having to cater increasingly for a younger age group whilst other agencies such as the Young Single Homeless have opened hostels specifically for this age category.

Some agency workers whom we spoke to were aware that the media images did not coincide with the picture they knew on the ground. A worker in a London night-shelter, for example, felt that the poster presently found in Underground stations quite seriously misrepresented the problem of running. As he said:

> You see on the Underground these posters which say 'Ring Home'. I think they give the impression that it is middle class kids who are running from home. . . . That's simply not the case. Most people we see don't have anyone at home who's the slightest bit interested in where they are.

In Wales, it was clear that many young people, on the run and without secure accommodation, had no home to phone, let alone to return to. Many came from care. Moreover, in Wales, most young people do not run to London but stay within their home town or county. The publicity centres on London, but our findings indicate that the problem exists throughout the regions, in both urban and rural areas. It appears that most young people are forced to leave their local area rather than being drawn by the bright lights of the big cities.

In Wales, it appeared that a high proportion of young people on the run and homeless came from local authority care. It also appeared that a high proportion of these young people were involved with petty crime, largely theft. These offences were committed, in some cases, before they left home or care but, more particularly, once they were without a stable base.

Although statistics are not kept systematically, by the police, it was felt that well over 50 per cent of runaways came from care. This was higher than the 34 per cent reported in the 'safe house' in London (Newman 1989). Estimates on the number of young people with a care background using hostels for young homeless people, again, reach 30 per cent in London (Randall 1988).

The police estimated that over 50 per cent of runaways from care had offended on the current or past run. Estimates of the extent to which young homeless people were involved in offending vary, but 30 per cent is given in one central London night-shelter (Randall 1988). An agency worker here felt that this figure would rise steeply after several weeks in London. In Wales we were told, in several of the hostels, that 'the majority' of the young people were involved in petty crime. Putting aside the problems of relying on estimates, these figures, of a care background and offending, are high.

Running from care has always been a problem. Young people run from secure units, from children's homes and from family placements. In the three children's homes we contacted, the number of total monthly runs in proportion to the number of inmates varied from 11 to 150 per cent, giving an average of 56 per cent.

Yet, although many assume that running is a product of the care system, most of the absconders we spoke to had already run from home *before* coming into care. Once in care, frequent absconding can be a factor leading to more secure confinement. It would appear that one of the main risks to these young people is to offend, to be caught and, eventually, to risk a custodial sentence, which can affect future prospects in a major way.

Two risks which are often mentioned, in the press and publicity related to young people living on the streets, are prostitution and drugs. In the Welsh research we found little evidence of structured prostitution, where money is exchanged for sex, although a number of agency workers had evidence that some young women exchanged sexual favours in return for food and shelter.

Drug use was widespread, but drug abuse and drug problems only affected a few. It is interesting that alcohol, which agency workers felt was a much wider and more damaging problem than drug abuse, is seldom mentioned in the press or in publicity, whilst prostitution and drugs often dominate such reports. The general public's interest in prostitution and the way in which an emphasis on drugs can divert attention away from underlying social and political problems is well known. Yet the way in which some agencies play down their clients' involvement in care and offending is less obvious. They may have in mind the good name of their project. They may be well aware that they must draw funds from a general public not normally sympathetic to law breakers. There are, perhaps, two other reasons for playing down an involvement with care. An admission that a high number of clients are in care means, on the one hand, that the problem will not easily go away. On the other hand, such an admission can narrow the problem and marginalize the client.

Other stereotypes associated with the homelessness of an older age group – such as alcoholism and psychiatric problems – can be translated into the perceptions of the young homelessness scene in an uninformed way. These are images which the agencies cannot always afford to deny as, particularly with the national restructuring of the resettlement units, money is available if the image fits. As one agency worker told us:

> Because there's a traditional, white, middle aged, male idea of what homelessness is, many projects still target their resources at these traditional groups. They are highly visible. . . . The police don't like them living on the streets. The City Council don't like them living on the streets so consequently anyone that does anything will get handouts.

One important outcome of these media images is that other categories of homeless young people remain largely hidden – young people in general, and young women and young people from ethnic minority groups in particular.

THE DISTINCTION BETWEEN RUNAWAYS AND YOUNG HOMELESS PEOPLE

In media and publicity images, which have been important in defining a social problem area, running and homelessness are often not clearly defined. However, there is a legal distinction between the two. This distinction rests on age and constrains the type of services an agency can offer. In looking at these two categories, it should be remembered that the research looked at young people 18 and under.

In simple terms, runaways have, by reason of their age (usually under 16), left home or care *illegally*. They are essentially on the run. Homeless young people have left home or care *legally* or been legally 'thrown out' at 16 or over but have no secure accommodation.

The two following quotations express well the situation of, first, a girl on the run from care and, second, a homeless boy. Kelly, now 15, had come into care at 11 after running repeatedly from home. She spoke of the danger of later runs from care:

> I broke my arm on the run. I was climbing a wall and I didn't realise how far down it was. I fell on my arm. They caught me then. They took me to hospital. [Later] I fell on glass and had stitches in my knee. I broke my ankle on the run. I jumped off a motorway bridge. There were police both ends and I jumped.

Kelly is not typical. She told us that she had not spent more than two weeks in the same place for the last three years. Kelly was an 'expert' at running and was called 'the road runner'. She told us about dressing for a run:

> You dress for going on the run in jeans, trainers and a few jumpers. They [the public] are walking round in short skirts and that. . . . When I get back [to the children's home], I go in the shower. . . . I take off my clothes and they lock them in the cupboard and my shoes so I can't go. . . . I've been though, in my nightie and bare feet.

James, who fits into the category of homeless, told us that he had been kicked out from home when he was 17 because of family arguments. The account of his first four nights sleeping rough are not untypical:

> I slept in a telephone box – sitting on the thing where they put the telephone book, with my feet against the door to stop myself falling off. . . . I slept in a bus shelter up in Brynhendy. I walked [15 miles], got 2–3 hours sleep then walked back just to keep warm, that is. I thought 'sleeping rough – no trouble' but then, it started to rain. One night it poured down in particular and I got soaked. I was wet for the next 2 days . . . I had 2 quid on me to last me 4 days and I spent it all on 10 cigarettes and a pie and chips on the first day which was all gone in a couple of hours. I had no food then for the next couple of days.

In many ways young runaways and young homeless people are in a similar situation. The immediate reasons for leaving home are often the same – namely, family breakdown or family arguments. Whether young people abscond from care or leave legally, they have few family resources on which to depend. The importance of such resources is well known (Hutson and Jenkins 1987). The outcomes of running from, or leaving home or care are often the same. Young people living away from a secure base are all at risk from the effects of offending, from dangers to their health and, ultimately, to their lives. They are, additionally, at risk from the alienation that comes from withdrawal from mainstream, adult life. Essentially the young runaway and the young homeless person end up in the same situation – looking for somewhere to sleep and a means of support.

However, despite this similarity, the law in Britain makes a crucial distinction between the two categories. British laws concerning the age of majority are complicated. Young people achieve their majority gradually. However, laws concerning under age juveniles are strictly enforced and adhered to by the authorities, who deal very carefully with minors.

The law, in Britain, is that a young person must be in the care of a parent, guardian or the local authority up to the age of 16. Between 16 and 18 young people can leave with the permission of their carers. The police have powers to detain anyone under 17 if they are believed to be beyond parental control or in danger. Seventeen is also the age at which most Care Orders expire. At the age of 18 a young person may, in theory, take out a tenancy. A young person may work at 16 or, if unemployed, receive an allowance if on a YTS scheme. At 18 an unemployed person may draw Income Support and Housing Benefit.

However, legal access to work, housing and state benefits at 18 does not mean practical access to adequate income and accommodation. At 18, young people need to have no access to accommodation, have not intentionally left accommodation and fit an exclusive priority such as pregnancy or mental illness in order to qualify as officially homeless at a housing department. Even after waiting several years on the housing waiting list, young people are often only offered 'hard to let' properties, if indeed they are offered anything at all (Youth Review Team 1987). In the private sector as well, young people are often regarded as 'bad tenants', often because of the unreliability of their Housing Benefit. Without the necessary bonds or deposits, many young people end up in multi-occupancy houses and in bed and breakfast. The young people considered in this chapter were often, in fact, sleeping on the floors of those at the bottom of the housing market.

Income for young people at the bottom of the labour market is precarious. Most of the young people we saw did not have jobs. If they did, these jobs were low-paid and insecure. Many were not even in a secure 'claiming' situation because this requires, in particular, a secure address. Income Support has, since 1988, been graded by age, thus making it increasingly difficult for young people under 25 and without a job to live away from a home base. Thus in practice, the age of majority is being raised from 18 to 25.

AGENCY DEFINITIONS OF CLIENTS

Agency workers appeared to be expressing one of two main viewpoints when they spoke of their clients and their situation. The difference between the two viewpoints rested on whether or not their clients had problems over and above their immediate rooflessness. Many project workers felt they were catering for essentially 'ordinary' young people. For example, in the quotation below, the temporary homelessness of the client is felt to be due to the normal process of growing up and leaving home in the absence of work and adequate housing provision. A youth worker said of his clients:

> They have mobility. They leave school. It doesn't matter to them where they sleep. It's part of staying out late, not getting a job, being a layabout. . . . It's not classed as homelessness. I see it as natural – like living with your sister because your mother's giving you gyp.

In contrast, the project worker quoted below saw her clients as essentially 'vulnerable', suffering from problems other than the lack of accommodation:

> They do have problems other than accommodation. It takes you weeks and weeks to get through. . . . But it's mainly a lot of hurt, a lot of anger and a lot of friction. . . . To be honest with you, it's rejection.

To a certain extent, of course, the different viewpoints reflect the actual clientele. The first speaker was a youth worker, the second a worker in an emergency accommodation project.

There may, however, be other factors behind the way in which these clients are characterized. The research findings suggest that the viewpoint prevailing in a project will depend on its history, the basis on which its funds are sought and its basic political and social aims. For this reason, it is important for the anthropologist to look up from the client to the service provider.

The following quotes, from two very different agencies, show again the difference between 'ordinary' young people and those with extra problems:

> People still tend to see it [homelessness] as youngsters from particularly inadequate families or with severe behavioural problems rather than it could be *their* kids. It's much more widespread than they realise.

> If young people have avoided social service intervention up to this age [15], it's hot in the kitchen but the problem is short term and it resolves itself. We [the Social Services] are looking at children with a history of intervention.

Again, of course, the different viewpoints partially reflect the 'objective' nature of the clients themselves, yet these viewpoints are also affected by the agencies' objectives and structure. For example, the first agency worker, stressing that homelessness is wider than most people realize, later stressed the need for young people to have access to mainstream services such as housing, health care and employment. Part, at least, of the work of this agency is to work as a political pressure group for change and better coordination of mainstream services. It is, moreover, essential to its cause that its clients should be seen by the policy makers and funders as 'normal' and 'ordinary'. Such an agency is likely to play down the care and offending involvement of its clients.

The second quote, of the 'children with a history of intervention', is from a worker in a Social Services Department. Social Services and some voluntary agencies have a long history of helping vulnerable young people. The *raison d'être* of their work rests on the 'vulnerability' of their clients. These agencies are likely to stress the need for special help for their clients. Moreover, they are likely themselves to be providers of such special help, often in the form of counselling. In addition to reflecting the history and basic aims of the agency, the differences in definitions of clients can also mirror differences in the expertise and training of the agency workers.

Moreover, what services can, economically or legally, be offered can also affect the way in which the client is defined. The laws of the age of majority form an important constraint on the provision of services to young people. In general, agencies cannot offer practical services such as accommodation and jobs to those under 16. In fact the London 'safe house' has had to work, officially, outside the law in offering emergency accommodation. All an agency can offer to young people under the age of 16 is care and counselling. If care and counselling is all that can, within the law, be offered, then it is not surprising that agencies working with runaways (minors) will stress their underlying, emotional and family problems which are, apparently, amenable to what they can offer.

It is obvious to any anthropologist that definitions can be used strategically. In this case agencies can find themselves in a dilemma, both if they stress the problems of clients or if they play down these problems. A normalizing approach to social problems is very much in fashion in social work today, and goes along with an unwillingness to intervene in people's lives and risk stigmatizing them. The advantage of such an approach is that it shows that a social problem is potentially widespread and can affect anyone in the population. The disadvantage of such an approach is that, if running and homelessness are part of growing up, then it can be difficult to justify intervention or gain funding from some sources. This approach could, in the last resort, leave young people at risk.

If, on the other hand, the vulnerability of the client is stressed, this approach also has its drawbacks. It may imply that homelessness or running is not a general problem but one which affects only the inadequate. This approach may serve to marginalize and stigmatize young people who approach these agencies. Wells (1980) goes so far as to suggest that every facet of youth homelessness is often reduced to a social problem in the search for funding. While we feel strongly that the current problems presented by young homeless people are serious enough to justify all the present publicity, we have already pointed out a possible overemphasis on drugs and prostitution.

As both viewpoints have certain advantages and disadvantages, it was not surprising that some agency workers switched from one viewpoint to another according to the audience, the situation and the strategy.

CLIENTS DEFINED, INTERNALLY, AS 'HIGH RISK' AND 'LOW RISK'

As well as defining clients as problematic or ordinary, often to an external audience such as the press, agencies appeared to make another distinction between clients. Some clients were referred to as 'high risk' or 'vulnerable'. Others were spoken of as 'low risk'.

This form of classification was made particularly clear to us when watching the workers in a London night-shelter refer young clients on to advice centres. This night-shelter was concerned mainly with young men coming into the capital to look for work. It worked mainly with two advice centres. One was always crowded and dealt with young people in groups. The second advice centre had more staff and could offer individual counselling. Most young people were sent to the first centre. However, the only girl and two young men, felt by the workers to be gay, were sent to the second, even though their situation was not apparently different from the majority of clients who were referred to the earlier advice centre. Thus, in their cases, 'vulnerability' appeared to be classified on the grounds of gender and sexual orientation, and counselling was offered as the main way of dealing with it. We are not implying criticism of such actions. Projects are essentially practical and decisions must be made. We are interested, merely, in the way in which clients were differentiated and classified in terms of vulnerability, and then processed through the system.

It is, perhaps, surprising that the majority of agencies hardly ever dealt with 'high-risk' clients. We found, for instance, significantly large numbers of projects which excluded hard-drug users or young people with a history of violence or sexual offences. Additionally, most of the agencies we spoke to excluded the mentally and physically handicapped, either formally or informally. Whilst this appears a paradoxical situation, it probably has much to do with the practicalities of running a project.

In the first place, agencies have to prevent potential disruption of their projects, and many do not have the 24-hour staff cover which is often necessary to deal with 'high risk' clients. Moreover, it was felt that such problems could be 'contagious' – particularly drugs and criminal behaviour – as this quote, by an agency worker, shows:

> We don't take the extremes of behaviour. . . . Drug problems, which we see as a long term problem, we're a bit cagey about – because that spreads like wildfire. So somebody who comes in without a problem, certainly goes out with one!

In the second place, problematic clients can give the project a bad name by, for example, alienating neighbours or attracting the police. As one worker said, speaking of 'high risk' referrals:

> By not accepting them, we're not saying that there's not a need for provision for those people. . . . It's necessary to keep the

reputation of the place going. . . . We need to protect the tenancy of the place in order for it to flourish, if you like. . . . It's like sowing the seed for better provision.

In a sense, then, there appears to be a three-tier classification operating here – the 'non-vulnerable', the 'vulnerable' and the 'highly vulnerable'. Clearly middle-range young people are the most suitable to deal with within homelessness projects. The 'non-vulnerable' present problems of having to justify intervention, whilst the 'highly vulnerable' present practical difficulties.

We can see that classification and definition can result from everyday, practical actions. These actions are performed, not with an eye to policy directives, but with an eye to getting through the day. This routinization can serve to sift and sort clients into categories (Howe 1985).

YOUNG PEOPLE'S DEFINITIONS

There is often a difference in perception between the workers and their young clients. In the following quotation an agency worker contrasts her view with that of the young clients:

It's whose perception really, isn't it? . . . It's either rejection from the family or anger at the care system, that's *my* perception. *Their* perception is much more practically based – there aren't any proper jobs for them; they haven't got anywhere to live that's suitable.

However, it would seem that young people do not always stand on the same side in the 'problematic' or 'ordinary' debate. First, in our research, we found that young people tended to emphasize practical, often short-term, problems – like a bed for the night – whilst some agencies stressed underlying problems. In these cases there could be a mismatch between what young people were seeking and what the agency was offering. We were told, by one worker, that young people acted largely as consumers wanting 'the keys to the penthouse flat'. Instead, agency workers required young people to participate – doing, at least, the washing up and, at most, entering into contracts whereby they were to show evidence of actively seeking work and accommodation themselves. The control implied in such contracts was often justified by defining the clients as 'vulnerable' and 'problematic'.

A study of young girls absconding from a children's home shows that the girls saw running as essentially non-problematic, a sensible strategy in fact to cope with separation and the frustration of institutional living (Ackland 1981). The staff, however, tended to see running as problematic – creating problems for them and indicating underlying problems in the girls themselves.

Our research presents an interesting contrast to this in so far as several agencies stressed the gains of running and homelessness – maturity, 'time out' – whereas it was the young people who stressed the risks to life and morale of an unsettled way of life. This shows, again, the way in which viewpoints can be switched and definitions used strategically.

DEFINITIONS AND GATEKEEPING

Definitions can act as gatekeepers because they determine who is included under a particular label. The way in which a problem is defined can help determine its size. This can be seen by considering the definitions of homelessness operated by Shelter and housing departments.

In the four counties we visited, the housing departments defined homelessness at one end of the spectrum; namely, young people were only classed as 'officially homeless', with a statutory claim for housing, when they had no access to secure accommodation, had not intentionally left such accommodation and fitted a priority category, such as having dependent children.

This narrow definition excluded most single homeless. It is likely that it also deterred people from presenting themselves at the housing department. Many know that they do not qualify for housing and so do not put themselves on the waiting list or, even, seek advice. With such a narrow definition of homelessness, the problem may appear to be small on both a local and a national basis.

At the other end of the spectrum, Shelter takes a broad definition of vulnerability and homelessness, effectively defining young people as homeless, and consequently vulnerable, if they are simply living in an unsatisfactory housing situation – be that sleeping rough, sleeping on a friend's floor or in an unsuitable co-habitating situation. With such a definition, youth homelessness becomes a significant problem in many parts of Britain.

In this context, definitions are used as gatekeepers. Shelter needs to broaden and highlight the problem of homelessness, whilst housing departments, with a dwindling stock of houses, need to limit demand.

In this respect, the definitions used reflect the structure, purpose and resources of the agencies involved.

An obvious outcome of operating different definitions – in this case, of homelessness – is the resulting disagreement between agencies, which can reach the level of opposition. A second problem, perhaps more serious, is the impossibility of nationally coordinated and centrally funded action when primary definitions cannot be agreed upon.

CONCLUSIONS

This chapter has not considered the reasons for the homelessness of young people or of running. It is often debated as to whether homelessness results from the personal problems and failings of the homeless themselves or from wider economic and political structures. There is a danger in this chapter that, in focusing on the 'problems' of young homeless people, the question of homelessness is moved away from the centre of housing policy, at the same time diverting attention away from employment and benefit issues. This is not our intention. Nor do we, in looking carefully at what agencies are saying, want in any way to criticize or cast doubt on present projects catering for young homeless people. We intend, rather, in hinting at the complex construction of definitions, to ask merely for an awareness of the way in which they are created and applied.

In focusing on the definitions of agency workers, we point out the importance of looking at the values and definitions of those intervening as well as the values and definitions of the clients on the ground. In looking at running and homelessness, we found two main viewpoints. On the one hand, some stressed that homelessness and running were essentially normal, presented practical problems and potentially affected a wide client group. Others, on the other hand, presented homelessness and running as essentially problematic, arising from underlying problems and affecting a small, vulnerable category of young people. It appeared that the way in which the problem and the client were defined depended less on the 'objective' characteristics of the client and more on the history, the political and social objectives, the skills, the resources and the funding base of the agency.

It is clear that the solution to a social problem is linked to the way in which it is defined. In the area of running and youth homelessness, there appear to be diverse definitions, both of the situation and the clients. Their diversity reflects, in part, the varied background of agencies working in this area and the day-to-day strategies which agency workers and clients must adopt in order best to use limited resources. Although different definitions can lead to a mismatch between need and provision and a lack of coordination, it is clear, from other chapters in this volume (for example, those of Gatter and Pottier), that different definitions do not necessarily lead to deadlock.

REFERENCES

Ackland, J. (1981) 'Institutional reactions to absconding', *British Journal of Social Work* 11: 171–87.

Agnelli, S. (1986) *Street Children, A Growing Urban Tragedy*, London: Weidenfeld (a Report for the Independent Commission on International Humanitarian Issues).

Howe, L. (1985) 'The "deserving" and the "undeserving": practice in an urban, local Social Security office', *Journal of Social Policy* 14: 49–72.

Hutson, S. and Jenkins, R. (1987) 'Family relationships and the unemployment of young people in Swansea', in M. White (ed.) *The Social World of the Young Unemployed*, London: Policy Studies Institute.

Newman, C. (1989) *Young Runaways*, London: The Children's Society.

Randall, G. (1988) *No Way Home: Homeless Young People in Central London*, London: Centrepoint, Soho.

Sereny, G. (1984) *The Invisible Children*, London: Pan Books.

Wells, K. (1980) 'I came for the experience', *New Society* 52: 214–16.

The Youth Review Team (leader P. Willis) (1987) *The Social Condition of Young People in Wolverhampton in 1984*, Wolverhampton: Wolverhampton Borough Council.

3 Anthropologists or anthropology?

The Band Aid perspective on development projects

Bill Garber and Penny Jenden

This chapter is in four parts. First, we outline the activities of Band Aid with respect to development projects in order to provide a context within which the remainder of the chapter can be understood. Secondly, by examining some of the criteria that Band Aid has used in selecting development programmes for funding, we hope to illustrate considerations – that is, areas of anthropological knowledge *par excellence* – which we feel are important, if not vital, to the successful design and implementation of development activities. Next we examine factors that constitute structural obstacles to the incorporation of anthropological (ethnographic) knowledge, and will then go on to consider examples of projects in which the need for an anthropological understanding has been recognized. Finally, through specific examples, we will consider the appropriateness and cost-effectiveness of the ways in which project personnel have attempted to acquire anthropological data and insights.

BAND AID: ROLE AND PROCESSES

Band Aid is a donor agency rather than an operational one. It provides funds for other organizations to manage or implement programmes in the field, particularly Non-Governmental Organizations (NGOs). These are essentially charity organizations, which are either local/indigenous NGOs (in which case they also may be community groups or associations) or international agencies such as Oxfam, Care, Save the Children Federation, and so on. Band Aid has also funded a number of projects that directly involve government departments and ministries.

The Band Aid portfolio has around 250 projects located in six African countries: Burkina Faso, Chad, Ethiopia, Mali, Niger and the Sudan. A broad range of different types of programme are

included in this portfolio, the majority being community development projects aimed to stimulate activities such as environmental
protection (reforestation, terracing, agro-forestry), provision of
primary health care, income generation, the development of portable
water sources, and the construction of small dams.

Projects submitted for funding go through the following selection
process:

1 Project proposals are submitted to Band Aid by various organizations. The project site and implementing agency are visited by
  Band Aid's field representatives, who often help to improve
  proposals before passing them on, with recommendations, to the
  secretariat in London.
2 In London the project proposals are submitted to an advisory
  committee, which will either:
  (a) reject the proposal;
  (b) defer a decision until more information is obtained (which the
      secretariat then sets out to obtain);
  (c) recommend that the project be funded to a certain level.
  The next step is for the programme to be submitted to the trustees
  for the approval of a global sum.
3 Before any funds can be disbursed, the secretariat has to take a
  number of further steps. For example, it will clarify the budgets,
  specifying which line items in each budget Band Aid is supporting,
  and will obtain from the implementing agency agreement on the
  financial and narrative reporting to be provided. It is only after
  these issues have been resolved that the first *tranche* of money for
  a programme will be released.

ANTHROPOLOGICAL KNOWLEDGE AND DEVELOPMENT PROGRAMMES

Having outlined the procedures used in selecting projects for funding, we can now consider what Band Aid advisers hoped to find in
project submissions. In doing so we shall illustrate the relevance of
certain anthropological types of knowledge and skills for project
implementation.

One of the things Band Aid sought to find in a given project
submission was an answer to the question 'Who is to benefit?' With
this question Band Aid wanted to ascertain whether the organization
submitting the proposal had a sociological analysis of the different
groups involved, of their interest *vis-à-vis* each other, and *vis-à-vis*

the planned activities of the project. In most cases though, given the operational context, Band Aid tried to establish whether project organizers had the means to develop such an analysis.

The advisory committee also scrutinized the programme documents for evidence that 'priorities' had been worked out democratically. It asked: What are the development priorities of the targeted communities (particularly the poorer and more vulnerable members of those communities)? How have the various social groups taken part in identifying these priorities? And exactly how will the proposed activities address these concerns? In addition, the committee wanted to be assured that project documents gave due consideration to a number of sociological concerns, asking, for example: how local drought-coping mechanisms had been or would be identified and strengthened; whether anything was known about decision-making processes within the different local groups; what the value and relevance was of indigenous technical knowledge (ITK); how local rights in land were distributed and allocated, and so on. To deal with such questions it is clear that one needs an understanding of local political processes; an insight, for instance, into how formal village or community meetings are run. One also needs the ability to interpret what people *say*, in order to 'read between the lines' and to sort out vested interests. In short, agencies need to have both an interest in ethnography and the skills to acquire it. When assessing proposals one is, in effect, trying to see whether a development agency has – or is developing – an ethnography of the people it is working with.

One of the biggest problems that development projects run into, we feel, is that they generally lack an adequate ethnographic or historical analysis of the very problems they set out to tackle. Thus, projects aiming to reverse the process of environmental degradation tend to use a crude Malthusian explanation in their analysis of how such degradation has come about, and use this crude explanation as the basis for their planning (see also Fairhead's chapter, this volume). Current social and historical determinants of land-use patterns, for example, are often only considered after development projects have been operating for several years or when the lack of understanding of these has visibly become a serious problem for implementation. It is often the case that significant amounts of effort and resources are expended before the initial ethnographic assumptions, which have been embodied in the design of the project, come to be reassessed. This lack of an ongoing ethnographic sensitivity from the outset can lead to a massive waste of resources and missed opportunities.

Another important issue the advisory committee addressed was project flexibility: how can one ensure that the management of a proposed programme is as flexible as possible? In order to avoid the implementation of a 'blueprint approach', it is vital that projects ensure that the various groups within a community will actively participate in implementing, monitoring, evaluating and (particularly) *evolving the project*. We would argue that the question of how the development projects themselves develop is vital in ensuring that technically and socially appropriate solutions are arrived at. This is the main point: solutions have to be arrived at; they are the end product of a process which entails working together with different groups of beneficiaries. This process involves seeking to understand various issues, such as the implications in practice of rights in resources, the rationale of local farming systems, the perspective of the different target groups, and numerous other ethnographic concerns.

While the various questions and issues are in and of themselves important, we will nevertheless argue that the issue of flexible management remains paramount. A project does not, and should not, have to start off with a full-scale 'traditional' ethnographic inquiry, but rather *acquire such understandings as the programme develops*. Furthermore, we feel very strongly that the only correct way for acquiring these understandings is by working closely with the various social groups involved.

The point we are trying to establish is that in order to be successful, development projects must require a flexible system which engages in a *learning process* by working with and coming to understand local groups, their inter-relationships and their points of view. This flexible approach to project management is intimately linked in with an anthropological or, perhaps more accurately, an ethnographic approach. This is not only because the issues being dealt with are, for a large part, ethnographic concerns, but also because the methods involved in this process are in themselves, to a large extent, ethnographical.

For the purposes of 'data' gathering and project design, it is commonly found that appraisal missions interact with the prospective beneficiaries on a formal basis, if at all, and often by means of questionnaires and formal meetings. This interaction is problematic in a number of ways, but particularly in that only certain kinds of people tend to attend and express themselves in these contexts, and only do so in limited ways. These types of interaction are further limited in that the agenda for discussion is normally determined by the agency itself and, more complexly, by the expectations local people have developed of the agency's own agenda (see also Griffith, this volume). We are not arguing that other forms of communication are problem-free; they are not. However, it should be recognized that interaction between projects and local people frequently leaves a lot to be desired.

While we emphasize the process of acquiring ethnography, we should make explicit that we are not suggesting the recreation of ethnographic 'databases' such as there existed in the colonial period. This is for a number of reasons, the most basic of which are:

1 Ethnography *per se* is synchronic, while the problems faced by poor people and development projects are dynamic. As such an *ongoing* ethnographic process is what is required rather than 'one-off'-style ethnographies.
2 The manner in which ethnographic sensitivity is incorporated into programmes is of key significance. As we shall show below, the central issue of 'Who does the ethnographic research and within what institutional context?' must be addressed.
3 It is important that the ethnographic process allows 'beneficiaries' to take part in the development of the project's activities. In this context, the ethnography will constantly be revealed as different groups make decisions with regard to activities and resources. If the ethnographic research is a separate process from that of decision making, there is a danger that ethnography will become a resource at the disposal of the project management for the manipulation of people.

FACTORS THAT DISCOURAGE THE ADOPTION OF A FLEXIBLE OR ETHNOGRAPHIC APPROACH TO DEVELOPMENT

Although we have argued that development projects should have a flexible or ethnographic approach, we must also stress that it is still rare to find such approaches in practice. In this section we will explore some of the causes that lead to projects being inflexible, having their own momentum and lacking in ethnographic learning.

The first point to note is that (nearly) all development projects have budgets, and that budgets usually imply fixed programmes to be run within a particular area and within a given time frame. The implied rationale is simple: how can one know what one is going to spend if one does not know what is going to be done where and when? This, of course, is a matter of degree. The more detailed a budget is (by implication), the more pre-planned, pre-specified and often fixed the proposed set of activities is going to be. So why do projects have specified budgets rather than simple global totals for unspecified expenditures and activities? The short answer is that donors will not give funds on that basis. While donors differ in the degree of specification they require in budgets, it is rare indeed to find one that will give out any significant sum without some budgetary breakdown. This in turn begs the question as to why donors, or for that matter the internal funding processes of the operational agencies themselves, are so reluctant to give out unspecified funds.

While flexibility depends on both the ideology of the organizations involved and the sources of the funds they are dealing with, it must be recognized that donor agencies also have to justify their allocations. It is an unfortunate fact that it is normally easier to justify expenditure on projects with clear goals, targets and fixed programmes of activity. Such projects at least appear to be doing something. Projects with fairly vague goals, targets and even more unclear ways of attaining them are hard to justify, for example, to a donor public which has been impressed with publicity emphasizing the calamitous nature of a situation and the required urgency of a response. In short, all along the line, because of certain understandings as to *what* the problems are, *what* aid is for, and *how* it is to be used, it is usually easier to sell 'hard' activities (for example, so many thousands of trees planted, so many miles of terracing, so many wells) than it is to sell vague talk about participatory processes or an ethnographic style of development.

With a fixed plan of activities and a pre-specified, detailed budget, it is much easier to assess whether or not money is being spent 'correctly'. Indeed, in terms of financial reporting, all that accountants are interested in analysing is the discrepancy between the projected and actual expenditure on the various line items in the budget. In other words, accountants look to see how closely a project has stuck to its pre-determined plan. If expenditure has gone according to plan, this is fine; if, however, there have been changes in expenditure, this variation has to be 'justified'. Changes away from the pre-planned activities (that is, flexibility) have to be explained and, in the case of more bureaucratic agencies and donors, will need to receive prior head-office approval (for instance, for changing expenditure from a training line item to expenditure on research). The corollary of this approach to fiscal management, in terms of assessing project progress and performance, is a concern with the meeting of 'targets'. The degree to which a project meets its pre-planned targets is seen by many agencies as the measure of its effectiveness. The consequences of this are not only that resources can be wasted but also that projects can become so committed to particular lines of action that they are unable to re-orientate activities and re-commit funds without serious loss of local credibility. This will be illustrated in the examples that follow.

We are not saying that this feature of reporting determines that projects become inflexible, but it is one of a number of factors which encourages it. It is a pressure on project managers and can encourage them to adopt a fudging approach to reporting, so that they can retain some degree of flexibility in the field. In practice, budgets can be re-worked, say annually, but these adjustments tend to reflect factors such as inflation of costs, fluctuating exchange rates, logistical problems and so on, rather than reflecting a re-orientation of project activities due to the ethnographic learning process.

A further factor which reinforces programme rigidity is the relationship between implementing agencies and host governments. The latter often insist on a very detailed specification of the agency's activities in their operating agreements, while donors themselves rarely, if ever, agree to provide funds until such agreements are signed.

Because of funding processes, the institutional context and issues of accountability, it is common for development projects to have pre-planned sets of activities that are worked out maybe as far as five years in advance. This implies that development problems and their solutions are already 'known' at the outset. This initial analysis of the situation then becomes enshrined and set in stone within the project document and its budget. 'The system' does not encourage what we regard to be essential for project success: a continual ethnographic learning process which closely involves the beneficiaries.

If one assumes that one has already correctly identified the problems and their solutions, then there is no point engaging in an ongoing learning process. The issue here is not just that poorly received ethnography is reified, but rather that the reification of any ethnography hinders or even prevents subsequent learning. This constitutes a further reason for not using ethnographic 'databases' that have been constructed separately from project implementation.

One area where the enshrining of simple, and perhaps unfounded, ethnography in projects contributes to their momentum is that of staffing. For example, if the initial ethnography a development agency has at its disposal indicates that the project requires an irrigation engineer and an agronomist, it will come as no surprise that five years down the road the community ends up with a small dam and market-gardening project. However, it may later prove to be that the community would have benefited more from the presence of a social forester and para-veterinary trainer.

Another factor (already touched on) which encourages inflexibility in projects is the structure of the implementing agencies in terms of the degree of centralization or de-centralization which they allow in their own decision-making procedures. One might also add as relevant the relationship of these agencies to their donors, and the nature of the donors concerned. For example, we know of one agency where key decisions in terms of budget changes (and hence changes in activities) can, because of the agency's internal structure, take up to eighteen months for the relevant committee to agree! Perhaps the best analogy for this situation is if one considers driving a car where there is a 20 seconds delay between turning the steering wheel and the actual turning of the wheels on the ground. Not only can it be hard for projects to learn the ethnographic lessons, but on top of that, responding to them can be a hopeless problem.

The final area we would like to consider with regard to the momentum of development projects is how the culture of the developers themselves becomes embodied in monitoring and evaluation procedures. Because of the training and the educational background of most people employed by development projects, there is, as mentioned above, a tendency for agencies to rely on survey/ questionnaire methods that are inappropriate for researching dynamic ethnographic decision making. And yet, it is these procedures that we at Band Aid are interested in. Part of the problem here lies in the fact that the concepts of 'monitoring' and 'evaluation' are, by and large, understood as being distinct. When the initial analysis or ethnography of a situation is enshrined in the project document in the form of a work plan, goals, targets and staffing, at what point does a project have the opportunity of updating its ethnography? It is unfortunately true that most of the regular, day-to-day monitoring procedures are concerned with issues related to meeting 'targets'; they do not really address questions as to the impact of project activities on different groups or whether or not the targets are actually worth meeting in the first place. Because of their formal organizational structures, development projects can really only attempt the necessary learning experience during the occasional evaluations – exercises that are by no means to be regarded as a substitute for the process of continual ethnography.

We will now discuss how the ethnographic process that we have in mind can more successfully be incorporated into development programmes.

ETHNOGRAPHY AND DEVELOPMENT PROJECTS: CASE STUDIES

In this part of the chapter we discuss some specific programmes in which the need for integrating an ethnographic understanding has been clearly recognized by project staff. Nevertheless, we want to argue that the ways in which this can be functionally achieved, within a reasonable time frame, are far from clear.

There is a popular idea in the aid world which holds that somehow, by working through local NGOs, it is possible to be several layers closer to the ethnographic reality and consequently, that such programmes are much more sensitive to that reality. In our experience at Band Aid this popular idea is a myth. NGOs have their own agendas and timetables, and these are not necessarily compatible with those of the groups they are trying to help.

The fundamental rationale underlying all development aid is that external funding or assistance can provide help to vulnerable groups and communities. Although this assumption can be challenged, we also believe (as do other contributors to this volume) that until we have really tried to make it work, we should not abandon the effort. Our discussion therefore takes as legitimate the political will to help, and focuses essentially on the methodology and mechanisms by which effective help may be achieved.

The first project we discuss is a soil conservation/re-afforestation programme in Ethiopia, which Band Aid has supported for some time. The agency implementing the programme became involved in the area during the drought of 1984/85, while distributing food aid. As the relief food requirement became less necessary, the organization attempted to transform the relief programme into a development project. Although it is very common for NGOs to become involved in development programmes as a result of initial emergency interventions, this kind of introduction does generate its own problems. For instance, it often becomes difficult for the agency involved to convince people that it is interested in promoting 'grassroots', self-help development initiatives when it has already shown itself to be capable of commanding vast resources and dispensing these free of charge. In this Ethiopian project the organization involved has tried to move from relief distribution to development via a food-for-work programme.

The objective of the project is to increase the productive capacity of the land and to enable the community to become self-sufficient in food production, principally through the rehabilitation of the degraded ecosystem and environment of Alaba *woreda* (an administrative unit). The area is mostly open plain surrounded by sloping hills extending over 68,000 hectares in the Great Rift Valley, and has a population of approximately 115,000. Elders of the area relate that some decades back the *woreda* was heavily forested and the economy heavily pastoral with very minor crop cultivation. Then, about thirty years ago climatic conditions started to change dramatically as a result, it is argued, of massive deforestation. According to the agency the reasons for this deforestation were: population growth, heavy grazing of steeper slopes, and the indiscriminate use of trees for firewood.

Measures to reclaim the heavily eroded and gullied soil have now been instigated by the aid programme. They consist of components such as soil and water conservation, construction of earth bunds, terraces, protection of hillsides through re-seeding and re-planting, re-afforestation through the establishment of community wood lots, alley cropping and the planting of trees around homesteads where tenure is reasonably secure for peasants. In cooperation with the local Ministry of Agriculture, the agency raises tree seedlings in a central nursery and negotiates with Peasant Associations, within a certain radius, to accept a tree planting programme on the Peasant Association land, for ultimate use as a community wood lot. Once the Peasant Association has agreed to offer a site, which is normally a relatively degraded one as there is little or no 'surplus' land in most parts of Ethiopia, the agency organizes a food-for-work programme. It supplies the seedlings, gives technical guidance during tree planting, and engages in discussion with Peasant Association members to determine the subsequent management of the wood lot. The Peasant Association has responsibility for recruiting the labour for the initial planting and will, it is hoped, also take the responsibility required for the ongoing management and care of the new resource. In this project the physical results after only eighteen months were certainly impressive.

The agency in question is highly geared to the meeting-of-targets management style described earlier. During a visit, we were in fact proudly shown various graphs and tables, which demonstrated that the numbers of kilometres of terracing, check dams and trees planted were significantly higher than the original goals set for the period. However, when we tried to discuss such issues as existing grazing practices, management of communal land, the beneficiaries' long-term plans for management of the new resource, and the ways in which benefits would be distributed within the community, village or Peasant Association, the answers to our questions were disappointingly vague. Indeed, in discussion the all-Ethiopian project staff pointed out that they knew little or nothing about the people with whom they were working.

While this ignorance had not constituted a problem during the food-for-work programme, which guaranteed the farmers' 'participation', the lack of understanding was now becoming a fundamental constraint, as the programme moved on to find ways of encouraging beneficiaries to take full responsibility for the management and distribution of the new resources. The project staff were aware of the problem. Clearly, the long-term benefits of the new trees and soil conservation works had not been sufficiently demonstrated, or been recognized by the population, for the latter to be prepared to plant and protect their own trees and community wood lot, or to consider fair systems of resource distribution *without being paid to do so*. With hindsight, the beneficiaries' reluctance to participate in the long-term goals of the project is not really surprising, since their development priorities had never been seriously identified. The area's problem and the solutions imposed had never been (and still were not) the subject of any local discussion or consultation with the beneficiary groups.

But the agency, a Christian one, has suggested that the *ignorance* of the farmers in this area is the primary reason for their lack of interest in the development initiatives advocated by the programme. The presumed ignorance came through in the original proposal the agency submitted:

Alaba is a highly traditional Muslim *woreda*, with customs dating back centuries, and is surrounded by non-Muslim (more 'modernised') communities on all sides (Kembata to south and west, Oromo to the east, and Gurage/Silti to the north). Before the revolution, any attempts at development were resisted, sabotaged, or outright destroyed by the communities' religious leaders (*sheikhs*). Only after the revolution have the MOA [Ministry of Agriculture] and other government agencies succeeded in organising peasants and effecting basic campaigns (e.g. literacy). The long-lasting effects of this age-old bias against education, enlightenment, and wider exposure will continue. To a very real extent, this is why Alaba required extensive relief during 1985 (they had developed fewer means to combat drought), and this is why development involvement is an ongoing requirement. . . .

The *sheikh*, as the traditional head man of the Muslims, enjoys significant economic and social advantages closely resembling former feudal patterns. His strategy in maintaining his lucrative position is to keep his people uneducated, ignorant, uninformed. . . .

The local government authorities have greater power and influence over the peasantry (and access to the peasantry) than does the *sheikh* and view the *sheikh* (quite properly) as a reactionary anti-modernizing influence. [They] would oppose any open relationship and involvement with him, and would again obstruct our work if we were viewed as supportive of the *sheikh*. . . .

The *sheikh* appears a highly exploitative self-interested person, willing to use his traditional position to coerce people for his economic advantage, and any strategy that enhances his ability to maintain such a position would be an oppressive one.

In part as a result of ongoing dialogue with Band Aid, the agency has now begun to recognize that its immediate analysis, quoted above, which is shared by local government in the area, is inadequate, and that if the project is to be beneficial and sustainable, it will need to arrive at a rigorous and sympathetic understanding of local power structures, land-use systems and perceptions of environmental degradation. (We will return to this later.)

The second project, also in Ethiopia, concentrates in the Gamu Goffa and Sidamo regions. These areas, both potentially productive, have not been self-sufficient in food production recently and have several pocket areas prone to and affected by drought. The objectives of the programme are to raise the farmers' capacity for food production, reduce their vulnerability to drought, improve the living conditions of families and strengthen the organizational and managerial capacity for self-reliance.

The programme essentially aims to provide a means whereby NGO assistance can be channelled to farmers through existing farmers' organizations, Service Cooperatives (SC) and Peasant Associations (PA), and works with and through Ministry of Agriculture (MOA) personnel at all levels. An important element of the programme is the emphasis given to training and support of MOA staff to enable them to respond effectively to farmers' needs and priorities.

To date nine Service Cooperatives have been identified by local MOA personnel as needing the type of support the programme can provide, and both MOA personnel and the SC/PA leadership have been assisted in formulating three-year proposals which are now being implemented. Inputs required vary in type, quantity and in terms of provision of each site – depending on the individual SC location, specification of need and management capacity. Project benefits include material and technical support for food production, environmental rehabilitation and conservation, and training for both government (MOA) staff and farmers' representatives.

Farmers, in discussion with MOA staff, are expected to identify their own problems and to suggest ways in which their needs can be met. The project then responds in trying to meet these needs through the provision of credits for oxen, seeds, tools and other primarily short-term rehabilitation inputs.

This particular programme has been the subject of a recent external evaluation, which arrived at the following conclusions:

The farmers attach less importance to and are less enthusiastic about longer-term activities than the short-term rehabilitation inputs. . . . Of course planning longer-term development is a much more complex matter than responding to immediate needs. The complexity can be exemplified in the whole question of credit for oxen. There is a desperate need for oxen in these drought-prone regions. Many animals died or were sold to provide cash for food during the recent drought, and their importance in helping farmers to prepare the ground for planting is such that obtaining replacements has become an obsession. Farmers, however, tend to underrate the degree to which oxen purchased on credit must be fully productive if the transaction is to be economic for them; and project staff tend to consider the economics only in terms of the additional crops that can be grown. Little attention has been paid to using oxen for other tasks when they are not required for cultivation. Neither has proper consideration been given to exploiting the increasing value of a young animal. A number of farmers have in fact been purchasing a young ox on credit and then selling it a year later when it has increased in value. The money obtained has then sometimes been used to purchase two young animals. This practice, not specifically encouraged by the project staff or the Service Cooperative, is [nevertheless] good business practice. This and other ways of maximising returns from investment in draught animals should be studied and propagated by the programme.

The conclusions of the evaluation report were discussed in detail, and with passion, at a workshop attended by farmers, SC leaders, the MOA, extension workers and donors.

It was agreed that the revolving fund for oxen credit had run into many problems. Donors were concerned to see specific funds go to the most disadvantaged within the communities, whereas the SC leaders (the managers of the funds) had a tendency to select their most credit-worthy clients. In fact, severe problems had arisen regarding repayment of loans, due to several factors. The major cause had been the death of many oxen, perhaps occasionally due to negligence but more often to disease and a lack of veterinary drugs.

The credit programme included an insurance scheme whereby each recipient paid a yearly premium of 5 Birr to constitute a fund for replacing animals lost due to normal causes. The high mortality rate in some SCs because of epidemics, however, has totally surpassed the capacity of the meagre insurance scheme to provide replacements. The tendency has been to erode the loan repayments fund in order to replace lost animals, thus jeopardizing the working of the revolving fund. Another reason for the low level of repayment has been the poor harvests in some areas. The credit scheme can function only if a marketable surplus is produced and the repayment schedule is based on realistic calculations of how much farmers will be able to produce beyond their families' subsistence needs. Ways in which oxen can generate funds (such as fattening and sale) must also be taken into account.

As stated above, during the workshop the oxen credit and insurance scheme had been the subject of hot debate. For example, the case was cited of one angry SC member proposing to the PA leadership that insurance should be paid only by those people whose animal died! Also, some SCs had had the experience of being in debt to their membership because of the high loss of oxen, since they had promised insurance payments from a fund which had been exhausted for some time and was unlikely to be replenished under the current conditions. After much discussion, it was concluded that a formal study was needed to produce an analysis and understanding of traditional insurance mechanisms, which certainly existed but about which the project staff were totally ignorant. Moreover, as the farmers themselves pointed out, different systems existed in different areas and important lessons could be learnt from knowing what happened elsewhere. In fact, the occasion of the workshop itself had provided the first opportunity for all farmers involved in the programme to meet one another, and they unanimously agreed that it had been a productive exercise.

From the farmers' point of view, the credit programme was one of the most significant aspects of the project. However, the fund had been limited to credit for the purchase of draught oxen, and this limitation was challenged by the various SC leaders. Some of the SCs, for example, were semi-pastoral, and credit for oxen was not a high priority. In these cases it was felt that credit should be made available for purchasing general livestock. Women also argued that they should have access to small loans to promote a variety of small business initiatives. The farmers' representatives felt that the actual operation of both the credit scheme itself and appropriate measures to insure borrowers should be left to the discretion of individual SCs, which could be relied upon to design and implement workable systems relevant to the local conditions. But the farmers' views differed from those held by the project holders and donors. The latter, although receptive to the farmers' arguments, were keen to develop a model which would be relevant for all sub-projects in the many different areas, and which would thus satisfy the donors' requirement for accountability. Interestingly, the leaders of the SCs acknowledged the need for accountability, but they were not convinced that an externally commissioned 'study' would be the most appropriate means by which this could be achieved; a scepticism we share, as will be seen later on.

The final project we want to consider is in Kordofan, Western Sudan, where ways need to be found to assist in the rehabilitation of pastoral groups severely affected during the drought years of 1984/85. During those years substantial numbers of animals had died or been sold at very low prices in return for grain. While herd losses seem to have forced many Kawahla pastoralists to become sedentary, others who were left with viable numbers of livestock preferred to migrate (farther south than usual) with the better rainfall in 1987/88. The latter have started to build up livestock numbers again, and have retained the traditional mobile pastoral system, which involves the movement of the camel, goat and sheep components of the herds. The interaction between newly sedentarized groups and those who were able to remain mobile is far from clear.

Traditional pastoral leaders (*sheikhs*) are categorically opposed to settlements, and to local irrigation schemes in particular, since these schemes encourage an influx of settlers from outside; settlers who allegedly destroy or appropriate for themselves the grazing resources of the pastoralists. At the same time, it appears that the pastoralists are dependent on these sedentary groups for certain goods and services; for example, to obtain labour for herding at different times of the year and/or bad years when certain animals have to travel far to find adequate pasturage.

Within the government there is still to be found an attitude, partially informed by political considerations, which discredits the nomadic pastoral system as both unproductive and destructive of the region's ecology (see also Seddon, in this volume). The view propounds that settlement, based on crop farming and local irrigation schemes along the *wadis*, is a remedy and the pathway to development.

Central government has tried to reduce the authority and influence of local *sheikhs* by setting up district and rural councils. But, although government administration is processed through these councils, even government officials agree that the traditional organizational structure is still strongly in place and that the councils themselves rely on the *sheikhs* and other traditional authorities at each level. In theory, all land belongs to the government and all decisions about land use are administered through the rural councils. In reality, though, it is through the local *sheikhs* that decisions about livestock movements and pasture allocations are made, and through them that disputes are settled. They also appear to have retained their influence amongst those groups who have been sedentarized.

The particular agency involved in this project is working with pastoral groups in other areas of the Sudan and the Sahel, and is committed to challenging the conventional view of pastoralism as an unproductive, ecologically destructive system. As such the project makes conscious efforts to work closely with local pastoral leaders and has already committed itself, in the initial stages, to a 'restocking' programme which involves the provision of a number of animals to families who had lost their animals during the drought of 1984/85.

Beneficiaries were identified in partnership with the local *sheikhs*. Essentially the agency was concerned to reach the poorest groups, and it does seem that those who received animals were those who were truly destitute. However, it has now also become clear that while such gifts may help to meet the immediate short-term economic needs of destitute pastoral families, the strategy is insufficient to bring about their effective reintegration within the wider (and extremely complex) pastoral economy. Initially, using information gathered during the re-stocking exercise, the programme implementors had hoped to develop an understanding of some of the processes leading to destitution, on the basis of which they hoped to develop appropriate interventions to retard and reverse these processes at a local level. (Most NGOs claim to be able to intervene only at a local level, although the objective is often to find appropriate kinds of intervention that have the potential for wider application and impact.) Unfortunately, in this case, the Sudanese project manager had tackled the research without any real direction or assistance. He had spent many long hours designing and filling in a questionnaire, painstakingly recording information, the validity and usefulness of which would have been challenged by any first-year student of anthropology, even when fresh from school. The questionnaire recorded information retrieved from pastoral families on a one-to-one basis; direct questions covered such issues as numbers of animals of different kinds owned, numbers lost in the drought, the income-generating activities different family members engage in, and so on. Each time the questionnaire had been administered, people's answers had been taken at face value by those collecting 'the data'.

Not surprisingly, there was a striking uniformity in the pastoralists' responses; a uniformity which raised more questions than answers. During our visit it became quite clear that the project manager had been unaware of the extreme sensitivity of the direct questions he was asking, nor was he aware that the responses were extremely difficult, in fact almost impossible, to accept. The crux of the matter is that *with minimal training*, this enthusiastic and committed project manager could have produced useful information on a range of project-relevant issues: livestock marketing, seasonal movements, gender, relations with non-pastoral communities, and so on. Had this information been collected, it could have helped inform the direction of meaningful activities in the near future.

Since then, it has been decided to abandon 're-stocking' in its present form and to develop a para-veterinary programme within the project area. This initiative has been warmly welcomed by the pastoral groups involved. This year's activities, however, are essentially geared to maintaining the agency's credibility and to monitoring the health of recently donated animals, in preparation for more relevant interventions in the future. Last year an important opportunity to learn more about these particular pastoralists was missed, while the conventional wisdom on the effects of pastoralism on the regional ecology (and in the national economy) was allowed to remain unchallenged. This time round the project manager should be better equipped to gather useful data.

THE ANTHROPOLOGIST IN DEVELOPMENT

In all these cases there has emerged a clear appreciation by the implementing agency or organization that:

1 simple delivery of resources (credit/trees/technical assistance) alone is not enough;
2 existing ethnography is inadequate, and a revised ethnographic understanding of the beneficiary population is critical if additional resources are to have any chance of producing sustainable benefits to vulnerable individuals and groups;
3 current staffing structures and methodological skills are inadequate to develop this kind of understanding.

As a resolution to these problems it has been proposed at one time or another that an anthropologist be brought into the programme to conduct 'studies' . . . The anthropologist as contemporary magician in the development world! . . . Can it really be that easy?

Let us look for a moment at what *mostly* happens when the 'professional' anthropologist arrives on the scene to get at the 'real situation' through short-term consultancy fieldwork. First, there is the tendency to work in isolation. Just as the forester gets on with the forestry, the water expert with the water, the administrator with the administration, so does the anthropologist get on with the anthropology. Consultations across the disciplines represented on the project are minimal. Secondly, the anthropologist's report to head office – written invariably in the language of head office – constitutes a kind of additional ethnography; that is, an ethnography different from the participants' own ethnographic understanding. As a result, the local project staff will be faced with two ethnographies: that of the anthropologist, and that of the communities with which they are in daily contact. Moreover, and this is our major criticism, whereas the viewpoint of the anthropologist may be integrated within the agency's overall decision-making process, it is extremely unlikely that any *anthropological understanding* will filter through to become *integrated into the day-to-day running of the projects themselves* – yet, this is where anthropological insights are most needed.

Although our verdict may be unfair to some consultant anthropologists, as is clear from several experiences recalled in this book, it is also our experience that the recruitment of an 'imported' anthropologist can be unnecessarily cumbersome, expensive, and in the end a probably ineffective way of going about retrieving basic ethnographic information. Even if that information is retrieved to satisfy head office, we still need to face the challenge that the information must be integrated into the programme in a manner which makes sense to the project participants. A possible analogy may be that of building a bridge. If your job in life were to build bridges, you would not be content just to send out a lorry with the necessary materials and expect a bridge to exist a year later. Within this analysis the role of the anthropologist can be likened to that of the structural engineer who, having been dispatched by the bridge builder, comes back and reports that the bridge is not built because there is nobody there to build it. The lorry driver could have provided that information a year earlier if he had been asked to check! In short, ethnographic information can be acquired on a day-to-day basis, starting from day one, and it is neither essential nor necessarily desirable that this should be done by professional anthropologists on short-term consultancies.

CONCLUSIONS

Development projects are about delivering resources, not about anthropological analysis; they have to deliver resources to exist. Although some agencies and organizations conduct initial 'feasibility' studies with the help of anthropologists, the ultimate goal remains the delivery of resources. Hence, most staff on a development programme are recruited on the basis of relevant technical expertise, related to one resource or another (health care, agriculture, forestry, veterinary care and so on). Anthropologists, when they are employed in ongoing development programmes, are most usually expatriates, and rarely do they participate directly in the delivery system. Rather, they are observers of the delivery process and, as observers, acquire their own particular understanding of what goes on. Because of their unique interests, anthropologists tend to be distinct from anyone else involved in the delivery.

Yet, even though development programmes are by nature delivery systems, they must surely develop the structural capacity to answer questions such as: are the 'right' resources delivered? Are they relevant to the situation? Do they have any long-term value? Do the intended beneficiaries (vulnerable groups) have access to them? Have they helped these groups to become less vulnerable? What else can be done?

In our experience most programmes are only able to answer the question 'Did we deliver?' so they must leave the answering of all other questions to external consultancies and/or evaluations. The information is then exported and discussed out of the area, with new 'solutions' being arrived at many miles from the programme, often in a totally different country.

But how can project staff begin to ask some of these vital questions themselves on a day-to-day basis? This is the ultimate question. At Band Aid we believe that this training component of a programme is as important as the delivery system itself: one concern makes little sense without the other. Functional mechanisms for encouraging feedback and genuine participation by beneficiaries (and non-beneficiaries!) must be developed beyond the level of mere rhetoric – for example, the rhetoric used in occasional meetings with village leaders. Special training for all categories of project staff, time and money for the regular sharing of information, and institutional space for continual ethnographic discourse within a programme should become legitimate aspects of every project. This is the area where anthropologists can make a really important contribution. They should focus on helping project staff and beneficiaries develop their own appropriate ethnographic understanding rather than 'doing it for them'. In the three examples discussed above, there were competent and committed local staff who could have made very constructive and immediate use of the kinds of training and orientation that any anthropologist could have provided in a short space of time.

It is not difficult to conclude from the issues we have raised that a fundamental constraint on development projects is the 'projectization' of development. Most of the problems we have described would not be relevant if we were engaged in supporting and facilitating certain ongoing 'processes' rather than 'projects', and if development agencies honestly accepted the proposition that vulnerable groups are capable of designing and managing their own development, given the necessary resources. The rhetoric of most agencies would have us believe that the participative approach is fundamental to NGO practice. As we have shown above, we have reasons to believe that this is the exception rather than the rule.

In Burkina Faso, Band Aid has now allocated limited funds to local committees to identify and finance development projects independently. This project fund *is* the project. Because of the decision to limit the level of funding to £1,000 per organization, most Western-style agencies operating in Burkina Faso are uninterested in submitting proposals, so the bulk of the applications are for very modest village-group initiatives. Already, the Band Aid advisory committee has allocated funds for a workshop during which the different groups will meet together and discuss their own programmes, compare problems and identify their own needs for technical assistance. No 'solutions' or 'objectives' have been designed *for* these groups, since the beneficiaries themselves are responsible for proposing their programmes and for attempting to find solutions. The artificial distinction between project staff and beneficiaries has disappeared as a result, and technicians are working directly for the community rather than for an external 'employer'. It is still too early to say whether this new experiment will prove significant in development terms, as certainly the issue of targeting the poorest and most vulnerable remains unaddressed, but it does promise to become an alternative to the 'resource delivery' mode of development and its many associated difficulties.

4 Anthropology and appraisal
The preparation of two IFAD pastoral development projects in Niger and Mali

David Seddon

THE ANTHROPOLOGICAL APPROACH AND DEVELOPMENT PROJECTS

All too often development projects designed and implemented by international aid agencies lack that crucial appreciation and under-standing of the dynamics of local economy and society that derives from what I call 'the anthropological approach'. Such an approach involves a detailed analysis of the complexities of local-level struc-tures and their operation, based on an adequate body of empirical material collected with due consideration for these complexities. It involves a recognition that economic or sociological models cannot simply be translated from one context to another and applied without local research if they are not to do considerable damage to local processes; although it also accepts that lessons can be learned by comparing between different social situations. One of the reasons that the anthropological approach is rarely adopted in the prepara-tion of development projects is the short-time period normally devoted to the identification, formulation and appraisal that together constitute the preparation phase of a project. Usually missions to undertake these elements of project preparation are in the field for weeks rather than months, and the kind of time period 'normally' devoted to anthropological study for academic research purposes – as much as a year or eighteen months – is deemed impossible. Another reason is that it is comparatively rare to find the personnel responsible for project preparation predisposed to adopting the anthropological approach by virtue of their professional training or inclination. Usually the mission personnel are 'specialists' whose focus is less on the complexity of the local social context than on specific and often narrowly defined economic or technical matters. It is even rarer to find development projects prepared and implemented by international agencies which adopt a participative approach; that is, one in which the local population is involved from the outset in a collaborative fashion in the conception and design, preparation and implementation of the project.

Many development projects, however, run into opposition, either overt or covert, from the local populations to be affected by intervening outside agencies. In addition, projects run into difficulties (all too often put down to some 'perversity' or 'inadequacy' or 'irrationality' inherent in local social and economic structures), because they fail to consider in sufficient detail the complexities of local social dynamics and fail to appreciate their significance for the design and implementation of a successful project. Although the anthropological approach and the participative approach do not of themselves guarantee a successful project, they nevertheless ensure a greater chance of success and effectiveness.

Although it is rare to find examples of the adoption of anthropological and participative approaches among the major international agencies, they *can* be found, and can be used to demonstrate what is possible if the right combination of preconditions is established. The crucial precondition is an agency broadly sympathetic to such approaches, prepared to recruit personnel to undertake missions in which such approaches are adopted, and ultimately willing to fund projects based on such approaches. Many non-governmental organizations (NGOs) have, over the past decade or so, acquired a reputation for being broadly sympathetic to the anthropological and the participative approaches to project preparation and implementation, but few NGOs can be regarded as major agencies either in terms of the size and scope of their projects or in terms of the funding provided. Broadly, the national aid agencies of the Scandinavian countries have shown a more positive attitude towards what might be characterized as grassroots approaches, and the same could be claimed for Canadian aid programmes, but I am not myself familiar with the detail of their activities and projects. One major international aid agency, however, with which I do have some familiarity, has over the last decade progressively developed a commitment to designing and implementing grassroots, 'user-friendly' projects, involving and benefiting particular disadvantaged groups of the rural poor, and has made its commitment increasingly clear both in its public statements and documentation and in the way its projects are designed. This is the International Fund for Agricultural Development (IFAD), based in Rome and established in 1976 as a 'fund for the rural poor' (IFAD 1984) with a mandate to explore new ways of mobilizing the poor, enlisting their participation and activating their productive potential.

During 1987 and 1988 I was involved as a consultant to IFADs Africa Division on missions to the Niger Republic and to Mali in connection with the preparation of projects for pastoral rehabilitation and development in the aftermath of the drought of 1984–85. Both the Niger and the Mali projects were conceived as a result of international concern regarding the situation of former pastoralists in the region, made destitute or near destitute by the loss of their herds and flocks and forced to migrate or to seek refuge, often across international frontiers (UNDRO 1987). The present chapter will provide, on the basis of first-hand experience, an account of the preparation of two projects involving an emphasis on both the anthropological approach and the participative approach. I hope that this may encourage *more optimism* regarding the potential for the application of these approaches – which I regard as essential for the effectiveness and sustainability of development projects – and for the involvement of those with training in social anthropology in the preparation of development projects initiated by major aid agencies. I also hope that the positive commitment of IFAD will encourage other donor agencies, particularly those with whom it co-finances projects, to reconsider their approach to development and development assistance. IFAD is explicitly committed to trying to influence the policies of other lending agencies and development institutions, through programmes of collaboration and co-financing that favour the rural poor. It should perhaps be added that involvement in essentially innovative approaches to project preparation *is* exciting, and that, if I seem excessively positive, the influence of this experience should be taken into consideration.

The projects whose preparation phases are discussed here are now being implemented, and are, as might be expected, encountering a variety of problems and successes, both anticipated and unanticipated. My more recent experience of project identification and preparation with IFAD and other agencies has underlined just how innovative was the combination of factors associated with the preparation of the Niger and Mali pastoral development projects.

THE INTERNATIONAL FUND FOR AGRICULTURAL DEVELOPMENT

IFAD was established in the aftermath of the UN World Food Conference in Rome in 1974. The Conference concentrated on the continuing problems of food and nutritional deprivation throughout the Third World, and particularly in sub-Saharan Africa, and recognized that these were not simply a result of failures in food production (that is, technical problems) but were the consequence of economic and social underdevelopment manifesting itself in chronic and acute poverty and deprivation. IFAD was established as an agency of the United Nations in 1976, and started operations in 1977. It has a special mandate to serve the rural poor and to encourage and promote improved food production to increase nutritional status and farm incomes among the rural poor.

IFAD is supported by contributions from developed countries, oil-producing developing countries and other developing countries. Despite the fact that contributions from these three categories of member countries are not equal, in the IFAD general governing bodies each category of member country has equal voting rights. This gives the developing member states two-thirds of total voting power. In practice, however, resort to voting has not taken place because there is a strong desire to reach consensus. In this IFAD differs significantly from, for example, the World Bank or the International Monetary Fund, although it is also essentially a bank, lending to developing countries. Loans from IFAD, however, are often at highly concessional rates. Its articles of agreement speak of its concern to collaborate wherever possible in the fight against poverty and hunger through the preparation and implementation of *appropriate investment projects* in developing countries.

The clearest recent statement of IFAD's orientation and approach is the annual report for 1988 (IFAD 1989). In his foreword to the report, the president of IFAD, Idriss Jazairy, suggests that over the last decade IFAD has played the role of catalyst in the effort to tackle poverty alleviation from the grassroots upwards, and remarks that the Fund's concern to analyse the determinants of rural poverty has inevitably led it to sharpen its participative approach. One of the reasons for this is the recognition that people's participation in projects effectively reduces the cost involved and helps make project activities sustainable. Thus

it is people's participation which provides the internal dynamic essential to the success of rural development and makes the pilot efforts of the Fund self-generating and in consequence highly replicable. For the smallholders, the landless, the nomads, agro-pastoralists, poor rural women and fishermen who constitute IFAD's main beneficiary groups, active involvement in the design, preparation, implementation and evaluation of projects has become the predominant factor in the alleviation of their poverty and in their attainment of a more productive life.

(IFAD 1989: 7)

The other reason is that

to IFAD, beneficiary participation is not only an instrument of development, it is also a development goal in itself. Along with the improvement in their material well-being, poor people are able to afford themselves a mechanism for democratic self-expression. This is why IFAD seeks to promote participation through grassroots-based democratic institutions.

(IFAD 1989: 8)

Much of what is called 'participative development' has its origins in the grassroots activities of NGOs working with the very poor. IFAD has sought not only to learn from this experience but to join forces with NGOs in overcoming obstacles to self-reliant grassroots development. In 1988, IFAD established the IFAD/NGO Extended Cooperation Programme (ECP), and already several projects have been initiated under this programme. The ECP is designed to support the kind of innovative pilot activities in which NGOs excel and which can provide a source of replication and investment for IFAD and other donors.

IFAD is, of course, a bank, and as such is concerned with the capacity of the projects, and the populations involved in the projects, to fulfil certain financial and economic criteria. IFAD projects have to be cost effective, although ultimately it is to national governments that loans are made and it is national governments, not local populations, that are obliged to repay the loans. It is often argued that there must be a trade-off between promoting the welfare of the poor and ensuring an economic pay-off or 'acceptable rate of return'. In many projects, including the projects established by IFAD, there is tension and even conflict between these two objectives; but there is no inherent and unavoidable contradiction between them. In IFAD's perspective and approach, the rural poor are not simply the rural poor; they are the producers who have the knowledge and experience of local conditions that most outsiders rarely acquire; and they are generally extremely efficient in their allocations of resources. An investment in the poor is an investment in potentially the most effective and efficient section of the population. What the poor do lack is access to and control over resources and the capacity to emancipate themselves from the physical and social constraints which impede their efforts at self-help. IFAD believes that 'banking on the rural poor' (IFAD 1987a) is a viable development strategy, which will help the poor to help themselves and actually repay their investment.

With respect to pastoral development in particular, a recent preliminary review of IFAD's involvement in livestock production and pastoral development (Seddon, Appendix in IFAD 1988a) suggested that the Fund's approach has changed over the last decade, from a more technical 'top-down' form of intervention designed essentially to improve livestock productivity to one more concerned with the encouragement of herders' associations to undertake their own economic development and environmental management, and hence with pastoral development in a broader, sociological as well as economic sense. The president, in his foreword to the 1988 annual report, acknowledges that 'IFAD's projects aimed at small herders and their livestock have similarly evolved under the impact of the participatory mode', noting, for example, that 'feedback has shown that women's groups in particular need assistance for small animal production – such as goats and sheep which they can easily manage – so that the Fund has begun investing more in research on small animals and its application in project components for poor rural women' (IFAD 1989: 10). The fact remains, however, that livestock projects have been given a low priority until relatively recently and have accounted for only a small proportion of IFAD's funding over the years. Between 1978 and 1983, out of a total of 111 projects funded, only 7 were in livestock development; between 1983 and 1987, only 8 out of 109 went to livestock projects; and the total for the period 1978 to 1987 was 15 (5.9 per cent of all projects), compared with, for example, 60 in agricultural development, 23 in irrigation and 59 in general rural development (IFAD 1988a: 109).

The annual report for 1985 draws attention to the problems livestock development projects in Africa and the Near East have had to face, and suggests that 'livestock projects have encountered implementation difficulties *due to an inadequate assessment, at the project design stage, of the socio-economic situation of pastoralists*' (IFAD 1986: 62; my emphasis). The two areas identified as posing particular problems were (1) difficulty in carrying out de-stocking policies to limit livestock numbers to the carrying capacity of the pastures, and (2) introducing small livestock keepers, habitually used to raising cattle for meat, to milk production and the associated collection and processing activities. However, both forms of intervention made basic assumptions regarding the dynamics of the pastoral economy and society which were ill-founded. There are indications that the difficulties encountered were still regarded within IFAD as being in some sense 'the fault of the locals' (for example, 'It has been found that these groups of people are unable to make necessary changes . . . in their traditional pastoral habits and life-styles' – IFAD 1986: 62), although it was gradually being recognized that 'a better implementation of livestock projects *requires careful project design based on an in-depth understanding of the socio-economic situation of pastoralists*' (IFAD 1986: 62; my emphasis).

Taking care to analyse local social and economic structures is not a luxury, nor even something that can be justified only on 'moral' or 'welfare' grounds; project effectiveness can be significantly enhanced by so doing. It was reported in 1986 that, in some of the projects, measures taken to tackle these problems had considerably improved implementation performance: 'in one project in Africa, arrangement for distribution of drugs and running of community pharmacies *improved considerably when responsibility for these activities was entrusted directly to the beneficiaries themselves through the herders' association*' (IFAD 1986: 62; my emphasis). IFAD's 1988 annual report on 'Livestock and pasture management' recognized explicitly that

> over the last four years there has been a significant shift in the way IFAD has approached the livestock sector. In addition to support-ing livestock as an exclusive activity, attention has been paid to assisting the whole agro-pastoralist sector on which large numbers of the rural poor depend for their subsistence. In this context, IFAD's approach has evolved from seeking to increase the pro-ductivity of livestock raising as such to a broader integrated strategy. This encompasses the carrying capacity of the pastoral land, while ensuring at the same time proper management of resources.
>
> (IFAD 1989: 77)

Given the approval for several pastoral development projects in 1987 and 1988 (including the Niger and Mali projects), the report added, significantly, that 'IFAD's most recent projects have seen a further evolution in this approach' (IFAD 1989: 77).

The particular problems of Sahelian Africa have been well recognized by IFAD; in 1986 it established a Special Programme for Sub-Saharan African Countries Affected by Drought and Desertifica-tion (SPA) designed to assist recovery from the major drought of

1983–85. The SPA involved both short-term and medium-to-long-term measures aimed at sustained growth in food production and rehabilitation of the resource base of IFAD's beneficiary groups – identified as 'the smallholders, the landless, the nomads, agro-pastoralists, poor rural women and fishermen' (IFAD 1989: 7). Short-term interventions are planned to rehabilitate the production capacity of the rural poor and, where appropriate, to complement ongoing 'structural adjustment' programmes with measures designed to protect the rural poor against the adverse effects of budgetary cuts affecting rural support services and to maintain or reinforce and extend, in particular, credit provision and/or the flow of input supplies (see Seddon 1990, on IFAD and 'structural adjustment'). Long-term interventions focus on environmental and institutional components. Soil and water conservation; small-scale irrigation schemes; agro-forestry; improved land, pasture and livestock man-agement; applied research and extension are the major elements included in efforts to rehabilitate and enhance the production base of smallholder and pastoral production. These efforts have been complemented by the strengthening of local institutions and the promotion of producers' groups and the informal sector (IFAD 1989: 24). Three Special Programme projects – in Mauritania, Niger and Mali – have included components specifically designed to address the problems confronting pastoral populations and to take into consider-ation the lessons learned about the 'problems' of pastoral develop-ment over the past ten years. It is on two of these three that I shall concentrate.

APPRAISAL AND PROJECT PREPARATION

In the IFAD project cycle, there is a formal sequence, from identi-fication to formulation, to appraisal and then to implementation. During implementation, monitoring and evaluation (M&E) also takes place. Often, however, specific project identification is pre-ceded by a general identification, usually although not always made during a Special Programming Mission (SPM) to the country con-cerned. The SPM is designed to provide up-to-date information on the general situation within the country and to identify, in a general manner, a range of possible projects for subsequent specific identi-fication. Appraisal comes before implementation and is an essential part of the preparation of projects. Initial identification is followed by detailed formulation, conception by design; appraisal involves a careful assessment of the project as specified by the formulation mission and a consideration of both the design of the project and the costs provided in order to appraise its viability and likely effectiveness. At all stages, the mission findings and their reports are subject to comment by IFAD staff, whether informally or formally through a Technical Review Committee (TRC). The project, once prepared and appraised, has subsequently to pass through a Policy and Project Review Committee (PPRC) chaired by the president or his representative.

This chapter is as much about the anthropology of appraisal as about the relationship between anthropology and appraisal, and examines both with respect to two pastoral development projects, in Niger and Mali respectively, which have now been approved and funded by IFAD.

A crucial determinant of the way in which a development project is prepared is the personal and professional orientation of the personnel involved in its conception and design. In IFAD, each project is the responsibility of a specific project controller within a regional division (for example, Africa or Asia) who may have one or more countries under his or her jurisdiction and several projects. Both Special Programming Missions (SPM) and general identification missions may establish a range of possible projects for IFAD consideration, but the views of the project controller are important in the identification and conception of a project, in part because he or she is usually involved from the outset and is familiar with the country concerned (and government policy and practice) and so with the factors likely to affect project viability. Also, the project controller has a considerable say in determining the recruitment of consultants for the various stages in project preparation. The subject specialisms of the consultants selected and their personal and professional outlook will affect the way in which the team or mission as a whole approaches its task.

Often the initial choice of the team or mission leader – the individual responsible for leading the mission in the field and for producing its final report – is critical, since the terms of reference (TOR) of a team leader may establish the framework within which he or she works and the mission as a whole operates. The mission leader's orientation and inclination can have a substantial impact on the way in which the mission approaches its task and on the character and recommendations of its report. Project controllers share, more or less, the general orientation and commitment of IFAD; their selection of the team leader will be the result of many variables, including an estimation by the project controller, the division director and others concerned.

In many international agencies and even in NGOs (although to a lesser extent), team leaders tend to be technicians (engineers or agronomists) or economists, partly perhaps because the dominant conception of development projects is still often that of infrastructural, strictly agricultural or economic development. Even in IFAD, this tends to be the case; economists predominate, and it is rare for other social scientists to be selected as team leaders, although the participation of social anthropologists and rural sociologists is becoming more common (usually under the broad label of 'socio-economist'). In the case of both the Niger and Mali projects, the team leader of the identification, formulation and appraisal missions – who was in fact the overall team leader for both projects – was an individual with a doctorate in social anthropology and with a great deal of experience, gained during extensive fieldwork and through involvement over several years in pastoral development (see Swift, various publications). Swift was selected as a consultant for the preparation of these two projects precisely because he was familiar with the local economy and society of the regions within which projects were being considered, and also because he had been involved in the international agency discussions concerning the post-drought refugee problem in the Mali–Niger–Algeria area (UNDRO 1987). He had, I believe, considerable latitude in the selection of other team members, and in the process of selection was clearly at pains to put together teams which included other individuals sharing his own broad approach to development in general and to pastoral development in particular.

It was important to select team members according to the specific characteristics and needs of the local economy within which the projects were to be introduced. Given the importance for the Fund of cost effectiveness and the general concern to devise projects which stand up to rigorous appraisal in economic and financial terms, the involvement of a financial analyst was necessary for the preparation of both projects. In the case of Niger, because of the importance (known to the team leader) of animal disease as a major constraint on production, a veterinary expert was included, while for Mali it was estimated that such expertise was not crucial. For Mali, where the potential for the rehabilitation of oases was thought to be considerable, an expert on palm trees was included; in the case of Niger, where previous government policy had envisaged the resettlement of destitute herders around permanent water sources to cultivate out-of-season crops, it was regarded as desirable to include someone with the skills of an agricultural economist. Both projects also required

broader economic expertise to consider not only production potentials but also alternative economic activities for those unable or
unwilling to maintain a pastoral existence, including participation in
dynamic regional markets.

Significantly, preparatory missions for both projects also included
an unusual number of individuals with a broadly anthropological
background, fieldwork experience, and familiarity with pastoral
societies and pastoral development. Some were expatriates with
extensive experience of fieldwork in the regions concerned (for
example, Angelo Maliki, who has a doctorate in social anthropology
and extensive field experience in Niger, Mali and Chad – see Maliki
Bonfiglioli 1981, 1984, 1988a, 1988b); some had considerable relevant anthropological and rural development experience elsewhere
and at least a familiarity with pastoral economies and societies (like
myself, see Seddon 1981, especially chap. 3); some were Nigerien
and Malian nationals with equally appropriate qualifications. The
latter included natives of the regions within which the projects were
to be located. The selection of national social scientists with good
local knowledge and contacts as members of the various preparation
missions was a crucial feature of both the Niger and the Mali projects,
and was agreed by IFAD at an early stage without argument.

The teams, therefore, were selected with a general concern for
the anthropological approach and were predisposed to adopt that
approach despite the presence within the teams of 'specialists' whose
personal and professional orientation might not otherwise have
encouraged them to work within such a framework. In the case of
both projects, not only the team leader but several other members
were explicitly committed to 'the participative approach'. Having
worked with herders' groups within the proposed project areas in
the past (and being familiar with other work on local herders' associations; for example, Aronson 1985; EUROACTION-ACORD 1987,
1988; Garba *et al*. 1984; Marty 1985; Thébaud *et al*. 1983; White
1984a, 1984b), and having demonstrated their commitment to promoting herders' associations as a key to successful local participation
in projects, several members on both teams were able to encourage
the initial conception and design of the projects on the basis of a participative approach (see Swift 1984; Swift and Maliki 1984a, 1984b).
In so far as these individuals were familiar with the complexities and
specific features of local economy and society, and in so far as one
of them was also overall team leader, they exerted a strong influence
on the orientation and terms of reference (TOR) of the preparation
missions and thus on the design of the projects.

Another significant feature in the preparation of both projects was the high degree of continuity and indeed overlap between the formally distinct preparation stages of the project cycle: identification, formulation and appraisal. Not only was there a considerable continuity of personnel through all three phases, but in the Niger project the formulation and appraisal phases were also run together during a single mission. This meant that, instead of the usual disjunctures between the three key phases of preparation, a cumulative development of fundamental conception and design could take place over a reasonably lengthy period of time (at least a year in the case of the Mali project preparation). There was also some overlap in personnel between the Niger and the Mali preparation missions, facilitating a transfer of experience and ideas from one situation to another within what is, after all, essentially a culturally as well as an ecologically continuous region.

In the last few years, partly in response to a perceived need to combine careful anthropological and sociological investigation with the demands of project timetables, there has been a dramatic growth in the use of various 'Rapid Rural Appraisal' (RRA) techniques (for example, *Rapid Rural Appraisal Notes*, produced by the IIED; McCracken *et al.* 1988). Whether such techniques can be expected realistically to provide the kind of understanding required for preparing and developing the kind of collaborative (participative) and essentially open-ended projects envisaged in this chapter remains debatable. All too often development agency missions ignore sources of information other than those generated by other agencies, projects or government departments. Where rapid rural appraisal is supported only by official documents and reports, there is a strong likelihood that less immediately apparent but possibly crucial aspects of local economy and society will remain inadequately understood and that the necessary foundations for a successful project will be lacking. Only where a pre-existing corpus of sociological and broadly anthropological knowledge is available to be drawn upon by preparation missions, as was the case with the missions I was involved in, can rapid visits produce reliable information on local social and economic dynamics.

GENERAL PROJECT IDENTIFICATION

Although IFAD's SPM to Mali in 1979 had indicated that the poverty of the pastoralists in the north of Mali merited IFAD attention, it was not until the mid-1980s that a specific project was identified in that region. In December 1986, a four-man United Nations inter-agency mission, led by Fabrizio Gentiloni of the UN Disaster Relief Office (UNDRO), and including IFAD (Jeremy Swift), the FAO (Gregori Lazarev) and the World Food Programme–WFP (Jamie Wickens), collaborated with the governments of Algeria, Niger and Mali to consider the situation of refugees within the region in the aftermath of the 1984–85 drought, and to establish what might be done to ensure their return home and their reinstatement. While it was recognized that relief measures – such as food aid – would be necessary in the short-term, it was agreed that the medium-term objective should be to promote the reconstitution of the local economy, and the longer-term objective to improve the food security and resource base of the local population. Algerian authorities prioritized the repatriation of Nigerien and Malian refugees from camps in southern Algeria, whereas the primary concern of the governments of Mali and Niger focused on the refugees' rapid and sustainable reabsorption into productive activities.

In December 1986 the three southern Algerian camps of In Guezzam, Tin Zaouatine and Bordj Badji Mokhtar contained some 11,450 displaced persons, of whom around 8,000 (70 per cent) were from Niger and 3,450 (30 per cent) from Mali. In May 1985 the number of displaced persons had been as high as 20,000, but a gradual process of return had reduced the numbers as those who believed they would be able to maintain a livelihood in their country of origin once again departed. The displaced persons were pre-dominantly of Arab, Touareg or Daoussaq origin (20 per cent, 70 per cent and 10 per cent, respectively); those from Niger came mainly from the two districts of Tahoua and Agadez, those from Mali were largely (90 per cent) from the region of Gao, with a minority (10 per cent) from the region of Timbouctou.

The UN inter-agency mission concluded that a lasting solution to the refugee problem would only be found through the economic and social development of the regions from which the refugees had moved in despair and, in particular, through the improvement of their food security. The mission therefore proposed the identifica-tion of specific projects in the north of Mali (within Gao region essentially) and in north-central Niger (in Tahoua and Agadez districts). As regards Mali, which was the particular concern, it was felt that the northernmost border district (*cercle*) of Kidal deserved special attention, being an area of extremely limited development activity which nevertheless demonstrated development potential, while other interventions might be appropriate in the *cercles* of

Menaka and Ansongo within the context of the planned development project in north-east Mali (*Projet Mali Nord-Est*). Between 1979 and 1986 the districts of Tahoua and Agadez in north-central Niger had been involved in two USAID livestock development projects – the Niger Range and Livestock Project (NRL) and the Integrated Livestock Project/*Projet Élevage Intégré* (ILP/PEI) – but these projects had run into various difficulties (only in part because of the drought) and had been halted. It was considered possible that IFAD might be able to identify a project which built on the experience of these projects but avoided the mistakes they made. The IFAD representative on the inter-agency mission had been closely involved with the USAID projects and was familiar with both their strengths and their weaknesses (Swift 1984).

The starting point for both the Niger and the Mali projects was the identification of a need for long-term economic and social development and for improvements in food security in areas where semi-arid to arid climatic conditions prevailed, and where the dominant mode of existence was based on pastoral production. Despite some interest in the potential for small-scale agriculture around permanent water sources (Niger) and in oasis rehabilitation (Mali), the general thrust of the preliminary identification of 'need' was towards a programme of post-drought reconstruction involving essentially pastoral rehabilitation and pastoral development.

There was a generally shared belief among the agencies and the governments concerned that pastoral rehabilitation and development was possible, given appropriate assistance and intervention. The importance of this should not be underestimated, for it is a commonly held view that the experience of the last decade or so in Africa (with major droughts in the early 1970s and in the mid-1980s) demonstrates the non-viability of existing systems of production and modes of existence in 'marginal areas'. Both the Niger and Mali projects were designed on the premise that pastoral reconstruction is not only perfectly possible in the post-drought situation (even without external assistance – see Spencer 1978: 77–8; IFAD 1987b, vol. III: 25) but is essential if large-scale destitution and hardship is to be avoided. Furthermore, the frequently expressed view that such reconstruction inevitably threatens environmental degradation was rejected in favour of an approach which regarded the relationship between human population, livestock population and physical 'carrying capacity' as dynamic and capable of rapid fluctuations, up as well as down (see Livingstone 1985: 18–23; Sandford 1982, 1983), and as something to be examined in each case, not predicted a priori.

The inter-agency mission in December 1986 was able, on the basis of a three-week visit, to make general recommendations (as indicated above). It was also able to sketch out in preliminary fashion the elements of future project intervention (which were to provide the framework for subsequent identification missions by IFAD), and to initiate short-term relief measures and preliminary project activities even prior to those identification missions. The participation in this inter-agency mission by the subsequent team leader of the Niger and Mali projects made it possible for the mission, first, to develop in a short time a clear basis for subsequent interventions and, secondly, to ensure continuity of conception and approach throughout the ensuing phases of project preparation. Even during such a short visit, time was spent with local development committees and local representatives in the region of Gao, and particularly in the *cercle* of Kidal, as well as with the local government authorities. Visits were also made to remote locations to observe and to discuss with locals the potential for project activities in their locations. Care was taken, even at this early stage, to meet and discuss with representatives of those who might be involved in the proposed projects. In addition, discussions were held with other major donor agencies, and with higher-level government officials.

The inter-agency mission, like the subsequent IFAD missions, was indeed extremely brief. Nevertheless, given the expertise and knowledge of local conditions (and of the literature) and given the importance accorded to the work of this mission by the relevant authorities (in all three countries), who were prepared to make information available to the mission, three weeks was considered sufficient to draw general conclusions as to what was to be done, and to produce a preliminary outline of future interventions. It is generally the case that donor agency missions are brief – often absurdly brief, even to those without knowledge or experience of the anthropological tradition of lengthy fieldwork. It is also generally the case that such missions spend most of their time discussing only with higher-level government officials and drawing upon government and other donor agency documents and data. In contrast, in the cases under discussion, these cruder restrictions were avoided by the selection of key personnel with detailed knowledge and experience of local conditions; by drawing on a rich body of field studies and field experience (see References);[1] by discussing intensively with locals within the project areas, and by ensuring considerable continuity between the various phases of project preparation. Only when full use is made of such existing 'knowledge' is 'rapid appraisal' effective; where such a background does not exist, or is not drawn upon, use of 'quick' techniques is of questionable validity and becomes 'dirty'.

For Mali, proposals by the inter-agency mission (contained in Appendix A of UNDRO 1987) concentrated on the *cercle* of Kidal, with specific interventions to assist in herd reconstitution, the rehabilitation of selected oases as part of a limited programme of agricultural diversification, the improvement of pasture and water management and use, and the development of local institutions such as herders' associations to strengthen the existing cooperative structures and activities. The mission recognized that more detailed work would be required to develop these proposals but it made its own recommendations and identified specific immediate activities. These included a limited programme of herd reconstitution with the assistance of the World Food Programme (WFP), the establishment of a working group under IFAD auspices and including the WFP, FAO, UNDRO and several NGOs (EUROACTION-ACORD, OXFAM and Band Aid) to coordinate activities, experiments with various kinds of public works and with technical innovations for oasis development, and preliminary studies. IFAD agreed to provide US $130,000 under its Special Operations Fund for technical assistance to initiate some of the proposed activities, notably pilot herd reconstitution. For Niger, IFAD decided, following the inter-agency mission, to send a further mission to undertake the specific identification and appraisal of a pastoral development project in Tahoua and Agadez districts, to be integrated within the Niger Special Country Programme already in preparation. The hope of being able to present the Niger Special Country Programme to the IFAD Board in December 1987, together with the knowledge that a great deal of background for any proposed pastoral development project in those districts existed and could be drawn upon, encouraged the merging of what are normally distinct phases in project preparation in a single mission during May–June 1987.

THE ECONOMIC AND SOCIAL CONTEXT OF THE NIGER PROJECT

The Niger Republic is a land-locked country in the West African Sahel, covering a total area of 1 million sq km. The population was estimated in 1986 at 6.6 million, growing at an average of 2.7 per cent a year. Because a large part of the country is arid, average population density is low. The country can be divided into several ecological zones: in the north, the arid Saharan and Sahelo-Saharan zone, where rainfall is insufficient for crop production and the dominant activity is nomadic pastoralism; the Sahelian zone, with rainfall below 350 mm, where limited agriculture is possible and transhumant pastoralism predominates; and the semi-arid (Sahelo-Sudanian) zone, where average rainfall is between 400 and 600 mm and where the dominant production system may be characterized as agro-pastoral. Further south are the Sudanian zone, with rainfall between 600 and 800 mm, where settled agriculture (millet, sorghum, cowpeas, maize and groundnuts) predominates and livestock are kept on a more restricted basis, and the Sudano-Guinean zone, with rainfall over 800 mm a year where crops like manioc, mangoes and vegetables are grown. In general rainfall decreases from south to north. The agricultural sector as a whole contributes around half of GDP (47 per cent in 1985) and about 91 per cent of the labour force is employed in this sector. Uranium is the major foreign exchange earner, generating about 70 per cent of export revenues; but live animals and animal products account for most of the rest. Livestock production is a crucial part of the economy, contributing nearly one-third to rural GDP; pastoral producers constitute some 20 per cent of the population. However, the sector has been particularly vulnerable to rainfall variations and to drought over the last fifteen years, with the most recent drought in 1984–85 resulting in very high losses of animals and the impoverishment of a significant proportion of the population reliant on livestock as a mode of existence. As a consequence, large numbers of poor herders no longer had sufficient animals for self-sufficient production, and experienced increased vulnerability to ecological and economic fluctuations.

Experience with livestock development in Niger has been disappointing. A long-standing emphasis on cattle vaccination has kept rinderpest and some other diseases under control, but has not dealt with the diseases of other species and has absorbed most of the livestock service resources. An extensive programme of drilling boreholes with high-capacity pumps (since the 1950s) has brought into production formerly underused pastures, but has disrupted traditional systems of land tenure and land use for limited gains, and has encouraged environmental degradation around new water points. Government ranches have removed good pasture from the traditional pastoral economy but have failed to provide useful results with wider applicability in the arid and semi-arid zones. Livestock development projects funded by donor agencies (for example, USAID, the World Bank, and so on) have also experienced considerable difficulties.

Recently, however, the government, with support from various external donor agencies, has experimented with a different approach, based on the creation of small-scale 'community development' institutions, the *Groupements Mutualistes Pastoraux* (GMP) or herders' associations. The intention is to give livestock producers' groups more responsibility and to equip them better to undertake their own development activities, including service provision, credit, cereal storage and marketing, livestock marketing and, eventually, pasture management. The new 'national livestock policy' was originally formulated at the Niamey workshop in February 1986 and incorporated into government policy in the new Five Year Plan. It endorses the idea that 'the rehabilitation of small herding households is the best way to reinstate efficient and ecologically sustainable livestock production' (IFAD 1987b: 17). In 1986 the government of Niger also negotiated a structural adjustment loan from the IDA (World Bank) and an IMF Standby arrangement. The government has reformulated its rural development policies and priorities within the context of the Structural Adjustment Programme (SAP). Broad reforms include: (1) reorientation of the investment programme in favour of grassroots development, (2) redefinition of research priorities, (3) a reform of agricultural marketing and price policies, (4) a reduction in the subsidies on farm inputs, and (5) initial reforms of the credit system. It was anticipated that the reorientation of rural development would result, among other things, in a substantial increase in the contribution of the livestock sector to national GDP, improve the state of the pastoral economy in the semi-arid and arid zones in particular, and raise income levels and standard of welfare among the rural populations in those areas. The official adoption in 1988 of a *Plan for Structural Adjustment* confirms this policy orientation. Implementation of the new policies in the area of pastoral development was to be the responsibility of a newly created Ministry of Animal Resources (MRA), responsible for all livestock development activities, including animal health and the central veterinary laboratory, production and some aspects of marketing.

In the arid and semi-arid areas of Niger, livestock production is undertaken predominantly by pastoralists – herders whose livelihood depends directly on animal production. Three types of pastoral production may be identified: *pure pastoralism*, characterized by an almost exclusive reliance on animals and animal products for household revenue (although not for food consumption); *pastoralism associated with dry farming*, characterized by a heavy reliance on pastoral activities for household revenue but in which rain-fed cultivation by, or on behalf of, the household also contributes an important share, and *agro-pastoralism*, where rain-fed farming is the main source of household revenues, with livestock producing important additional income.

In the early 1980s, the pastoral economy of the districts (*départements*) of Tahoua and Agadez in central northern Niger – where the IFAD pastoral development project was to be located – was dominated by pure pastoralism (*c.* 60 per cent of the population), with a minority of the population involved in pastoralism combined with rain-fed farming (*c.* 10 per cent) or in agro-pastoralism (*c.* 30 per cent) (Milligan 1982a, 1982b; Swift 1982, 1984). In the aftermath of the 1984 drought, the proportion of the population involved in pure pastoralism appreciably declined and came to constitute no more than half of the population of the 'pastoral zone' (Bourn and Wint 1986). The population consists of several language/ethnic groups: Touareg, Arab, WoDaabe, Fulani.

In the early 1980s all of those combining pastoralism with agriculture were Touareg, while the pure pastoralists were highly heterogeneous. The Touareg population comprised three major groups: the Kel Gress to the south and south-east of Tahoua, the Kel Dinnik to the north and east of Tahoua, and the Kel Ayr to the south and west of Agadez. The Kel Gress were predominantly agropastoralists (Bonte, various publications); of the Kel Dinnik just over half were involved in pure pastoralism and just under half in pastoralism combined with rain-fed farming; the Kel Ayr were mainly pure nomadic pastoralists (Swift 1984: *passim*). Among the pure pastoralists in addition to the Touareg, there was a very small minority of Arabs (about 2 per cent) and a large minority of WoDaabe/Fulani (around 20 per cent of the total population).

Among all of the pastoral groups crucial decisions regarding herd management were taken by co-herding groups consisting of several households, often closely related by kinship and affinity but also frequently linked by ties of friendship. The precise size and structure of these co-herding groups, however, differed depending on the ethnic group, and among the Touareg depending on the federation and sub-groupings within the federation (see Maliki Bonfiglioli 1984, 1987a on the implications of this heterogeneity for the creation of herders' associations).

In the early 1980s, the total livestock population of the region was around 700,000, of which the majority (*c.* 400,000) were small livestock (sheep and goats), with about 150,000 cattle, 60,000 camels and 84,000 donkeys. It has been suggested, that for pastoralists relying largely on camels and small livestock in the Agadez region, 'the herd size considered sufficient for an average family (for milk consumption and for sale at market to buy needed goods) consists of 3–4 donkeys, 6–10 camels and 30–40 each of goats and sheep per household' (Saenz and Worley 1985). Investigations among four WoDaabe herders' associations in the vicinity of Abalak, in the south of the region, during 1982, revealed that average herd size for cattle was 16.3, for sheep, 3.5 and for goats, 1.3, with donkeys averaging 1.7 and camels 0.7. This size of herd was considered insufficient to maintain an average household, and additional sources of income were required. The Niger Range and Livestock Project (established by USAID in the same region) estimated that, as a rough approximation, three Tropical Livestock Units (TLU) per person was the minimum herd size for subsistence purposes; this would give an average of about fifteen TLU per household – equivalent to about 150 sheep and goats, or 15 camels or 21–22 cattle (Swift 1984). In the early 1980s the average number of TLU per rural inhabitant in Tahoua district was greater than two, implying that an appreciable proportion of livestock owners were self-sufficient in livestock; in Agadez, by contrast, the average was between one and two, suggesting a significantly lower proportion of the population able to subsist on animal production alone.

The drought of 1984–85 substantially reduced the total animal population in the region as deaths and forced sales took their toll. In Agadez district, total livestock population in 1983 was around 326,000; in 1984 it had dropped to about 152,000, and in 1985 amounted to only 75,000 or so. In the sub-district (*arrondissement*) of Tchin Tabaraden in Tahoua district, the average herd in August 1984 of 13.2 TLU had declined by the end of the rainy season of 1985 to an average of 3.15 TLU; the proportion of cattle and sheep in the average herd and in the total animal population declined most dramatically. There was also a significant redistribution in the structure of livestock ownership throughout the arid and semi-arid zones, from poorer to wealthier pastoralists, from pastoralists to others (for example, merchants and government officials), and from the arid and semi-arid regions to the regions further south (and even abroad). A significant proportion of the pastoral population of Tahoua and Agadez districts, notably small herders, was drastically affected by the 1984 drought. In August 1985 it was estimated that some of those most acutely affected by the drought and associated loss of livestock were people living in the pre-desert scrub country of the Agadez district including mainly Touareg and some WoDaabe herders. In November 1985 it was reported that

> the majority of people originating from this area, estimated at about 20,000 individuals, are at present completely indigent, lacking any resources whatsoever. . . . The pastoralists not only suffer from seriously reduced levels of disease resistance, but are entirely dependent on food relief for their subsistence. . . . A large number, perhaps as much as a third, of these drought victims are stranded in towns (Agadez, In Gall, Arlit).

> (Saenz and Worley 1985)

In fact, a much larger area and population was affected. At the beginning of 1986 it was estimated that in the whole of Agadez district as many as 62,000 people were seriously drought-affected, while in Tahoua district the estimated number was 25–30,000. The majority of these near-destitute pastoralists were 're-settled' by the local authorities and relief agencies around permanent water sources and encouraged to practise out-of-season agriculture and seek alternative sources of revenue; food aid was provided in the meanwhile. Many others fled to the small towns of the region or went south out of the region and even abroad in search of the means of subsistence; a minority fled north to Algeria, where they found support in the camps near the border. Investigations carried out between December 1984 and September 1985 among this 're-settled' population in the sub-district of Tchin Tabaraden found an overall mortality rate roughly double the average national mortality rate; rates of infant mortality were double and child mortality rates four times the national rates (Metzel *et al*. 1986). Food aid continued to be provided in Tahoua and Agadez districts until late 1986, but no further distribution had taken place by May 1987, when the IFAD formulation mission visited the region. Even those temporarily 'settled' and near-destitute pastoralists, however, maintained their links with other, more fortunate friends and kinsfolk still involved in pastoral production; by no means all had given up hope of rejoining the pastoral economy, circumstances permitting.

THE PREPARATION OF THE NIGER PROJECT

Following further specification during spring 1987, the pastoral development project in central Niger was prepared during May–July 1987 at the request of the government of Niger and subsequently integrated into the IFAD Special Country Programme (SCP) for

Niger. The SCP involved three major components – the Small-scale Irrigation and the Soil and Water Conservation sub-programmes, which had been identified and prepared by IFAD missions during 1985 and 1986, and the Pastoral Development sub-programme, identified during 1986 and formulated during the mission of May 1987 and subsequent work in Rome. The results of the preparation stages were presented in a major three-volume report – *Niger Special Country Programme: Appraisal Report* – in December 1987 for consideration by the IFAD Board (IFAD 1987b). The project was approved as part of the Special Country Programme on 3 December.[2]

The telescoping of the various phases of project preparation was in part a function of the concern on the part of IFAD to have the Niger Special Country Programme ready to go to the Board by December 1987, and in part a consequence of the very substantial body of experience and information already available from the studies and the activities of the USAID livestock development projects in the districts of Tahoua and Agadez between 1979 and 1986, with which the IFAD mission leader was fully familiar (Swift 1984). Under these rather exceptional circumstances, the IFAD mission to central Niger in summer 1987 was able to combine several phases in one. Indeed, an early task of the mission was to review the experience of other livestock and pastoral development projects in the region and elsewhere in Niger, in order to be able to make proposals which drew on recognized potential and avoided recognized constraints and problems. (The main livestock development projects in the region had all experimented to some degree with herders' associations, or *Groupements Mutualistes Pastoraux* – GMP.) The best documented of these experiments was that of the successive USAID projects, which had created ten pilot associations in 1982 (Swift 1984; Swift and Maliki 1984a, 1984b). On the basis of this review, it was concluded that the main reason for the lack of success of other livestock development projects was the failure to create an appropriate and reliable institutional framework involving both herders' associations (GMP) and the project in a multipurpose and *collaborative* organization. This was in contrast to the comparative success of small-scale attempts (for example, by OXFAM and the American NGO, the Cooperative League of the USA – CLUSA) to provide credit for herd reconstitution or for pastoral production more generally. The small schemes emphasized close cooperation with the representatives of herders' associations or with small, relatively heterogeneous 'functional groupings' composed of co-herding groups of kinsfolk and friends (Swift and Maliki 1984a, 1984b; Maliki Bonfiglioli 1987b).

The overall objective of the project proposed was to help poorer herders re-start pastoral production in the region in a productive and ecologically sustainable manner and to reduce their vulnerability to future droughts and other shocks. The project would last three years, as the first phase of a longer-term commitment by IFAD. The specific objectives would be: (1) to create and/or strengthen local-level organizational structures – the herders' associations (GMP) – so as to improve herders' ability to manage economic activities and physical resources and to negotiate on more equal terms with the government and other outside agencies, such as the project itself (seventy GMP of about thirty households each would be involved); (2) to initiate a credit programme which would help to re-constitute the herds of the selected GMP, to provide working capital to improve productivity and commercialization, and to enable herders to buy cereals at post-harvest prices and store them for dry-season consumption; (3) to provide selected GMP with a package of veterinary and animal production inputs to increase productivity; and (4) to conduct studies concerned with establishing the basis for long-term pastoral development ensuring economic growth, environmental sustainability and basic food security within the region, and for monitoring and evaluating the effects of the project throughout its life.

The major components of the project would be: (1) the organization and training of herders' associations (GMP); (2) the provision of credit to GMP, for herd reconstitution, for production and marketing, and for the establishment of cereal banks; (3) the provision of assistance to improve animal health, including training of volunteer veterinary auxiliaries nominated by GMP support to existing government animal-health services and facilities; (4) the initiation of public works programmes with a food-for-work element (with WFP support); and (5) the carrying-out of various studies, such as a base-line socio-economic survey, a study of markets and marketing, studies aimed at contributing to government initiatives to define a new rural land tenure and land-use code, and applied research to help define a food security strategy for the pastoral zone, as well as other investigations concerned primarily with improving agricultural and livestock production.

At the heart of the project was the idea that all activities would, from the outset, involve the selected herders' associations (GMP) in the fullest possible way. As a result, the framework for implementation and specific components (already devised) would be kept under review and subjected to modification as the project evolved; that is, as the crucial development agents – the herders themselves in their cooperative institutions – became better equipped and capable of taking on more of the activities envisaged.

Experience in Niger (and elsewhere) has demonstrated some of the difficulties in creating or making effective community development institutions among pastoralists. In Niger's pastoral societies, the traditional lineage and status group structure is in most cases neither appropriate nor effective for this purpose. There are substantial differences between and within ethnic groups in the way these structures operate, ranging from some very hierarchical Touareg to the very egalitarian WoDaabe. However, the failure of most development programmes to identify a traditional structure appropriate for modern development does not mean that there are no effective cooperative groups which might be encouraged to take on new development activities. Pastoralists do work together on many essential tasks, especially in relation to the management of herds, water and pasture, and sometimes in marketing. Evaluation of the experiments already undertaken – for example, the creation of ten pilot herders' associations in the Tahoua–Agadez region under the auspices of the Niger Range and Livestock Project (NLR) – enabled several problems to be identified: the relationship of the herders' associations to the traditional political framework on the one hand, and to the government on the other; the difficulty in designing a single community structure appropriate to the very diverse ethnic, status/class, social and economic groups in the region (particularly problems affecting the role of women and of Touareg 'ex-slaves' (*eklan*)); and the relationship with government technical services unfamiliar with and often somewhat hostile to the idea of effective voluntary/community development workers in education, health (animal and human), livestock production, agriculture, and so on (see Aronson 1985; Swift 1984; Maliki Bonfiglioli 1984, 1987a, 1987b; White 1984a, 1984b). The drought of 1984–85 undoubtedly set back the development of the pilot herders' associations created in the early 1980s. But if problems were identifiable and difficulties visible, a positive evaluation in 1984 (Garba *et al.* 1984) and the investigations of the IFAD mission encouraged the view that the IFAD project would, nevertheless, be well advised to build on the experience of herders' associations and seek to strengthen them to provide the foundation for pastoral development in the region.

The conclusions of the mission were presented during the summer of 1987 to a Technical Review Committee, and the first two volumes (the main report and its supporting annexes) of the Appraisal Report of the Special Country Programme, including the Pastoral Development sub-programme, were produced in August. The working documents relating to the Pastoral sub-programme supporting the conclusions of the main report were produced in December 1987. In its thirty-second session, held at the beginning of December, the IFAD Executive Board approved the project as a part of the Niger Special Country Programme.

THE ECONOMIC AND SOCIAL CONTEXT OF THE MALI PROJECT

Mali is a land-locked country in the West African Sahel, adjacent to the Republic of Niger. It is 1.24 million sq km in area, with a population of around 5.5. million. It is largely arid; only about a quarter of the country is potentially agricultural land and only 11 per cent is currently cultivated. The arid zone – defined by rainfall of less than 600 mm – covers more than half of the total area of Mali. It includes a desert zone (with less than 100 mm) and a north Sahelian zone (between 100 mm and 600 mm). The arid zone incorporates all of the north and east of the country and large parts of the centre, with very low population densities in the north and east (fewer than 6 people per sq km). Pastoralism on its own and in combination with agriculture is the main economic activity over most of the land areas. Livestock production accounts for a fifth of GDP and is the main activity of the regions of Timbouctou and Gao, which together make up a large part of the arid zone. The main livestock systems are defined, on the basis of the contribution of livestock to household budgets, as *pastoral* or *agro-pastoral*. Before the 1984 drought about one-third of all cattle and somewhat less than one-quarter of all sheep and goats were produced within the agro-pastoral systems; the pastoral systems of northern Mali accounted for about 45 per cent of all cattle, 65 per cent of all sheep and goats and 100 per cent of camels.

Kidal *cercle* is within Gao region in the north of Mali. It is fully within the arid zone, being Sahelian in the south and sub-desert in the north. The economy is almost exclusively pastoral; 90–95 per cent of the population is rural and directly involved in livestock production. Before 1973, camels, cattle, sheep and goats were all herded together, with donkeys for transport; cattle herding was largely eliminated in that drought, and there are currently few cattle in the *cercle*. Traditionally, livestock were sold in Algeria to the north and goods bought there with the proceeds; but this trans-Saharan trade with areas to the north has been severely limited in recent years, to the detriment of the people of Kidal. The great majority (around 90 per cent) of the population of Kidal are Touareg of the Kel Adrar confederation, although nomadic herders of other Touareg confederations and other ethnic groups, especially Arab Kunta from Bourem, also use Kidal pastures for part of the year. The Kel Adrar are organized according to the basic social and traditional framework of most Touareg groups: a horizontal division into major clans or fractions (which form the seven basic administrative units), and a vertical division into traditional social classes. Of the traditional Touareg social classes, Kel Adrar society contains *ilellan* ('free'), *imghad* ('vassal'), *ineslemen* ('religious'), *inhaden* ('artisan') and *eklan* ('slave' or 'Bella') groups. But the traditional Touareg social stratification was never particularly well developed in Kidal (Swift 1981) and Kel Adrar society always had fewer 'Bella' groups than other Touareg confederations in Mali. The social structure of local Touareg society has undergone substantial change over the last decades, largely as a result of successive droughts. A much larger section of society is living on or below the poverty line; there has been increasing strain on traditional family and clan systems of self-help and redistribution in favour of the poor; some households have diversified into market gardening with a resulting partial sedentarization at oasis sites; others have simply abandoned the pastoral or agropastoral mode of existence and have moved to makeshift squatter settlements around the small urban centre of Kidal or around towns further south in Gao region or elsewhere; many young men have left on wage labour migration, often abroad, increasingly on a permanent basis; family structures have come under stress and the traditional clan has declined as a major locus of decision making regarding pasture management and the use of resources generally. Traditionally, although Kel Adrar clans were not territorial units (because of precise rules about the ownership of water rights), the grazing areas of different clans used to be well defined and clans used to operate within such areas as effective managers of the physical resources: pasture, browse, water sources, wild grasses, trees and so on. However, these traditional provisions for physical resource management and conservation by local 'users' groups' have not been supported by government and there is no clearcut legislation enabling local groups to exercise their traditional rights over local resources. Nevertheless, in practice, co-herding groups do continue to provide a relatively coherent basis not only for animal husbandry but also for land use and resource management.

Just as traditional systems of control over resources and patterns of production have changed, so too has the distribution of livestock ownership. Before the 1973 drought, an average-to-wealthy family would have had 50–60 sheep and goats or some equivalent combination of animals. Substantial animal sales and deaths occurred in 1973, and many households were made destitute. By 1983 many households had recovered some degree of self-sufficiency, although at a lower level than before 1973. Heavy losses occurred again in 1984, leaving most households unable to survive on the basis of their herds. A rough estimate of the situation in 1987 suggested that 10 per cent of households had 20–40 sheep or goats, while a small proportion also had small camel herds. These would be able to maintain a pastoral existence. But 20 per cent of households had only 10–20 sheep or goats, with 1–2 camels; 60 per cent of households had fewer than 10 sheep or goats, with a minority having only 1 or 2 animals; and 10 per cent of households had no animals at all. These figures suggest that Kidal is one of the poorest *cercles* in Mali.

The poverty in livestock is particularly serious in view of the permanent risk of further drought, the virtual lack of alternative economic activities within the *cercle*, the restrictions on trade to the north and the geographical isolation of the *cercle vis-à-vis* the south, which makes transport both difficult and expensive. Cereal prices are much higher in Kidal than in Gao or other markets along the Niger, while livestock prices are lower. The pastoralists of Kidal are obliged to sell their livestock (and to a lesser extent animal products) to obtain grain; the adverse terms of trade affect them severely. There was a variety of barter and gift exchanges in the traditional (that is, pre-1973) Kidal pastoral economy, with varying degrees of reciprocity and levels of expectation of return. It is not clear how far these forms of exchange would constitute a mechanism for redistribution in a situation of generalized poverty. In 1987 a major source of grain was the World Food Programme, and government provided food aid. The traditional drought-coping strategies of the Kidal population were inadequate to deal with the two recent droughts (1973 and 1984). The first response – to sell animals and build grain reserves – failed because animal prices collapsed while grain availability declined and prices soared. In 1973, herders then migrated south in search of pastures only to find that competition for the remaining pasture was acute. In 1984, despite the drought, pastures in Kidal were adequate, but pastoralists from the south migrated northwards, increasing the demand on Kidal pastures which were quickly exhausted. Many pastoralists then moved further north to end up in the Algerian camps.

The main vulnerable groups in the aftermath of the 1984 drought were those households with insufficient animals to maintain a pastoral existence; and these amounted to some 90 per cent of the total population. Within this general category of 'vulnerable households', there were particular types of household and individual especially at risk: female-headed households (an increasingly common type); displaced persons living in 'shanty-towns' or elsewhere; old and sick people and their households; children under 5 years, and pregnant or lactating women. Displaced persons were a particular category of the poor. Food aid distribution during the 1984 drought by the government encouraged concentrations of destitute households around the towns of the Gao region, including Kidal itself; others went north to Algeria where, even in late 1986, despite a significant gradual return, an appreciable number remained. It was with this large category of 'vulnerable households' unable to maintain a pastoral existence that the Mali project was to be primarily concerned. The objective was to prepare a project which would not only provide mechanisms for improving the welfare of the local population but also, in collaboration with local groups and associations, to help re-establish and develop the pastoral economy and other complementary activities, improve food security and enhance the local capacity to manage local resources.

THE PREPARATION OF THE MALI PROJECT

As already indicated above, the broad identification of a pastoral development project in the northern Gao region of Mali, with a concentration on the *cercle* of Kidal, had been made during the inter-agency mission of December 1987. At that time the project was referred to as 'The Post-drought Income and Food Security Programme Mali'. Following this preliminary identification, the government of Mali formally requested IFAD assistance in financing a development project in Kidal *cercle*, to rehabilitate pastoral production and improve its productivity, to diversify and extend agriculture, to improve local development structures and services, and to reduce risk from further droughts. All of these interventions would be with the general objective of expanding economic activity in the *cercle*, improving food security, and encouraging the return of emigrants from the area to their homes with confidence in their ability to sustain an adequate livelihood.

IFAD responded by putting together a team for a specific identification mission in May 1987, to elaborate on the preliminary proposals and to provide the detailed background necessary to formulate the project. The identification mission to Mali coincided in time with the formulation/appraisal mission to Niger, and the same person acted as overall team leader for both projects, dividing his time between the two, and handing over, in his absence, to an acting team leader. The acting team leader on the Mali identification mission was a Malian, a Touareg, a native of Kidal *cercle*, and a socio-linguist. During its period in Mali the team worked closely with other donor agencies, notably the World Food Programme (WFP) and UNICEF, and with non-governmental organizations, notably EUROACTION-ACORD, as well as with government officials and with local development committees. In particular, it worked closely with the *Direction Régionale d'Action Coopérative et de l'Élevage* (DRACOOP).

The report of the identification mission took longer than expected to put together, and although it was initially hoped that preparation and appraisal could take place during 1987, in fact these phases were delayed until 1988. Recommendations were presented to the president of IFAD in March 1988 for approval of preliminary funding under the Special Operations Facility (SOF) – a special facility for providing funds for preliminary studies and other activities even prior to full approval of the project. It was originally anticipated that before the summer of 1987 the first Board presentation would take place, at which the overall strategy and the framework of the programme would be described, along with a first tranche of programme activities, consisting of components which could be prepared and appraised in 1987. Further preparation work would be undertaken during the implementation of the first tranche. Together with the results of pilot activities, this would provide IFAD with a basis for deciding on the need and the scope of any subsequent tranches to be submitted to the Executive Board. In the event, the presentation to the Board was re-scheduled for December 1988, due to late completion of the identification mission report. As a result of the delays it was proposed that, although the approach proposed for programme phasing and tranche funding remained valid, a further mission should formulate in detail the components of the project, to be appraised in July 1988 for the December 1988 Board. The formulation mission would visit the field in May 1988. In the meanwhile, activities to be covered under the SOF – which could start at once – would include: pilot herd re-stocking; pilot support services to oasis agriculture; a pilot soil and water conservation scheme and range management; a pilot village development fund to finance training and the promotion of rural enterprises in favour of destitute persons in Kidal *cercle* and those returning to the *cercles* of Menaka and Gao; and preliminary studies and surveys.

In fact, on the basis of the recommendations of the inter-agency mission in December 1986, and the identification mission of May 1987, a pilot programme of herd reconstitution had already been initiated in July 1987 in Kidal *cercle* with funding from IFAD, the WFP and Band Aid. This programme involved the allocation of free food to local pre-cooperatives, who would then sell the food relatively cheaply to the local population and thereby accumulate a fund with which livestock (sheep and goats) could be purchased for distribution, on the basis of a concessional loan, to selected disadvantaged herders within the cooperative. It was planned that 350 herders and their families would receive these livestock loans – which would be worth 150,000 FCFA each but consist in effect of five goats, five sheep and a donkey. The project was to be managed by the selected local pre-cooperatives under the guidance of the DRACOOP, and with the assistance of the WFP and the cooperation of the regional and local development committees.

The first part of this programme was evaluated in January 1988 by the WFP, and resulted in minor modifications with regard to the transport of foodstuffs to the *cercle*. On the whole, the first part of the programme – the provision of foodstuffs and their sale to local pre-cooperatives to constitute a basic fund – had gone smoothly and the local population was well pleased. The second part of the programme – the organization of the purchase and allocation of the livestock constituting the loan for herd reconstruction – was evaluated by the DRACOOP and the WFP in April 1988, just prior to the IFAD identification mission in May. The evaluation highlighted, for example, that a few pre-cooperatives had shown themselves less than capable of managing their part of the programme, and suggested some modifications to the original programme. In general, though, the programme had gone well, and 159 herders and their families had received loans (totalling 1,749 goats and sheep).

The decision to collaborate with local pre-cooperatives and to encourage the development of these institutions as the basis of the herd reconstruction programme was a crucial one. Since the 1973 drought there had been a programme of cooperative rehabilitation in the Gao region, carried out by the DRACOOP and assisted by EUROACTION-ACORD. (Activities in Kidal started in 1981). In 1978 the programme was re-orientated from a predominantly short-term rehabilitation perspective to a longer-term development perspective involving production, income generation and service provision. Since then, cooperative programmes had included bulk buying of consumption goods, herd re-stocking and cash loans to members, construction of buildings, tracks and wells using cash-for-work, primary health care for people and animals, literacy and pasture management. Functional literacy programmes and the bulk buying of foodstuffs for re-sale to cooperative members have been the most successful of these activities. Evaluation of the cooperative programme as a whole in Gao region revealed some problems, notably with regard to the management of the cooperatives themselves and the low level of effective official support from most technical services (Marty 1985; EUROACTION-ACORD 1987, 1988). The IFAD identification mission concluded, on the basis of its investigations, that

> despite these difficulties, the Gao region pastoral cooperatives have had some important successes. Although technical results have been mixed, cooperatives are clearly the key to pasture management, if they are given more sustained support and long-standing land-tenure anomalies are removed. Most economic activities, especially restocking and animal production credits, have reached poor cooperative members despite shortcomings in accountancy and management. Although many people, especially women, do not attend cooperative annual general meetings and are not well informed about cooperative affairs, the cooperatives have encouraged greater democracy through public debate about activities and through effective decentralisation of decision-making and technical training.
>
> (IFAD 1987a: 13)

The identification mission came to the conclusion that pastoral cooperatives covering all the inhabitants of one sub-district (*arrondissement*) were, nevertheless, somewhat unwieldy and that further decentralization to smaller 'functional groupings' might be helpful. It observed that

> the division of each *arrondissement* cooperative into several co-operative sectors, already well under way in Kidal, is a first step in this direction, and the Kidal Development Project in the first

instance would work with six of these cooperative sectors in the most densely inhabited *arrondissements*.

(IFAD 1987a: 14)

But it also pointed out that

smaller functional cooperative groupings exist in the Kidal pastoral economy, especially at the level of pastoral camps and larger production and consumption groupings on the bases of kinship and friendship. Agricultural production at oases has also created small new functional groupings. These types of group offer the Kidal Development Project a potential to build effective participatory institutions at the local level.

(IFAD 1987a: 14)

The identification mission emphasized that the two major objectives of the project would be (1) to help strengthen and develop local associations and (2) to provide credit to assist in herd reconstitution and the effective rehabilitation of the pastoral economy to ensure increasing productivity and household incomes. There were also to be several other components, including credit for cereal banks for food security, soil and water conservation measures, interventions designed to improve agricultural productivity in oasis sites, assistance to the health and education services and a number of studies to define appropriate longer-term development and food security strategies.

The provision of credit would take a number of different forms. Highly concessional credit would be provided, along lines similar to the programme already in operation on a pilot basis since July 1987, to aid in herd reconstitution. Production credit would be provided on somewhat harder terms to those with viable flocks and herds to encourage increasing output and off-take as the basis for commercial pastoral production and to improve herders' incomes. Credit would also be provided to local cooperative sectors to establish revolving funds for the bulk purchase of cereals to create cereal banks for cooperative members. All credit would be channelled through the cooperative sectors. Underlying the mission's emphasis on credit as a key mechanism for revitalizing the local pastoral economy was the premise, based on detailed experience and analysis, that in most years local pastoral systems are not only resilient but extremely efficient and productive. Credit to purchase sheep and goats, which reproduce fast and are (particularly in the case of goats) relatively drought-resistant, would enable herders to re-stock quickly, to regain basic viability, and to begin the process of building up larger mixed herds. Improvements in marketing would aid herders to increase off-take, both generally and when needed for rapid destocking, which would enhance not only household incomes, but also the herders' capacity to vary herd size in accordance with climatic and resource changes.

The IFAD identification mission returned to Rome in May–June 1987 and began to prepare its report. The final report was ready early in 1988 after unexpected delays; it was a substantial and detailed document, amounting to over 300 pages. During March and April 1988 IFAD staff considered the report and developed the programme for the next stages in the preparation of the project. A meeting of the Technical Review Committee was held on 11 May to review the Identification Report, and a number of issues were discussed, including the nature of local cooperative groupings, the environmental implications of herd reconstitution, the problems of livestock marketing, soil and water conservation, and the scope of the project. With respect to this last, it was noted that a modest pastoral development programme had recently been approved for IFAD assistance in Niger and it was suggested that the Mali project should adopt the same flexible, essentially 'pilot' approach to pastoral development in Kidal. In general, it was agreed that the broad project aim should be to provide a sustainable system of farming and livestock-keeping for the existing population, thus preventing out-migration. A secondary, but important objective should be to provide assistance to returning refugees. It was agreed that a formulation mission would be sent to make its own investigations, to pave the way for programme appraisal by streamlining the identification mission's proposals, and to formulate preparatory activities for SOF funding.

The formulation mission which visited Mali in May–June 1988 included several individuals who had participated in the earlier identification mission (including the team leader and the acting team leader from the previous mission); it also included one person, in addition to the team leader, from the Niger formulation/appraisal mission (the acting team leader of that mission – me). Like the identification mission before it, the formulation mission spent a relatively short time (three to four weeks) in the project area, but was able to take advantage of the growing documentation on (and analysis of) developments in the region over the previous few years. The mission also benefited from previous experience gained by team members, from that of other persons attached to the mission once in Mali (such as seconded personnel from UNICEF and

EUROACTION-ACORD, now ACORD, actively involved in development activities in the area), and from government departments (notably the DRACOOP and the *Service d'Alphabétisation Fonctionelle* – SAF, both of which seconded personnel). Like the identification mission before it, this mission too benefited from meetings with the regional and district development committees and their members, and with 'officials' and members of the local cooperative sectors.

Field visits were an essential part of the mission's work. The formulation mission broadly confirmed the approach and key elements identified as the basis of the project by the previous identification mission: the involvement from the outset of local cooperative sectors and, where possible, grassroots functional groupings; the crucial role of credit, for herd reconstitution (particulary targeted at the most disadvantaged households and at women), for production and commercialization, and for the establishment of cereal banks; the importance of functional literacy training and health support; the potential for careful oasis rehabilitation; the possibility of engaging the local population in public works directed towards the management of local physical resources, including soil and water conservation and pasture protection and enhancement; and the need for improvements in the structure and organization of livestock marketing.

The formulation mission was able to develop and refine several of the proposed activities of the project and to provide detailed costings for a full cost/benefit analysis and financial assessment (IFAD 1988a and b). The individual responsible for the financial analysis, who participated fully in the field visits of the formulation mission, was to lead the formal appraisal/evaluation mission on behalf of the West African Development Bank (BOAD), the cooperating institution commissioned to undertake that task.

The results of the formulation and appraisal missions were combined in a final presentation to the IFAD Board in December 1988. The Kidal Food and Income Security Project was approved and initial project work began in 1989.[3]

NOTES

1 The references contain a select number of key texts not otherwise referred to. A more extensive bibliography can be obtained from the author.
2 The total project cost was estimated at US \$20.9 million; IFAD provided the lion's share of the loan at around US \$13.3 million on highly concessional terms – fifty years for repayment including a grace period of

ten years with a service charge of 1 per cent a year – plus a grant equivalent to US $0.7 million.
3 The total cost was estimated at US $14.8 million, of which UNICEF would co-finance US $0.40 million, the WFP US $0.34 million, ACORD of the UK, US $0.25 million, and the Islamic Development Bank US $2.50 million. The government of Mali would contribute US $0.16 million and the beneficiaries of the project US $0.15 million. The loan amount was equivalent to US $10.15 million and the grant amount equivalent to US $0.85 million; the terms were highly concessional. A brief summary of the project is provided in the IFAD 1988 annual report (IFAD 1989:110).

ACKNOWLEDGEMENTS

I am grateful to Dr Jeremy Swift and to Mr Bahman Mansuri (Director of Africa Division at IFAD) for their comments on the second draft of this chapter. My thanks also to the members of the seminar organized at the School of Oriental and African Studies by Dr Johan Pottier, and to those who participated in the follow-up workshop, for their comments on earlier presentations.

REFERENCES

Aronson, D. (1985) 'Implementing local participation: the Niger Range and Livestock Project', *Nomadic Peoples* 18: 67–75.
Baier, S. (1980) *An Economic History of Central Niger*, Oxford: Clarendon Press.
Bernus, E. (1975) *Les tactiques des éleveurs face à la sécheresse: le cas du sud-ouest de l'Air, Niger*, Paris: ORSTOM.
—— (1981) *Touaregs nigériens: unité culturelle et diversité régionale d'un peuple pasteur*, Paris: ORSTOM.
Bonte, P. (1973) *L'Élevage et le commerce du bétail dans l'Ader Doutchi Majiya*, Niamey and Paris: Études Nigériennes, no. 23.
—— (1975a) 'L'organisation économique des Touareg Kel Gress', in R. Cresswell (ed.) *Eléments d'Ethnologie*, Paris: Ed. Armand Colin, pp. 166–215.
—— (1975b) 'Esclavage et relations de dépendance chez les Touaregs Kel Gress', in C. Meillassoux (ed.) *L'Esclavage en Afrique précoloniale*, Paris: Maspéro.
—— (1977) 'Troupeaux et familles chez les éleveurs sahéliens', in *Systèmes pastoraux sahélians*, Annexe 2, Rome: FAO, pp. 43–87.
Bonte, P., Bourgeot, A. and Lefebure, C. (1979) 'Pastoral economy and societies', in *State of Knowledge Report on Tropical Grazing Land Ecosystems*, Paris: UNESCO.
Bonte, P. and Echard, N. (1975) 'Histoire et histoires. Conception du passé chez les Hawsa et les Twareg Kel Gress de l'Ader', *Cahiers d'études africaines*, 16 (61–2): 237–96.
Bourn, D. and Wint, W. (1986) *Pastoral Conditions in Central Niger Following the 1983–84 Drought*, Jersey: Resource Inventory and Management Ltd; Addis Ababa: ILCA.

Burnham, P. (1980) 'Changing agricultural and pastoral ecologies in the West African Savanna region', in D. R. Harris (ed.) *Human Ecology in Savanna Environments*, London: Academic Press, pp. 147–70.

Dupire, M. (1962) *Peuls Nomades: étude descriptive des WoDaabe du Sahel Nigérien*, Paris: Institut d'Ethnologie, Travaux et Mémoires de l'Institut de l'Ethnologie LXIV.

—— (1970) *Organisation sociale des Peul*, Paris: Plon.

—— (1975) 'Exploitation du sol, communautés résidentielles et organisation lignagère des pasteurs WoDaabe (Niger)', in T. Monod (ed.) *Pastoralism in Tropical Africa*, London: Oxford University Press, pp. 322–37.

EUROACTION-ACORD (1987) *Programme de relance du mouvement coopératif en sixième et septième régions de la République du Mali*, Rapport d'Evaluation, ACORD/Direction Nationale de l'Action Coopérative (DNACOOP), Bamako: EUROACTION-ACORD.

—— (1988) *Rapport d'Exécution du Programme d'Appui aux Éleveurs (Mali II) pour l'Année 1987*, Niamey: EUROACTION-ACORD.

Garba, I., Vu Thi, P. and Shaw, P. (1984) *Evaluation of 10 Pilot Cooperatives*, Tahoua, Niger: Projet Élevage Intégré.

Hill, A. G. (ed.) (1985) *Population, Health and Nutrition in the Sahel*, London: Routledge and Kegan Paul.

Hopen, C. E. (1958) *The Pastoral Fulbe Family in Gwandu*, Oxford: Oxford University Press (reprinted 1970).

IFAD (1984) *A Fund for the Rural Poor*, Rome: IFAD.

—— (1986) *Annual Report*, 1985, Rome: IFAD.

—— (1987a) *The Poor are Bankable: Rural Credit the IFAD Way*, Rome: IFAD.

—— (1987b) *Niger Special Country Programme: Appraisal Report*, Rome: IFAD.

—— (1988a) 'Pastoral development in arid zones: problems and potentials for sustained productivity – lessons from the policy and practice of IFAD', Rome, IFAD, *Staff Working Paper*, Africa Division.

—— (1988b) *Kidal Development Project Identification Report*, Rome: IFAD.

—— (1988c) *Kidal Food and Income Security Programme Formulation Report*, Rome: IFAD.

—— (1989) *IFAD Annual Report, 1988*, Rome: IFAD.

ILO (1968) *Projet de rapport au gouvernement de la République du Mali sur l'intégration et la sédentarisation des populations nomades maures et touaregs de la sixième région administrative*, Geneva: ILO, D 34/1968.

Irons, W. (1979) 'Political stratification among pastoral nomads', in L'Equipe Ecologie et Anthropologie des Sociétés Pastorales (eds) *Production Pastorale et Société*, Cambridge: Cambridge University Press; Paris: Editions de la Maison des Sciences de l'Homme, pp. 15–28.

Keenan, J. (1977) *The Tuareg: People of Ahaggar*, London: Allen Lane.

Livingstone, I. (1985) *Pastoralism: An Overview of Practice, Process and Policy*, London: FAO, a study prepared for the Human Resources, Institutions and Agrarian Reform Division.

McCracken, J., Pretty, J. and Conway, G. (1988) *An Introduction to Rapid Rural Appraisal for Agricultural Development*, London: IIED.

Maliki Bonfiglioli, A. (1981) *Ngaynaaka l'élevage selon les WoDaabe du Niger*, Nyamey: Ministère du Développement Rural (MRD).

—— (1984), *Bonheur et souffrance chez les Peuls nomades*, Paris: Comité international pour la langue française.

—— (1987a) 'Herders' associations in Mali', Paper presented at the OXFAM Arid Lands Workshop, Cotonou, Benin.

—— (1987b) 'Project Habbanae in Niger', Paper presented at the OXFAM Arid Lands Workshop, Cotonou, Benin.

—— (1988a) *Dudal: histoire de famille et histoire de troupeau chez un groupe de WoDaabe du Niger*, Cambridge: Cambridge University Press; Paris: Editions de la Maison des Sciences de l'Homme.

—— (1988b) 'Management of pastoral production in the Sahel: constraints and options', in A. Maliki Bonfiglioli, *Desertification Control and Renewable Resource Management in the Sahelian and Sudanian Zones of West Africa*, Washington, DC: World Bank Technical Paper, No. 70.

—— (with White, C., Loutan, L. and Swift, J. J.) (1984) 'The WoDaabe', in J. J. Swift (ed.) *Pastoral Development in Central Niger*, Niamey: Ministère de Développement Rural, pp. 255–529.

Marty, A. (1975) *Histoire de l'Azawak nigérien de 1899 à 1911*, Paris: Mémoire de l'Ecole des Hautes Etudes en Sciences Sociales (EHESS).

—— (1985) *Crise rurale en milieu nord-sahéliaen et recherche coopérative. L'expérience des régions de Gao et Tombouctou, Mali, 1975–1982*, Tours: Université de Tours, doctoral thesis.

Metzel, J., Shaw, P., Vu Thi, P. and Garba, I. (1986) *Rapport du Recensement de Base: Ingall-Abalak-Dakaro*, Tahoua: PEI/MRA.

Milligan, K. (1982a) *Aerial Survey of Human, Livestock and Environmental Conditions in a Central Region of the Pastoral Zone of Niger*, Niamey: USAID, Final Report.

—— (1982b) *Wet Season Aerial Survey of the Human and Livestock Populations and Environmental Conditions in a Central Region of the Pastoral Zone in Niger*, Niamey: USAID, Final Report.

Nicolaisen, J. (1975) 'The historical change of Tuareg social organisation', *Ethnos*, 1–4: 291–97.

Oxby, C. (1986) 'Women and the allocation of herding labour in a pastoral society', in S. Bernus, P. Bonte, L. Brock and H. Claudot (eds) *Le Fils et le neveu: jeux et enjeux de la parenté touarègue*, Cambridge: Cambridge University Press; Paris: Editions de la Maison des Sciences de l'Homme.

—— (1987) 'Women unveiled: class and gender among Kel Ferwan Twareg (Niger)', *Ethnos* 52 (1–2): 120–36.

Raynaut, C. (1975) 'Le cas de la région de Maradi (Niger)', in J. Copans (ed.) *Sécheresses et famines au Sahel*, Paris: Maspéro, pp. 5–43.

Saenz, and Worley (1985) *Internal Report*, Tahoua, Niger: PE1 Mimeo.

Sandford, S. (1982) 'Pastoral strategies and desertification: opportunism and conservatism in dry lands', in B. Spooner and H. S. Mann (eds) *Desertification and Development: Dry Land Ecology in Social Perspective*, London: Academic Press.

—— (1983) *Management of Pastoral Development in the Third World*, London: John Wiley & Sons.

Seddon, D. (1981) *Moroccan Peasants*, Folkestone: William Dawson.

—— (1990) 'IFAD and "adjustment"', Paper presented to the workshop on Structural Adjustment held at the University of East Anglia, May 1990.

Spencer, P. (1978) 'Pastoralists and the ghost of capitalism', in S. B. Westley (ed.) *East African Pastoralism: Anthropological Perspectives and Development Needs*, Addis Ababa: ILCA, pp 71–92.

Stenning, D. J. (1959) *Savannah Nomads: A Study of the WoDaabe Pastoral Fulani of Western Bornu Province*, London: Oxford University Press.

—— (1971) 'Household viability among the pastoral Fulani', in J. Goody (ed.) *The Development Cycle in Domestic Groups*, Cambridge: Cambridge University Press, pp. 92–119.

Swift, J. J. (1973) 'Disaster and a Sahelian nomad economy', in D. Dalby and R. J. Harrison Church (eds) *Drought in Africa*, London: School of Oriental and African Studies, pp. 71–8.

—— (1975) 'Pastoral nomadism as a form of land-use: the Twareg of the Adrar n Iforas', in T. Monod (ed.) *Pastoralism in Tropical Africa*, London: Oxford University Press, pp. 443–54.

—— (1977) 'Sahelian pastoralists: underdevelopment, desertification and famine', *Annual Review of Anthropology* 6: 457–78.

—— (1979) *West African Pastoral Production Systems*, Ann Arbor: Center for Research on Economic Development, University of Michigan.

—— (1981) *The Economics of Traditional Nomadic Pastoralism: The Twareg of the Adrar n Iforas (Mali)*, University of Sussex, D.Phil. thesis, reproduced by University Microfilms International, Ann Arbor, Michigan.

—— (1982) *NRL (Niger Range and Livestock Project) Final Report*, Niamey: USAID, NRL, first discussion draft.

—— (ed.) (1984) *Pastoral Development in Central Niger*, Niamey: Ministry of Rural Development (MRD) and USAID, Report of the Niger Range and Livestock Project.

Swift, J. J. and Maliki, A. B. (1984a) 'Preliminary evaluation of a pilot programme to create herders' associations in the pastoral zone of central Niger', Tahoua (Niger): Discussion Paper, Niger Range and Livestock Project.

—— (1984b) 'A cooperative development experiment among nomadic herders in Niger', London: ODI Pastoral Development *Network Papers*, September.

Thébaud, B. (1987) *Élevage et Développement au Niger. Quel avenir pour les éleveurs du Sahel? Réflexions sur les causes de la crise pastorale à partir de la situation de l'élevage dans l'est du Niger*, Geneva: ILO Publications.

Thébaud, B., Sylla, Djeidi and Nieuwkerk, M. (1983) 'Document de base pour le rapport d'évaluation du programme de relance coopérative en 6è et 7è régions du Mali', Bamako: ACORD, Rapport d'Évaluation.

Toulmin, C. (1983) 'Economic behaviour among livestock-keeping peoples', University of East Anglia: School of Development Studies, *Development Studies Occasional Paper* No. 25.

UNDRO/FAO/WFP/IFAD (1987) *Personnes déplacées du Mali et du Niger dans les camps du Sahara algérien: perspectives de réinstallation définitive des personnes d'origine malienne*, Rapport de la mission interorganisations (UNDRO-FAO-PAM-FIDA) 1–21 December 1986, UNDRO/87/1, 1987.

White, C. (1984a) 'The WoDaabe', in J. J. Swift (ed.) *Pastoral Production in Central Niger*, Niamey: MDR/USAID, pp. 292–430, 462–529.

—— (1984b) 'Herd reconstitution: the role of credit among WoDaabe herders in central Niger', London: *ODI, Pastoral Development Network,* Paper 18d, 13 pp.

5 Development in Madura

An anthropological approach

Margaret Casey

This chapter discusses my involvement in a tubewell irrigation project in Madura, Indonesia. Development of the project began in 1979; wells were drilled, irrigation systems constructed and water management associations formed throughout the island. The original aim of the project was to increase agricultural production, mainly of rice. Given that Madurese society is male-dominated, an assumption seems to have been made that most Madurese farmers would be men. Madurese women are, however, highly visible in the fields today and make an important contribution to agricultural production. Since little was known about their actual involvement, particularly in decisions concerning agricultural practice, certain members of the project staff increasingly came to feel that women were not sufficiently integrated into the development project. My brief was to conduct a study of Madurese women in agriculture in general, focusing on women's roles in decision making and production, and to make recommendations as to how the extension programme might become more effective in conveying advice to women.

In the following pages I will describe how I prepared myself to work in Madura, and present background information on the island and the project before describing the study I conducted and its implications.

METHODOLOGY I: SECONDARY SOURCES

Madura, an island which lies off the north-east coast of Java, is traditionally known within Indonesia for the proud and aggressive character of its inhabitants, for its hot, dry climate and barren soils, and more recently, in the context of the tourist industry, for its bull races (*kerapan sapi*). This stereotyped image was the sum of my knowledge of Madura before I commenced research. I had first been approached concerning the possibility of undertaking the study in early January 1989; at the beginning of April I was advised that the Indonesian government had approved my nomination, and in early May the Overseas Development Administration (ODA) approved the assignment. The departure date was then set for 18 May. The length of the proposed study had been extended from one month, to six weeks, to two months. The suggested Terms of Reference (TOR), received in mid-April, indicated that a 'farming systems' survey of an informal nature was required, with a focus on specific areas of technical interest. The latter included land ownership, production arrangements, women's roles in marketing produce, in seed selection, storage and purchase, and women's attitudes and decision-making influence in the adoption of cash cropping and irrigation. The TOR also suggested that research be conducted in up to six locations across the island. I was in the final stages of completing my Ph.D. thesis (which examines the involvement of women in the economy of a weaving village in West Sumatra, Indonesia), so it was not until the thesis was submitted and the final go-ahead given in early May that I turned my full attention to the task of locating secondary material. I obviously needed to find out as much as I could, and quickly, in the fortnight which remained before my departure.

A starting point was the firm of consultants who were employing me. On visiting their offices, I found a whole shelf of monthly reports, annual reports, special bulletins and manuals. I studied and made notes on a number of these. I also talked to an economist who had made a short input to the project earlier in the year. This proved extremely helpful in fleshing out a picture of tubewell irrigation in Madura. Whilst in the office, I was somewhat perturbed to be handed a copy of a revised TOR from the South East Asia Development Division (SEADD) of the ODA, which laid stress on structured interviewing of stratified samples – a departure from the 'farming systems' survey advocated in the draft TOR drawn up by project staff in Madura. Which method was I supposed to employ?

Leaving this problem to one side, since it seemed that I was not going to find an answer in England, my second task was to locate monographs on Madura. I learned that until recently there was comparatively little ethnographic information on Madura and that which was available was largely in Dutch. Under the auspices of the Madura Research Project, which was set up to redress the paucity of data available on Madura and the Madurese, fieldwork was carried out by a number of Dutch Ph.D. students in the late 1970s and subsequently published in the 1980s. Of these volumes, I found the works of Jordaan (1985) and Niehof (1985) to be of immense value. Not only did they provide a great deal of factual and relatively up-to-date information on Madura, but their accounts of conducting research gave me an invaluable insight into the reality of living and working in Madurese villages. My appreciation of Madurese culture was facilitated particularly by Niehof's lucid and insightful analysis. When I later awoke in Madurese villages to a cacophony of cattle, poultry and the early morning call to prayer relayed at volume over the omnipotent loudspeaker, I was to recall Anke Niehof's 'Story of the Imam's loudspeaker' (1985: 17–20) with some sympathy. I also read articles and books on rice production, women in agriculture, women in development projects, irrigation projects and so forth.

I made contact with a number of persons who had utilized an anthropological approach in development work. Their areas of expertise covered various kinds of projects and encompassed different parts of the world; all were helpful and encouraging. Not least, they stressed to me the importance of clarifying the TOR I was engaged to work under. This was a point which I was already beginning to appreciate, given the late revision to my own TOR. I was also fortunate to meet the sociologist who had been working on the Madura project. My visit had been scheduled to coincide with his next input, so that I might benefit from his advice and experience. Meeting him in London, before my departure, was a bonus.

Finally, I made strenuous efforts to brush up my Indonesian. Although *Bahasa Indonesia*, the national language, is used in schools and government throughout the archipelago, there are estimated to be over 250 distinct languages. I knew that for the most part I would not be able to communicate directly with Madurese women, since many do not speak *Bahasa Indonesia*. I had been told that I would have a Madurese-speaking woman counterpart, and felt it important that I should be able to communicate with her as easily as possible.

I shall now present a picture of past and present Madura, which is based on my readings of secondary materials. The description of Madurese history relies heavily on Niehof's accounts (see Niehof 1982: 257–60; 1985: 23–9). My purpose here is to underline the fact that Madura is not, and was not, an island of uniformity. It is made up, as we shall see, of regions with distinct patterns of social organization, with varying climates and differing agricultural traditions. The possibilities for different constraints which might determine the effectiveness of development schemes are thus apparent, and constituted pointers for the kinds of questions I wanted to incorporate into the survey I was going to conduct.

HISTORICAL BACKGROUND

The name 'Madura' originally referred to the western half of the island, which consisted of several small principalities which were united at the end of the fifteenth century by the Prince of Plakaran. His son converted to Islam (as did many rulers in the archipelago at this time) and later established a rigorous Islamic rule. The pattern of events in the eastern half of the island are obscure. During the seventeenth century, however, hegemony was established over the whole of the island by the Mataram dynasty; subsequent uprisings exacerbated the antagonisms between east and west, and the East Madurese rulers allied themselves with the VOC (the Dutch East India Company). VOC control over the whole island was achieved in 1743 when West Madurese rulers also made alliances with the Dutch.

From 1743 until the late nineteenth century, when the island came under the direct rule of the Dutch government, Madura was not incorporated into a 'Culture System' as were Java and other parts of the Dutch East Indies. Given Madura's topography, there was no prospect of developing plantations; the only local industry of any importance was the salt industry. This aside, Madura was important for the soldiers it provided under contract to the colonial army (Madurese soldiers were known for their ferocity and bravery). In return for supplying contingents of drafted 'recruits', local rulers were given a free hand to enhance their personal power at the expense of the indigenous populace.

Madura was heavily dependent upon the food-producing areas of Java, particularly for rice, even though agriculture was the livelihood of most Madurese. Maize was an important crop, as was fruit production around Bangkalan in the west; tobacco was only culti-vated around Sumenep in the east. Other areas of economic activity were fishing, animal husbandry, the freight trade carried by *prahu* (traditional boats), and the salt industry. However, bad harvests and heavy taxation contributed to the deteriorating economic situation in the early years of the twentieth century. A Madura Welfare Fund became operational in 1937 but ended with the Japanese invasion in 1942. Despite the years of colonial subjugation endured under the Dutch, the Japanese occupation is still recalled by the Madurese as a time of terrible hardship and oppression. Many villagers died of illness or starvation, whilst others were carried off as *romusha* (involuntary workers).

At the end of the Second World War the Madurese economy was

in ruins. Desperate attempts during the colonial period to overcome the combined effects of a dry climate, infertile soils and increasing population pressure had resulted in a process of deforestation, erosion and soil exhaustion. An observer concluded in 1949 that Madura offered few possibilities for development because of its poor soils, its lack of minerals, and its unfavourable position with regard to energy and transportation. The returning Dutch were not welcomed, although, after the withdrawal of the colonial troops, plans were made to establish the island as one of the states in a Dutch-inspired Indonesian Federation. However, demands for economic assistance, for social and political reform, plus dislike of colonial rule and a growing solidarity with the movement for Indonesian independence led to Madura's incorporation into the province of East Java. The Madurese regencies which had been set up under the Dutch became part of the Republic of Indonesia.

PRESENT-DAY MADURA

Madura belongs to the administrative provincial unit of East Java. The former regencies – from west to east, Bangkalan, Sampang, Pamekasan and Sumenep – constitute four of the twenty-nine *kabupaten* (administrative districts) of the province. The population of Madura, according to the 1980 census, is about 2.7 million, with a low growth rate of 1 per cent, partly because of migration. Average population density is 557 persons per sq km. The majority of the population is dependent on subsistence level agriculture, the size of the average land holding being 0.1–0.2 ha. A 1982 land-use survey pointed out that only 14.1 per cent of all land in Madura is used for wet rice cultivation (*sawah*), whilst the corresponding figure for the province of East Java is 28.5 per cent. Compared to the rest of the province, Madura has a low level of education, literacy rate, per capita income and development. As in the past, there is still some animal husbandry, fishing, salt and tobacco production; there are also a few industries, such as tiles, bricks and textiles, in the centrally located villages of Sumenep.

From her fieldwork conducted between 1977 and 1979, Niehof (1985: 28) notes that a number of developments had occurred. First, productivity in the fishing industry had increased due to technological innovations. Secondly, tobacco cultivation, which in the past was confined to the Guluk-Guluk valley in Sumenep regency, had also expanded significantly. In the regency of Pamekasan, for instance, the area for tobacco cultivation almost doubled in the ten-year period between 1964 and 1974, from 5,792 ha to 10,623 ha. In 1976 more than 26,000 ha of tobacco were planted by smallholders, almost 50 per cent of the East Javanese and 20 per cent of the total Indonesian smallholders' tobacco acreage. Most of the Madurese tobacco comes from the regencies of Sumenep and Pamekasan.

Aside from this economic division between tobacco-growing areas in the east and non-tobacco-growing areas in the west, there is also a cultural division between the densely populated fishing communities on the coast, known as *orang pengghir sereng* (people who are reportedly impertinent, licentious and immoral in character), and the scattered farming groups in the countryside, known as *orang ghunong* (characterized as backward, stupid and dirty – largely because of the unavailability of water). There are also discernible cultural differences between east and west. The Madurese draw a distinction between the *halus* (refined) culture and language of East Madura and the *kasar* (coarse) forms found in West Madura. Sumenep is sometimes likened to Solo (a royal city famous for its influence on the arts and culture of central Java), implying a similarity with the capital of highly refined Javanese culture and reflecting the diverse history of the areas.

Stemming largely from economic reasons, but also tied in with social factors, is the prevalence of migration amongst the Madurese. Migration seems to have been a feature of Madurese socio-economic life for centuries; an observer recorded high numbers of migrants to Java after the transfer to direct rule. The lack of suitable land for agriculture meant that alternative forms of income earning had to be found. Migration may be permanent, as is illustrated by the high numbers of Madurese living in Java, particularly in the coastal towns and cities of East Java. However, seasonal migration is also significant, particularly from the west of the island. In the nineteenth century it seems that many Madurese worked on the plantations in East Java on a seasonal basis. Others worked as coolies in the port of Surabaya, whilst some were involved in the trading of cattle to Java and Kalimantan. Estimates from the late nineteenth century suggest that 40,000 migrants went to Java once or twice a year by *prahu*.

The ethnicity variable is no longer included in post-war censuses and population registration. Thus it is difficult to determine how many Madurese are living outside Madura. It would seem from the relatively low rates of annual population growth in Madura, and from the low sex ratios, that seasonal and permanent migration are still important. The prevalence of Madurese men migrating to East Java and beyond to find employment as *sate*-sellers (vendors of skewered meat barbecued over an open fire), *becak* drivers (pedicab drivers), coolies, and so forth, on a seasonal basis, is an aspect of life to which I shall be returning later.

So far I have only described the economic aspect of Madurese social structure. However, as Niehof (1982: 267–70) notes, other aspects of indigenous social organization are crucial to the understanding of Madurese life and must also be considered when studying the rural areas of Madura. The economic, religious and kinship networks which exist in Madura often overlap and their relevance for rural development may vary. I want to turn now to these aspects of social organization.

The important settlement unit in Madura is the *tanean*, which consists of one or more houses, kitchen(s), cattle sheds and a *longgar* (prayer house). The *tanean* is occupied by an extended family who are linked not only by kinship ties but also by bonds of economic and social interdependence and cooperation. It is a semi-autonomous unit which lies amongst the fields and is often bounded by hedges or fences. *Tanean* do not appear to have been linked together territorially. In the 1930s a Dutch scholar ascribed the individualism which is often said to be a feature of the Madurese character to be an expression of the predominance of the *tanean*-based kinship tie over any potential village tie.

Unlike Java, and other areas of Indonesia, the village (*desa*) in Madura is not a cohesive unit but an externally imposed unit. The village is sub-divided into *kampung* – which is confusing, because the Madurese also call a cluster of *tanean* a *kampung*. The latter does not, however, correspond to the administrative division termed *kampung* and is less firmly integrated than the *tanean*. The village head (*kepala desa*) is known locally as *klebun*, but he is not regarded as a community leader as is the case in other areas of Indonesia. He is elected by villagers but is often perceived to be little more than a government official who is responsible for collecting taxes, maintaining law and order and implementing government programmes. Of course, sometimes a *klebun* may be extremely influential, but this is more a function of his personality and other factors than an extension of his position as village head.

The impact of Islam on Madurese culture is manifold. The Madurese are known for their strict adherence to Islam, a fact which has had political consequences. Niehof (1982: 257–8) notes that in the 1971 elections 66.8 per cent of Madurese voted for the orthodox-Islamic party *Nahtadul Ulama*. Religious education has played a prominent role in maintaining this pre-eminence. A research project conducted in 1974 found that Madura had 12,221 *madrasah* and *pondok pesantren* (religious schools), with only 865 elementary schools and sixty-two schools for secondary education. The religious teachers known as *kiyai* occupy a strategic role in village life. As head of a *pesantren*, a *kiyai* establishes a close relationship with his students (*santri*), which continues throughout their lives. This relationship often assumes a patron–client tie, with *santri* remaining loyal to a *kiyai* in return for protection. A *kiyai* may thus build up a powerful political and economic position. Women may also become religious teachers (*nyai*), but they do not seem to assume the importance which *kiyai* achieve. Niehof (1982: 171) notes that many Madurese villagers regard the *kiyai* as a legal representative of Islam and as such capable of conducting weddings, even though according to the Indonesian government's marriage laws of 1975 all Muslim marriages have to be conducted by the religious official. *Hajis* (those who have made the pilgrimage to Mecca) may also command a great deal of power and respect. Koran reading groups (*pengajian*) are often the only village-based organization in which a significant number of women are involved.

Other individuals who occupy prominent positions within Madurese villages include *orang blater* or *orang berani* (literally translated as 'brave men'), and *dukun* (a person who has mystical powers). *Orang berani*, by means of their exceptionally aggressive character, may wield considerable social and economic influence within the village and may also be prominent in political affairs. *Dukun* are consulted on a variety of matters: for traditional medicines, on the most suitable date for a wedding ceremony, and to fix dates for other auspicious moments in an individual's life.

Finally, it is a facet of Madurese character that one's honour must be defended at all costs. This is true of all rural areas, but particularly so in West Madura. The tradition of *carok* (revenge killing with a sickle-shaped knife) is the ultimate and, within the community, legitimate means by which an insult may be avenged.

Thus a number of considerations may possibly hinder the successful operation of a community-based project: the balance of power held by local leaders, particularly Islamic leaders, against whom officials may be reluctant to precipitate anti-government feelings; the lack of organization at the village level, which is not conducive to government administration; migration patterns; and attitudes towards external intervention which have been developed over centuries of interference by outside forces. That these factors do affect a project was made plain by the Sociology Adviser in the 1986 Annual Report; he states that in one village in West Madura, where an *orang berani* had become the *klebun*, his personal opposition to the tubewell project had ensured that the whole village had also opposed it. Further progress at that time was made impossible. In other cases, disputes over village boundaries cause problems as to who has the right of access to tubewell irrigation. Those who actually own the land may live outside the village boundary and are thus not represented on water management associations. Disputes also seem to have arisen over tubewells in relation to the appointment of tubewell operators, involving different factions within a village. Such conflicts are often perceived to be internal affairs, however serious they become, and government officials are again reluctant to become involved.

I shall turn now to the Madura Ground Water Project – to the reasons for its inception, how it was financed and implemented, and the role of sociology in the project at the time of my appointment.

THE PROJECT

In the Regional Development Plan of East Java for the period 1979–84 (Indonesia's Third Five-Year Plan) high priority was given to Madura. The Indonesian government, with the assistance of international agencies, directed its efforts to the development of Madura.

It is in the context of Madura's poverty and lack of resources that the Madura Groundwater Irrigation Project (MGIP) has been developed. The island is some 160 km long, up to 38 km wide and covers an area of 4,382 sq km. It is rugged and hilly but not mountainous, the highest point being 470 m above sea level. The general structure is of an easterly dipping anticline with the axis running through the centre. A 50- to 300-m thick limestone formation outcrops as prominent escarpments to the north and south. The limestone soils offered but marginal potential for agriculture in the past, as we have seen; however, the limestone formation itself holds the only real potential for groundwater abstraction for irrigation. To the north and south of the limestone ridge lie alluvial plains.

The climate is essentially tropical, but Madura has a more pronounced dry season than neighbouring Java, with droughts of four to six months. Dry season I falls between April and July, while dry season II falls between August and November. The wet season falls between December and March. However, the length of the seasons may fluctuate from year to year and from one area of the island to another. Rainfall varies significantly between different parts of the island, generally increasing away from the coast and from east to west. The mean annual rainfall varies from 1,250 to 1,750 mm in the east to 1,750 to 2,100 mm in the western inland area.

The project was originally designed to intensify wet rice (*sawah*) production. Soils were classified according to their suitability for wet rice, the classification being generally assumed to indicate a general suitability for irrigated development. This emphasis was in accordance with the aims of the Indonesian government's then agricultural policy to achieve national self-sufficiency in rice. One of the main changes envisaged as a result of groundwater development on Madura was the conversion of *tegal* (unirrigated land), previously supporting a rainfed cropping pattern of *padi gogo rancah* (dry land rice) and/or maize, to land suitable for wet rice. The aim was to grow two irrigated wetland rice crops. Such a change in land use was expected to result in a very large increase in agricultural production and be one of the major benefits of any groundwater development.

The project was implemented through the Indonesian Directorate General of Water Resources Development (DGWRD) by the Directorate of Irrigation II (DOI II). The executing agency within the DOI II is the Groundwater Development Sub-Directorate (PAT) which has Groundwater Development Project (P2AT) offices at provincial level and in the actual areas of operation. As P2AT is a government agency, it has to work through the existing apparatus of civil adminstration, from *kabupaten* to *kecamatan* (adminstrative sub-district) to *desa* (village). The Madura project comes under the jurisdiction of the East Java Groundwater Development Project Executive Board in Surabaya (BP P2AT Jawa Timur), which oversees all the groundwater projects in the province.

Financial support has been provided from the ODA (for the services of the principal consultants), from the European Economic Community (for the services of local consultants, technical assistance programmes, procurement of equipment and construction contracts) and also from the government of Indonesia. Liaison is maintained with the EEC and ODA mainly at Directorate General and Directorate level. Responsibility for the project was handed over from the EEC delegation in Bangkok to the Delegation in Jakarta on 28 November 1986. The principal consultants are Groundwater Development Consultants (International) Ltd (GDC) of Cambridge, United Kingdom, whilst the local consultants are Indec and Associates of Bandung, Indonesia.

Following reconnaissance studies and investigations from 1972 onwards, to determine the scope for development, the project has been implemented in four phases to date:

Phase 1	February 1979 – April 1982
Interim Phase	May 1982 – February 1984
Phase 2	March 1984 – February 1987
Phase 3	March 1987 – October 1990

Phase 1 consisted of a combined investigation and implementation programme during which design criteria were formulated and the necessary operation, maintenance and agricultural extension organization established in preparation for full-scale development. In the event, the late arrival of equipment and the subsequent delays in installation of new pumpsets necessitated an Interim Phase. By March 1984, forty-eight tubewells were in operation, irrigating some 1,660 ha. This represented about 30 per cent of the total development potential identified in the Phase 1 Final Report (February 1982), based on the estimated area of suitable land and availability of water in the development zones. Each tubewell typically serves a command area of between 30 and 60 ha and is divided into irrigation blocks, usually seven in number.

The extent of the potential aquifer was further delineated by hydro-geological studies conducted during Phase 2. The island's division into zones reflects the original selection of hydro-geological units. Aquifer properties and recharge estimates were also investigated further. Phase 2 involved the drilling of forty-eight tubewells, bringing the total irrigated area by March 1987 to some 3,400 ha. During Phase 3, a further thirty tubewells have been drilled, bringing the total to 126. The irrigation systems for the tubewells drilled during Phase 2 were also completed. The total designed irrigated area for the project as a whole is 4,633 ha.

The project is also concerned with the training of operation and maintenance staff, the consolidation of agricultural extension work, and the strengthening of local institutions. One of the key activities in this respect is to provide assistance in the formation of farmer water-users' associations (*Himpunan Petani Pemakai Air*, usually known as HIPPA), and in making these more effective. Support is recognized to be essential in areas such as Madura, where farmers have little or no previous experience of irrigation. The aim is to hand over the running of the wells to the individual HIPPA and the local government after two years of support (costs of diesel, operator's salary and so forth), although this has not always been possible. By the end of 1989, seventy wells had been handed over.

An extension to the current phase is being negotiated and seems likely to be forthcoming. The aims of this phase will be to complete ongoing HIPPA training and crop-demonstration programmes for the last batch of wells to be commissioned, and to try and improve logistical and financial support for the HIPPAs on a pilot basis.

SOCIOLOGICAL COMPONENT OF THE PROJECT

It was noted by the ODA Social Development Adviser, following his visit to Madura in 1985, that the original proposal for the MGIP had suggested that studies be conducted by a socio-economist over a three-month period to gauge farmer response. This proposal was subsequently modified by the Social Development Adviser to cover selection of sites, water charges and extension, and to clarify the effect of land tenure, cropping patterns and institutions on farmer response. Under these modifications, a sociologist or anthropologist would undertake this work over a six-month period.

The sociology programme was established in April 1985 with the appointment of a GDC Sociology Adviser (a man) and two Indec sociologists (also men). The GDC adviser made three inputs during 1985–86, whilst the two Indec sociologists were in post for twelve months. Following the recommendations of the Social Development Adviser, the sociologists focused upon the planning and design of new tubewell irrigation systems on the island.

A procedure had been drawn up after the Social Development Adviser's visit by project staff, whereby approximately three days would be spent at each new site and data would be collected on social structure, especially on kinship patterns, settlement units, religious groups and other village-level organizations. It was also the aim to cover such spheres as the strategy of mixed cropping, harvesting systems, non-farm incomes, market structure, the attitudes of farmers to tubewell irrigation, migration patterns, land ownership and village boundaries. The three-day survey would be backed up by three meetings in each village at which the views of farmers would be sought. Before these meetings were set up, a visit would be made to each village head to explain the objectives of the project, and it would be the responsibility of the village head to invite 'relevant farmers' to the meetings. Contact would also be made with officials at higher administrative levels – the *kabupaten* and *kecamatan* – and *Dinas Pertanian* (the Agricultural Service).

The focus of discussions was on the proposed areas to be irrigated, on possible canal alignments and block boundaries, and the final layout of the irrigation system. It was hoped that in holding these meetings as many interests as possible would come to be represented in the HIPPA and that any social factors which ought to be incorporated into the design of irrigation systems would be identified. The village studies were to be conducted by one of the Indec sociologists, whilst the GDC sociologist was to be responsible for reviewing the results of the programme, dealing with any problems occurring after the installation of pumps, and for report writing. The sociologists were expected to cooperate with the Design, Water Management and Agriculture sections of the project.

The above procedure was instituted too late to be incorporated into the 1984–85 programme, and since some work had already been undertaken in villages falling into the 1985–86 programme, the first two meetings were compressed into one. The procedure was implemented in 1986–87 for the Phase 3 drilling programme, although due to staff shortages the number of meetings was reduced from three to two. The three-day village studies were rarely undertaken because the Indec sociologist was heavily involved in the consultation meetings.

The Social Development Adviser had also pointed out the need for an extension strategy which incorporated women (see Conlin 1985: 16). Whilst recognizing that time constraints might make this difficult, he was of the opinion that a 'small supplementary study' might be considered for the future. However, his recommendations concerning the study of the impact of tubewell irrigation on women were not taken up. In the MGIP annual report (1986: 158), the Sociology Adviser stated that 'At present a further study is not considered necessary. . . . If time permits, further investigations of these points may be carried out during the remaining inputs . . . but at present have a low priority.' The sociology programme was originally scheduled to finish in 1986 but was subsequently extended. During Phases 2 and 3 the Sociology Adviser has currently made a total input of 7.5 man-months, with 1.0 man-month outstanding as of December 1989; following the end of the two Indec sociologists' input, one was retained for a further six months. Besides participating in the programme of site selection and evaluation, the sociologists also focused on those areas where take-up of tubewell irrigation facilities had been poor, particularly in West Madura. This involved the use of agricultural demonstration plots, videos and posters in an effort to increase farmer interest and involvement, plus the physical rehabilitation of irrigation systems (that is, lining tertiary canals, defining irrigation blocks and so on).

The primary aim of the sociology programme, as stated in the MGIP annual report of 1986 (1986: 154), was to ensure 'that all the parties and interests may be consulted . . . avoiding the alienation or exclusion of some elements from tubewell development at an early stage'. Although stress was placed on involving farmers, the participation of women in agriculture was not considered. The possibility that women might be farmers and as such should play a role in the procedure of meetings outlined above was not entertained. Moreover, in the efforts made to present the project as the responsibility of farmers, rather than an external imposition, the failure to involve women was a double omission.

The Social Development Adviser's recommendations had been echoed by a SEADD Natural Resources Adviser in 1986, but no new initiatives were made. An impetus to the study of women was provided by the appointment of a new agriculturalist to the project in mid-1987. A brief survey of women in agricultural production was subsequently undertaken by the Indec sociologist in October 1987 on the north coast of *kabupaten* Bangkalan. Although a woman student was employed on the survey, she was not deployed in the field but fulfilled an administrative role, and the Indec sociologist did not spend any nights in the field (see below). The ensuing report raised many more questions than it answered. The agriculturalist argued forcibly for a further study to be undertaken, offering to give up part of his allocated input so that the financial factor could not be used as a stumbling block. However, it was eventually agreed that the study should go ahead utilizing savings in the 'visiting specialists'' input in the ODA consultancy contract.

An explanation is necessary here concerning the appointment of a sociologist/anthropologist to conduct the study. It was not the case that project staff decided to opt for an expatriate sociologist-anthropologist from the outset; in fact, it was a last resort. A number of Indonesian institutions and individuals were approached concerning the availability and suitability of a woman to undertake the research. Given the tight schedule, it proved difficult to find someone who was able to do the research. Methodology proved to be another problem; one woman who was available was a fervent adherent of the quantitative approach, and informed the project members who were interviewing her that she would require at least one month to conduct the pilot study for her proposed questionnaire.

There is a wide gap between the admittedly less well-defined qualitative (or ethnographic) approach and the quantitative approach. The latter produces masses of data and utilizes the latest statistical packages; it is, in short, often perceived to be more tangible and 'scientific'. However, the results of such studies do not necessarily increase our understanding of the particular problem under investigation. This does not mean that the qualitative approach is necessarily superior; it too has its drawbacks (see White 1982: 1). Preconceived ideas may merely be reinforced by spells of participant observation. Nevertheless, the qualitative approach is potentially an invaluable tool in helping to break down barriers between the 'observer' and the 'observed'. It may lead to insights as to why certain things happen in a certain way which a formal questionnaire, however rigorous, might identify but fail totally to explain.

The proposed study was not intended to be a quantitative survey of the roles of Madurese women; it was felt that what was required was a specific study of a qualitative nature. It was in this context, having failed to track down a woman who had the time and inclination to undertake such a study, that the project staff turned to overseas candidates. Through a series of chance meetings my name was nominated.

Since I have touched on the employment of indigenous personnel, it is as well to mention at this point another factor which has to be taken into account. My initial surprise at the stipulation in the TOR that I stay in villages overnight (how else would I conduct the study?) was subsequently explained by project staff. They told me that in their experience, Indonesian social scientists were often loath to stay in villages at night. It is important to remember that higher education is a goal which many aspire to in Indonesia but only an elite few achieve. Thus those Indonesians who have achieved the equivalent of an M.A. or Ph.D. may be reluctant to spend nights in a village, since day-to-day life in a rural area is not perceived to be commensurate with their status. In the context of the MGIP, a highly educated Javanese may have found the prospect of enduring physical hardships in a Madurese village not to his or her liking.

METHODOLOGY II: PRIMARY SOURCES

Although I had received the amended TOR in early May, project staff had not received the information until 17 May, three days before my arrival on the island. It was felt by project staff and myself that the alterations departed somewhat from the intended purpose of the study; the project's requirement was for qualitative information of an explanatory nature, as mentioned above. Such results might only be achieved, we felt, by means of informal, participatory research, rather than from a questionnaire survey and formal interviews. In any case, the time allocated for the study would not have permitted the sort of extensive survey and sampling which appeared to be envisaged in the amended TOR. What was required, we felt, was an anthropological approach rather than a sociological approach, since the emphasis was on understanding relationships between social groups and institutions rather than on the collection of statistical data.

Following discussions with the Sociology Adviser and the Agriculturalist, the TOR were subsequently re-negotiated with the South East Asia Development Division in Bangkok. It was agreed that four periods of fieldwork would be conducted in villages across the island and that a rapid informal participant-observation approach would be utilized. The advantage of this type of research, as I have indicated above, is that it yields a considerable amount of data on interpersonal relations, on gender roles, on figures of authority, political differences and so on, within a particular locale. This information is essential in projects which require community partici-pation. If a systematic survey is required at a later date, the data gathered from the informal participatory study forms an invaluable base from which meaningful questions may be framed.

With the TOR ascertained, I was able to concentrate on how I would conduct the study. I had been informed that I would have a Madurese-speaking woman as a counterpart, but in the eventuality I had two counterparts. One was a young Madurese woman who had a degree in sociology, and the second was an Indec woman agricul-tural field assistant from West Sumatra who was just beginning a long-term assignment to MGIP after completing an M.Sc. degree in Java. Although our relative youth as a team might have worked against us, I felt that I was fortunate on a number of points.

First, both women tackled the fieldwork with youthful optimism and a sense of adventure. They raised no objections to being taken away from the project headquarters for a week at a time, an aspect of the research which might have proved problematic with an older woman. This is not to suggest that we sailed through the periods of village research; we did encounter problems in the field, some of which were overcome whilst others proved intractable. Some villages we were genuinely sorry to leave, because we had formed close attachments with the villagers, whilst one village was left with no regrets. However, I felt that the youthfulness of my counterparts allowed them a degree of flexibility which might well have been missing in an older person.

Secondly, and this point is also related to age, is the question of methodology (particularly in the light of the anthropology versus sociology problematic outlined above; see also Gatter, this volume). I had drawn up a preliminary checklist of topics for discussion. My counterparts were initially highly suspicious of this checklist (and my explanations of participant-observation) and could not envisage how we were going to return to Pamekasan with any data at all. They made a number of attempts to turn the checklist into a formal questionnaire. Obviously, my success in eliciting information was going to depend heavily on my Madurese counterpart, since she was the one who would communicate directly with women villagers. It was essential that she understood why I proposed to use this form of methodology so that when we began the village studies we operated as a cohesive team, not split by misunderstandings and misgivings. After many talks between me, the Sociology Adviser (who, as a man and senior sociologist, commanded a great deal of respect), and the Agriculturalist (who was intimately involved with many aspects of the project, not just agricultural matters, and was immensely popular), both counterparts became amenable to, if not wholly appreciative of, the informal approach I intended to use. Subsequently, over the course of time spent in the four villages, my Madurese counterpart became very adept in the participant-observation method; my Indec counterpart also adapted well to the requirements I made of her. In my opinion her further training made her less flexible; she was used to formal surveys, to having a clear and definite role, and seemed to find the qualitative approach unsettling. Given these facts, I felt that I was fortunate again in my counterparts; if I had worked with an older woman, more experienced in the use of quantitative methods, I might well have encountered greater resistance to my own preferred methodology and the whole study might have failed.

When I arrived at the project headquarters in Pamekasan I had six days to study secondary sources, visit tubewells in various zones, discuss possible village sites, obtain authorization to reside in the selected villages, find suitable accommodation in the villages and, as discussed above, re-negotiate my TOR, draw up a checklist and persuade my counterparts of its utility. The back-up provided by project staff was amazing; I recalled the frustrations and delays which I had experienced before I was able to commence fieldwork proper for my Ph.D. thesis, and could only be thankful that the bureaucratic side of conducting field research was completely taken off my shoulders.

Four villages were selected for fieldwork; these villages spanned the island, from the drier eastern areas where tobacco is an important cash crop, to the wetter west, where migration is more prevalent and where efforts are being made to establish *polowijo* crops (in the Madurese context, crops other than rice), as cash crops. We were able to spend a week in each village conducting informal discussions with women. On our arrival in each village, it was necessary to have a formal meeting with the village head. Subsequent relations with village heads varied; in one village we did not see the man again until our departure, whilst in the other villages we met up at intermittent intervals as we conducted our research. We tried to set up a meeting with village women on the same day as our arrival if this was feasible, or the following day if this was not practicable, in order to alleviate as far as possible any suspicions or misapprehensions regarding our purpose in conducting research.

We directed our efforts to meeting women wherever they happened to be – transplanting rice seedlings, weeding tobacco plants, finding fodder for cattle, planting groundnuts, performing the myriad of tasks subsumed under the label 'housework', and so forth. The interviews were generally conducted in Madurese, largely because most women did not speak Indonesian but also because it was the language they were most familiar with. When we came upon a group of women and found that someone did speak Indonesian, the Indec counterpart would conduct an interview either by herself or with me. The study included women from different areas of the village, of different age groups or marital status, and with varying access to land and income-earning activities. The working pattern of our day typically fell into two parts, from 7 a.m. to midday and from 2 p.m. to 5 p.m. This was supplemented by visits to or from those women who lived close to the *tanean* in which we were residing, plus discussions with the men and women members of our *tanean*. These occasions were often extremely relaxed and yielded all kinds of information.

It proved possible to focus on particular topics as and when they arose, which would have been difficult if we had been administering formal questionnaires. Such topics typically concerned issues of local interest; thus in one village discussions frequently centred on tobacco, whilst in another women were keen to talk about *polowijo* crops. In the west, male migration and the opportunities to earn additional, non-agricultural incomes proved popular topics of conversation, whilst animal husbandry was much discussed in the fourth village. Thus key topics were identified by the women themselves and subsequently explored within the specific context of each village study.

One problem we encountered in each village was in persuading men that we wished to talk with women; wherever we were, men would appear, intent on telling us 'what we really wanted to know'. Men were keen that we should receive the 'right' answer to our questions, and obviously felt that their womenfolk might misinform us and that this would have repercussions for the village as a whole. An otherwise satisfying discussion with a woman would often come to an abrupt end when a man appeared, because women seemed reluctant to talk freely with men present (although there were exceptions). The first time this happened I let the discussion proceed; later, as it became obvious that the man concerned was not going to have his say and go but would stay on the scene as long as we did, I was forced to intervene and state my case as politely as possible. My Madurese counterpart was naturally reluctant to breach Madurese manners by asking a man to be quiet; as a foreigner I was able to make this kind of interjection without jeopardizing the study. Some men (and women) found these incidents amusing, although possibly for opposing reasons. I must confess that occasionally I had to resort to flattery in order to proceed; I would tell the man or men in question that the authorities knew that men were knowledgeable about irrigation, the use of pesticides, the availability of new strains and crops and so forth, but the point of the present survey was to find out what women knew or did not know so that they might receive advice geared specifically to their needs. I wanted to spend as much time as possible with women without alienating or antagonizing men, since this might have unfortunate consequences for the women concerned and also for the future success of the extension programme. This meant that sometimes I had to exercise a great deal of patience, which, given the time constraints, was not always easy.

The aim was to complete three interviews daily; the length of each interview varied considerably. On average we conducted twenty interviews in each village. I had hoped to be able to meet women at night, in their own homes, but given the isolated nature of *tanean* in rural Madura this was not always possible or feasible. However, lamplight permitting, I was able to discuss with my counterparts any problems or new ideas which had surfaced during the day and to transcribe the interviews into English.

At the end of each village study, approximately four days were spent in Pamekasan analysing the data, discussing the findings with project staff, writing a preliminary village study and preparing for the next village. The final week was spent in completing a draft report; it was essential to have this written before my departure because SEADD had requested that on my way back to London I should stop over in Bangkok to be debriefed.

FINDINGS OF THE STUDY

The introduction of tubewells and the adoption of new farming technology has had a significant impact on traditional cropping patterns in Madura. With the availability of irrigation water it is now possible to grow three crops in many of the command areas. Tobacco has flourished as a cash crop in the drier east, whilst in Central Madura there is now a greater diversity of cash crops, including tobacco, chilli, cucumber, shallot, water melon and soya bean. In West Madura, the cultivation of rice, groundnuts and maize, together with small amounts of mungbean, cow peas, sesame seed and sweet potato, is combined with animal husbandry. Migration by men is still a feature of life in the western part of the island. Proximity to the port of Kamal and to East Java and the unsuitable climate for tobacco production mean that many men still look to migration for their livelihood. In East and Central Madura, however, it is no longer imperative for men to find work elsewhere since the growth of tobacco as a cash crop has opened up new opportunities for income-earning. In one of the villages studied, a number of men had given up their jobs as *becak* drivers and *kaki lima* (street hawkers) and become actively involved in the cultivation of crops, even though the tubewell had only been in operation for a year.

The village case studies established that Madurese women make a central contribution to various stages of agricultural production. All the women interviewed named farming as their principal source of income. Although men prepare the land for crop cultivation (namely, ploughing, hoeing and harrowing the soil), women are generally responsible for a large proportion of the ensuing activities. Whether it is rice, tobacco, maize, or other *polowijo* crops which are culti-vated, the labour inputs for planting, transplanting, weeding and harvesting are supplied by women. They also provide labour under the *gotong-royong* system, whereby family members and neighbours come together and work as a group on each person's land in rotation, with no wage involved. This is an important form of labour for many small farming enterprises, since a large group may be assembled and the work completed in a short span of time. Women are usually responsible for supervising waged labourers in the field and for providing food and drinks to waged and unwaged labourers. The tasks of drying and storing seed and grain and of marketing agricultural produce also fall to women.

A significant proportion of women in the village studies participated in multiple income-earning activities, which varied according to local topographical conditions and proximity to market centres. These activities included cattle husbandry, poultry raising, trading in fish, fruit and other goods, making a variety of snacks, working as masseuses, and so on. Further, most women were involved in nonproductive activities. It falls to women to prepare and cook food, obtain water for bathing and cooking, collect firewood for cooking, to care for children, keep the house and yard swept clean, and so forth.

The establishment of tubewell irrigation systems, together with the introduction of high-yielding rice and maize varieties, new cash crops, and the availability of fertilizers and insecticides, would appear to have altered the balance of power between men and women. It is important to bear in mind that farming in Madura is based on the *tanean*, and that women members traditionally played a key role within this unit. In the past, women learned farming techniques and practices from their parents so that there was a smooth transition of skills and knowledge from one generation to the next. Women were intimately involved in the various stages of decision making and production, and because their menfolk were often absent from the village in search of work, women were directly responsible for all aspects of farming. The method of acquiring knowledge from firsthand experience still prevails. However, it would seem that women are being denied access to the information needed to operate the new technology because they are not included in the extension programme. The institutionalization of information – on the use of tubewell water, new strains and crops, credit arrangements and so on – seems to have brought about a sharper differentiation of 'male' and 'female' spheres of activity and influence.

It was clear from the findings of the study that the extension programme was missing a significant proportion of farmers because it was not making direct contact with women farmers. The extension services exist to disseminate technical assistance, to advise farmers on land preparation, on the availability of alternative crops and new seed varieties, the use of fertilizers and so forth. However, extension messages have been targeted at men; it is men who are invited to attend the preliminary meetings and who are subsequently invited to form the HIPPA. In the four villages studied, there were no women officials on the HIPPA; the *ketua kelompok* (heads of the irrigation blocks) were also all men. Invitations to meetings with Agricultural Field Assistants are usually only extended to men. A considerable number of women farmers said that they had never met or spoken with an extension worker, either from P2AT or the Agriculture Service. Videos were produced by P2AT (on tubewell agriculture and water users' associations) and shown in villages as part of the HIPPA training programme. Few women had seen these videos, despite the fact that in a rural area the showing of a video would be quite a social event. Women did not feel that they could simply turn up when they had not been invited. It seems that the only women who are at liberty to attend meetings are divorcees, widows and those whose husbands are incapacitated. Even within this minority group, few actually attend because they feel uncomfortable attending what is, in effect, a gathering of men.

According to Madurese *adat* (custom), men are perceived to be the head of the household whilst women are traditionally associated with cultivating the land, becoming wives and mothers, and holding the *tanean* together. This is reflected in the fact that a daughter may, in some areas, inherit twice as much as a son, because as a man the latter is free to leave the village and find work elsewhere. Both men and women are involved in decisions concerning the choice of crop to be planted, the purchase and application of fertilizers, the use of tubewell water and the sale of crops. Women are also household managers, responsible for the day-to-day running of the household, a fact which is directly related to the cultural association of women with food. By making men the target for extension messages (even in areas where they were absent from the village for long periods), they have been elevated above the *tanean* milieu in which they exist.

The extension programme, then, is skewed in its approach to farmers; services have been directed towards men, who have been identified as effective farm managers, and the knowledge which men acquire (or have access to, since not all men fully understand the extension messages) does not seem to filter through to women easily. Women are at a distinct disadvantage because they do not have ready access to the knowledge on which to base their choices. For example, a number of women in the survey did not know very much about pesticides because their husbands took care of this aspect of production. Although women were observed applying pesticides in the field, when questioned they did not know the brand name, the costs involved, or the optimum amount to use. Other women informed us that they did not use pesticides because they were afraid of

damaging the crop and of poisoning themselves and their livestock
(the leaves from various crops are used as fodder). They preferred
to let any infestation take its natural course. That women have
continued to participate in the decision-making process, albeit on a
diminished scale, is a measure of their tenacity and enthusiasm to
pick up information despite being virtually ignored by the extension
programme.

Leaving gender differentiation to one side, I want now to look at
the impact of tubewell irrigation on other aspects of village organization. The family unit has traditionally been an important source of
mutual help and cooperation for its members. It is from within the
cluster of *tanean* that an individual may seek interest-free loans to
buy seed and draw labour under the *gotong-royong* system. However, with the introduction of tubewell irrigation, the new crops and
varieties of rice and maize require greater expenditure on chemical
fertilizers and pesticides. Traditional kinship networks are no longer
always adequate to provide the cash flow required. This has meant
that in some villages small farmers have had to turn to wealthy
individuals for loans to purchase seed and fertilizers, to pay water
charges, and so forth. These same individuals may also be prominent
in buying up quantities of agricultural produce from small farmers.
This was illustrated well in one of the villages where a *haji* who
bought up a high percentage of the chilli crop (known locally as
lombok) was nicknamed 'Haji Lombok'. These wealthy individuals
may also be the proprietors of *kios* (village shops) which sell feed,
fertilizer, pesticides, farming tools, and a variety of household items
such as sugar, soap and oil. The *kios* undoubtedly provide a con-
venient service, making it possible for small farmers to purchase
small quantities of goods on a credit basis. However, at the same
time, small farmers are increasingly enmeshed in a patron–client
relationship, becoming even more dependent on a handful of individuals for inputs, credit and the marketing of produce. It would be
extremely difficult for small farmers to disentangle themselves from
this situation.

Women have traditionally been involved in small trading. The
expansion of tobacco production in East and Central Madura has
meant that the dynamics of economic networks have changed from
a range of local, personal contacts to a hierarchical structure which
extends beyond the local and interlocal markets. Agents of the
large *kretek* (tobacco mixed with cloves) cigarette companies from
East Java often buy the tobacco crop whilst it is still in the field,
thus cutting out the small trader altogether. Sometimes a wealthy

individual will make arrangements to buy the tobacco crop of a number of villagers, and then sell to the agent. Tobacco has proved to be an immensely popular and successful cash crop in East and Central Madura. It is from the sale of the tobacco harvest that debts which have accrued throughout the year are paid off. Any surplus cash is used to buy gold or cattle (as a form of insurance against hard times in the coming year), to pay for house repairs, school fees, medical costs and so forth. Post-harvest is also a popular time for wedding festivities.

In an effort to develop a comparable cash crop in the west of Madura, the emphasis has been on promoting a diverse range of *polowijo* crops, and promoting new strains of rice and maize. However, the failure to date to establish such a cash crop may be interpreted as a blessing of sorts since it has enabled women to maintain and in some cases expand their traditional trading roles.

Intercropping is traditionally practised in Madura. But farmers commented that when rice is intercropped with *ardjuna* (a high-yielding strain of maize which the government is promoting), the rice crop is often poor because *ardjuna* absorbs a lot of water. When *ardjuna* is intercropped with groundnuts, the yield from the ground-nut harvest is low because *ardjuna* absorbs more nutrients from the soil than the local variety of maize. Women are reluctant to give up planting maize because it is a staple food crop; on the other hand, they also wish to continue planting groundnuts because the latter is an important source of cash. Some women have attempted to solve the problem by intercropping the local variety of maize, which is a much smaller plant, with groundnuts in the main body of their plot of land, and planting small amounts of *ardjuna* around the perimeter of the plot. The *ardjuna* cobs are then sold, whereas the local maize is stored.

Many women farmers informed us that the seed from *ardjuna* does not store well. Further, the taste is not liked. Maize is a staple foodstuff in Madura, traditionally eaten mixed with rice. The problems surrounding indigenous ideologies of food, and the risks involved in planting a new variety or new crop, are difficult to pin down. The presence in Madurese kitchens of *lumbung* and *jurung*, large containers used to store rice and maize respectively, are indicative of the value placed on storing agricultural produce for the forthcoming year.

There are obviously different perceptions concerning the utility of tubewell irrigation. In West Madura, for example, the government has prioritized the production of cash crops (although, as we have seen earlier, its original aim was to ensure self-sufficiency in rice production) and promoted new, higher-yielding varieties of maize which do not conform to villagers' requirements. Farmers, on the other hand, see irrigation water as a means of ensuring that they are self-sufficient in foodstuffs. Only when this basic need is satisfied will the possibility of cultivating cash crops be explored. Many express a natural anxiety that if they switch to new crops or varieties they may face disaster if the crops fail. Part of the answer would seem to lie in directing the extension programme to those who are directly involved in producing, storing, preparing and marketing agricultural produce; that is, to women farmers.

RECOMMENDATIONS AND CONCLUSIONS

Phase 3 of the project is coming to an end, although the tubewells should be in operation for another twenty to thirty years. P2AT will at some point in the future withdraw and pass on the responsibility of technical services to the local government. The latter will be responsible for implementing future extension programmes. If previous work is to be consolidated and improved upon, the scope of the programme must be broadened to incorporate the roles of women in agricultural production and decision making. If men continue to be singled out as recipients of the extension services there will be a corresponding loss of socio-economic status for women. The extension programme would obviously be much more successful if directed towards both men and women. Ways must, therefore, be found of communicating extension methods to women as a group.

In the recommendations made in my report, I suggested that specific steps be taken to involve women in the extension programme. One of the major obstacles in such an endeavour will be in making contact with women, for it is clear that women are not represented in village-level institutions. As a consequence of this isolation, women have had little opportunity to develop leadership skills. When developing and adapting the existing extension programme, the various cultural constraints which women face must be acknowledged.

I felt that training and institution building will be key factors in reaching rural women in Madura. As a preliminary to implementing any programme, it will be useful to ascertain the numbers of men and women employed as Agricultural Field Assistants by the Agriculture Service. There are innate problems in trying to use men Assistants to approach women farmers in the Madurese context. In discussions with the Agricultural Field Assistant in one village, it was apparent that the man was aware of the gap in the extension service as regards women. He felt that he could not approach women farmers as a group. Efforts will have to be made to recruit more women staff, with priority being given to Madurese speakers, who may then be trained and deployed to work with rural women. As a corollary to this, men extension workers should receive some re-orientation training to make them more explicitly aware of the scope of women farmers' activities and problems. The Agriculture Service possesses the infrastructural capabilities of reaching village women and working with them, and efforts should be made to encourage adminstrative officials to put pressure on, and support, the Agriculture Service in mobilizing its undoubted potential to maximum effect.

In the drive to increase contact with women farmers, I recommended that women should be invited to special explanation meetings, that they should be integrated wherever possible into the water-users' associations (HIPPA), and that women's farmer groups should be set up. Efforts should also be made to involve more women in demonstration plots, so that they may learn at first hand about new crops and strains, recommended cropping patterns, inputs, water management and irrigation practices. I also felt that greater use should be made of extension materials. Because the majority of women in the survey did not appear to have seen the P2AT videos, it would be helpful to show the videos in selected areas at times which suit women. As regards posters, I suggested that they be displayed at various points around the villages, and not just at pumphouses. A likely site might be rice mills, which are a popular congregation point for women. I also suggested that a poster be designed which was specifically targeted at women, to emphasize the fact that tubewell irrigation is not the preserve of male farmers but is there for the benefit of the whole community.

If information is to travel beyond a small number of women, then contact groups must be set up with precise objectives. Existing women's organizations might prove useful here. Family welfare programmes – Pembinaan Kesejahteraan Keluarga (PKK) – have focused on the centrality of women's roles within the family, on health care, on the preparation of food, and so on. However, those who might benefit most from such programmes do not have the time to participate and often feel that the subject matter is irrelevant to their lives. If programmes were initiated which cover the other side of women's roles – namely, their involvement in farming activities – it might be possible to involve more women. A woman speaker from the Agriculture Service or P2AT could, for instance, discuss the extension literature and posters (which would also help to bridge the problem of illiteracy). An example of what might be possible in the future is provided by the family planning – Keluarga Berencana (KB) – programme; strong grassroots organizations have developed as a consequence of the visits to PKK meetings by family planning specialists. I recommended that a pilot PKK modification scheme be set up in a village in West Madura to offer advice and assistance on agricultural production.

My findings, that Madurese women are active participants in many aspects of agricultural production but have not generally been consulted in the planning or implementation of the project, are predictable enough and are not peculiar to Madura. During the past two decades many authors have documented similar situations in various parts of the world (see, for example, Nelson 1981). What is surprising, given this wealth of information, is that projects are still designed and implemented with little if any consideration of the roles and status of women within a specific locale.

One problem is that the contributions of technically trained team members – hydrogeologists, soil specialists, engineers and agriculturalists – are usually perceived to be more tangible than those of an anthropologist. Once a budget has been drawn up and the inputs from various specialists have been allocated, the working schedule is difficult to rearrange. In the case of the Madura Groundwater Irrigation Project, as we have seen, sociological inputs had been made since 1985. The failure to integrate women into the project may be partially explained by the fact that research into women's roles and status has entered the development sphere rather late. This is changing. That I was brought in at the end of Phase 3 (despite the fact that, as one official commented, 'It is a bit late in the day for this kind of input') indicates that the need for anthropological research by women and into issues which affect women is beginning to be appreciated. A second, related problem is the common attitude that it is impossible to contact women in an Islamic society; this is obviously an attitude-related problem, and not a fact.

The kind of anthropological engagement I envisage, which is stressed by other contributors to this volume, involves an ongoing participative approach which both anticipates and is responsive to change. In this sense, I argue that anthropology is a potentially valuable and flexible component of project design, implementation and management. I fully support the argument that, wherever possible, indigenous staff should be employed. That this is not always feasible or advisable may prove to be the case, as my own involvement in the Madura Groundwater Irrigation Project illustrates (both indigenous and expatriate sociologists were employed before my input was made, as we have seen). Obviously, special training in anthropological techniques for indigenous staff is a way in which knowledge may be transferred. In engineering this transfer, I feel that the professional anthropologist has a definite role to play. In my own case, my association with a young Field Assistant will hopefully mean that she will have learnt from the experience and will be able to put those skills to further use.

REFERENCES

Conlin, S. (1985) 'Report on three water resources projects in Indonesia', London: Overseas Development Administration.

Groundwater Development Consultants (International) Ltd (1986) 'Madura Groundwater Irrigation Project Annual Planning Report', Cambridge.

—— (1987) 'Madura Groundwater Irrigation Project 1986/1987 Annual Report/Workplan. Volume I Main Report', Cambridge.

Jordaan, R. (1985) *Folk Medicine in Madura (Indonesia)*, Leiden: Doctoral thesis, Rijksuniversiteit te Leiden.

Nelson, N. (ed.) (1981) *African Women in the Development Process*, London: Frank Cass.

Niehof, A. (1982) 'The island of Madura: a deceptive unity', in O. van den Muijzenberg, P. Streefland and W. Wolters (eds) *Focus on the Region in Asia*, Rotterdam: Study Group on Tropical Asia-Kota, pp. 255–73.

—— (1985) *Women and Fertility in Madura*, Leiden: Doctoral thesis, Rijksuniversiteit te Leiden.

—— (1987) 'Madurese women as brides and wives', in E. Locher-Scholten and A. Niehof (eds) *Indonesian Women in Focus: Past and Present Notions*, Dordrecht: Koninklijk Instituut voor Taal-, Land- en Volkenkunde 127, Foris Publications. pp. 166–80.

White, B. (1982) 'Quantifying time-allocation, domestic authority and agrarian change: notes on recent research in Indonesia', Paper presented at the Methodology Workshop: Research on Rural Women, Brighton: Institute of Development Studies, University of Sussex, mimeo.

6 Project appraisals
The need for methodological guidelines

Geoff Griffith

The need for project appraisals in which anthropologists, or people using anthropological approaches, play an important part is clear enough. Not so well defined are the methods most appropriate for such appraisals, the roles anthropologists have in preparing the ground for anthropologically informed appraisals, and how their particular skills can best be used to improve the quality of those project appraisals to which they contribute.

There is a growing literature (much of which passes me by, as the Maldive islands has no academic library), relating both to agricultural development, with 'Farmer First' (Cernea 1985) and Rapid Rural Appraisal (IIED 1988–89), and to culturally adapted market research (CMR) (Epstein 1988). Although this literature is presently leading the way in the development of reliable methodologies, much work remains to be done before clear guidelines will emerge as to the best (anthropological) ways in which project appraisals can be carried out.

The central focus in the literature is the necessity for development professionals to reverse priorities and take into account, in the first instance, the opinions and expectations of village-level project partners. This has two implications. First, it is necessary to search out and listen to the mass of the rural poor, who are the intended participants in development efforts. This must happen at the earliest possible opportunity and has to be the major consideration in drawing up plans for development projects. Secondly, the involvement to date of professionals in development has primarily been to give information to rather than learn from potential project partners. It is thus necessary to develop a 'new professionalism' (Chambers 1986) to respond to the challenge.

Most literature tends to focus discussion on methods used in particular projects, thus aiming to promote wider understanding of approaches used for specific issues. Although it is virtuous, the specific focus is often of little value to the appraiser entering a situation quite different from those described. Also, access to literature is often restricted (one must know where to look), so there is no guarantee that future appraisers will find relevant material. Given these constraints, it seems necessary that, out of the growing mass of examples, a readily available set of guidelines should be drawn up which would at least reduce the likelihood of mistakes being made or important issues being neglected in the field.

A useful basis for working towards such a set of guidelines can be found in Epstein's manual for culturally adapted market research. In this manual, the disciplines of market research and social anthropology are combined to give fieldworkers a clear idea of which methods should be used when gathering data. The intention is to enable accurate answers for specific development problems to be obtained in a comparatively short time. However, the manual is designed as a guide for those who train future fieldworkers, and would need to be modified and built upon for it to apply to the somewhat different problems faced by project appraisers.

This is where anthropology has a major role to play. 'Listening to' and 'learning from' are concepts central to most anthropological fieldwork. Yet there appears (to many working in the field with an awareness of the issues) to be a long way to go before such concepts will be implemented as part of standard development methodology. At present these concepts are merely being paid lip-service. Of course, the time usually allowed for project appraisals means that tried and tested anthropological methods must be modified to match the needs of the cases in hand (see also Garber and Jenden, this volume). Making the major contribution to this modification process is an important task for those using anthropological approaches because it should facilitate more appropriate, sociologically sound, quick appraisals.

The following example, from the Republic of Maldives, illuminates some of the important issues that must be considered if the quality of appraisals is to improve. The appraisal chosen is based on the workings of several large, multinational NGOs, in 1989, and illustrates some of the difficulties faced by all (not simply anthropologists) who engage in project appraisals. The case study is followed by a brief résumé of some organizational and managerial problems which serve to make the job of the appraiser particularly difficult. Finally, practical suggestions will be made as to how the anthropological approach might help to develop and improve the methodology of the appraiser.

PROJECT AREA

The Republic of Maldives is a small country consisting of about 200 inhabited and 1,000 uninhabited islands spread over some 90,000 sq km of the Indian Ocean, with a total population of about 200,000. The area for which a project is being considered consists of a large number (at least 100) of widely dispersed villages, each of which is located on a separate island. The islands are extremely small (the actual size rarely exceeds 1.5 sq km) and often very difficult to either land on or leave. Islands are isolated both from the capital and trading centre, Male, and from one another, by often rough seas with dangerous currents that make transportation and personal contact with people from other islands extremely difficult.

The villages are generally small (the average population being much less than 1,000), with little in the way of facilities. Each island has an administrative office, an Islamic court and a school offering basic primary education. Many islands have electricity in the evenings, but the power supply is generally only enough to enable households to use light and very low-powered household appliances. The only inter-village communication channel (apart from travel by boat) is CB radio. Most radios are owned by the government, and are used by officials to enable normal administrative procedures to be followed on even the remotest islands. CB can also be used by individuals to convey messages to friends, relatives and business partners on other islands. However, due to various technical problems, it is a very unreliable form of communication. CB also inhibits because it offers no privacy to the user. It is therefore clear that the population of each island is extremely limited in its ability to communicate with the outside world.

The village economies are dependent primarily upon fishing, together with money and foodstuffs sent home by predominantly male migrant labourers who work in the city. Fishing is perhaps the only area of Maldivian life where the cash economy has yet to prevail. Most people do not own fishing boats but work as crew for others. The larger boats need five or six people to go on a day's fishing. The crew are rarely paid in cash. Normally, each person receives a share of the catch (the size of which is dependent upon the fishing capability of the boat concerned), which is used for home consumption or sold when there is a surplus. Non-migrant males who work as fishermen usually have some other means of earning cash, doing various part-time jobs, mainly in service industries, around the village. There is little or no full-time employment available except for the few government jobs found on every island.

A large number of the women left at home supplement the often meagre remittances sent by their migrant husbands: small sums sent at irregular intervals, together with some rice and flour. These women produce coconut-leaf matting and coir rope for use in the many tourist resorts that proliferate in the area close to the capital.

There is some commercial agriculture, but it is on a very small scale and relatively few people (6 per cent of the working population) derive the major part of their income from it. The main cash crops cultivated are banana, coconut, chilli peppers and various members of the cucumber family. The plots are extremely small, being measured in square metres (400 sq m would be quite a large plot) rather than acres or hectares. Planting takes place at the start of the rainy season in May, except for banana and coconut, which have many seasons. Crops are harvested during the drier season, which starts in August or September. Agricultural production relies heavily on regular rainfall, because the soil, which has no clay content, does not hold water. Hence, a short drought can have a catastrophic effect on the crops. Because there is no appropriate technology available to enable the lifting of water from wells and its distribution to the fields, commercial agriculture is a somewhat risky business. This also partially explains why there is very little home gardening.

It is interesting to note that there is virtually no staple food crop production. Rice and flour, the main constituents of the diet, are both imported; they are bought during visits to Male or in local shops. There are two reasons for this. First, such production would have to take place on uninhabited islands near the village, which would be problematic. The transport problems involved would make it extremely difficult for those most likely to be working there (villagers who do not own boats) to look after their crops. Secondly, in the eyes of the villagers, it is much easier to earn some money and buy rice. Hence, they do not want to grow staple crops.

There is no formal or informal market within a day's journey (in each direction) of most islands in the project area. In fact, the only real market is in the capital, Male. Village produce is therefore either sold to, or put into the custody of, the few small businessmen who are owners of large, motorized boats. They are able to travel for several days, or in bad weather weeks, to and from the market. These businessmen, few in number, sell the goods and charge commission on the items sold by them on behalf of the village producers. Businessmen then use the money so earned to buy imported items in the town, either for personal use or resale in the villages.

Migrant workers are dependent upon these businessmen for

foodstuffs and goods transported from the city back to their families. Likewise, since there is little or no bartering in the villages, non-migrants are totally dependent upon these businessmen (and cash) for acquiring goods. The businessmen, therefore, exercise a considerable degree of control over the village economies.

However, with the rapid growth in tourism, change is coming quickly to the Maldives. Migration is on the increase (in the atoll I am most familiar with it has increased by more than 50 per cent during the last three years) with far fewer males choosing to stay and work in their place of birth. Markets too are changing quickly. The demands of the tourists for fresh fruit and vegetables, nearly all imported, are slowly being reflected in changing consumption patterns, particularly in the capital. The increased affluence tourism now brings and the exposure of many young people to the outside world also mean that they are no longer satisfied to be 'small islanders': they want high fashion and the glamour of city life. Hence, the government has a policy of trying to make distant islands more attractive places to work and live in. It is in this context that the proposed development project was formulated.

THE PROPOSED PROJECT

Two large international NGOs (one concerned primarily with agricultural development, the other non-specific) were interested in promoting a wide-ranging loan programme in this area. The programme would, amongst other things, try to stimulate increased industrial and agricultural production; this was seen as a possible way of stemming the flow of young people out of the atolls. Although the NGOs had no permanent representatives in the country, they expressed an interest because the relevant government departments had drawn their attention to the possibility of such a programme during previous visits concerning other matters. Also, both NGOs had had discussions with another large multinational agency, already working in the country, on the feasibility of the scheme.

The three agencies then decided to undertake a joint preliminary investigation. Discussions were held and information was collected from several secondary sources. Through this, they identified a general need for loans in rural areas, of which agriculture would only be a small component. At this stage, though, there were found to be (unspecified) problems relating to the possible implementation of the loan scheme, which resulted in one large NGO pulling out, leaving the other organization (predominantly agricultural) and the NGO already working in the country to decide whether or not they wanted to carry on alone.

After some deliberation the two agencies decided to proceed to the next stage of the project cycle by agreeing to implement a loan scheme in which agriculture was only a minor component. The decision came as a surprise, to me at least. Why, I asked, did the NGO primarily concerned with agriculture agree to collaborate in a project which had little to do with its own interests? Why did it not withdraw at this stage? The answer is that NGOs are often diverted from their preferred areas of activity by the forces of circumstance within which they act. In this case, it seems that the desire to work with agriculture in the Maldive islands, even in a very minor way, was enough to keep the NGO interested.

At this point in the negotiations I began to take an active interest in this proposed scheme. As project coordinator for an already established (but unconnected) atoll development programme, I was myself planning to implement a loan scheme which would give loans in a way similar to that of two other existing loan schemes. Earlier, two small loan schemes had been set up by NGOs as part of their Integrated Rural Development Programmes, and mine would have been the third one. However, my scheme differed from the two in existence in that it would actively involve the poorest members of the community by offering small loans at half the normal rate of interest (6 per cent instead of 12 per cent) with no collateral. Punctual repayment would be encouraged, if necessary, by using the social sanction of friends and relatives, who would have to offer personal guarantees before the loan could be ratified. (The repayment rate in the Maldive islands, unlike in neighbouring countries, is something like 99 per cent.) It was on the issue of collateral that opposition to my scheme was voiced, because implementation of the scheme would have meant a change of policy for the government. Previous loan schemes had encouraged large loans for people with 200 per cent collateral; that is the most wealthy members of the island communities. Because the international NGOs were promoting a loan scheme more in line with existing policy, government was not prepared to allow implementation of my scheme until the outcome of negotiations with them were known. Hence, whilst my own loan scheme was delayed for several months, I keenly monitored the NGOs' progress with their project appraisal.

The two NGOs put together a team consisting of one foreign consultant, one ex-patriate NGO staff member and several government officials. These experts then attempted to assess in approximately two weeks (covering both fieldwork and consultation with other concerned parties in the capital) a situation which, as seems always to be the case in the Maldive islands, was quite unlike any they had previously experienced.

The appraisal team confirmed a demand for loans for a variety of purposes relating to income generation, and claimed, in line with government policy, that these loans would help to stimulate small business development, thus increasing village-based incomes. The point was also made that there was a need for special incentives (such as reduced interest rates) to encourage investment in agriculture, although this was recognized as being beyond the scope of the project. It was then suggested that some sort of wide-ranging loan scheme, involving the establishment of regional and mobile banking facilities, should go ahead. This was to be financed through a *combined* NGO and government fund.

As far as I can tell, the government was not at all happy with this proposal. First, the agriculture ministry objected to the high interest rates (12 per cent), because it feared that poor and marginal farmers would not want to commit themselves under such conditions. Secondly, the government knew that there was little likelihood of either staffing or running the new banking facilities. The national bank had been trying to set up regional banks for some time, but no one with both the qualifications and the desire to work away from the capital could be found to manage them. Thirdly, the idea of a combined NGO–government fund meant that the government contribution was too high. As a result, the proposal was mocked in many quarters and agreement was quickly reached (in about one week, after six months' delay) to scrap the NGO proposal and implement my own atoll-level loan scheme.

However, this is not the end of the story. I am aware that another team of experts from the large NGOs has recently visited the Maldive islands to reformulate the proposal. I did not meet them. Rumour has it that the dropped loan scheme is again a live issue, but this time there will be no mandatory agricultural component. The agricultural NGO is apparently giving its full support.

COMMENT

It is interesting to speculate about the position of the expatriate project appraisers, not because they were foreigners, but because their role was primarily to investigate, whereas that of the government participants was to secure for their country a loan scheme on the best possible terms. It is clear that the two expatriates (I had met and spoken with them) were highly competent and did their best to understand the issues before them. Nevertheless, in my opinion, they faced several difficulties which made accurate appraisal extremely difficult.

First, those conducting the appraisal were perhaps unable to pay sufficient attention to the ethnographic evidence. It is clear to those familiar with the area that many people who might require loans have very little access to the goods and services these could buy. This is particularly so in the case of agriculture. As already mentioned, there is little commercial agricultural production in the area. Even when individuals might wish to benefit from commercial agriculture, important items for which loans could be needed (such as seeds, fertilizer and equipment) are not available, neither in the village shops nor in the more distant market. Thus the problem of opening supply channels (among others) would have to be tackled before or at the same time as the loan scheme was initiated, if the scheme was to become practicable. This is not likely to happen.

Since there is no likelihood of agricultural supplies being generally available in the near future, it seems clear that the request for such loans originated from within government and not from the possible beneficiaries. However, this is not to say that villagers did not ask for such loans. The appraisers were taken to islands where they met island committee members – namely, island leaders and other wealthy businessmen – who had already been informed that a loan scheme might be in the offing. Since loans are a source of easy money, the committee members, when asked, naturally claimed to need loans of the type proposed. Under the circumstances, it was very easy to find a demand for loans by superficially questioning very few people.

It is only when the issue of *needs* is viewed from different perspectives that the practical problems relating to their identification become clear. But in a situation like the one here described, it can be very difficult for appraisers, given the constraints of time and guidance by officials who support the programme, to differentiate real need from one which has been cultivated by others.

Secondly, the project appraisal is only one part of an ongoing process, a dialogue of development. It is important to understand where the appraisal fits into this process and at what level the dialogue is taking place. For instance, if the appraisers had looked carefully, they might have found out that, whilst the demand for loans was considerable, there was little evidence to suggest that these would be used to develop agriculture. In fact, the demand for agricultural and other loans almost certainly originated from the concerned ministries whose officials felt this would be a good idea. The grassroots 'project partners' (villagers) had, as mentioned above, almost certainly not been consulted, but they had been given the idea that they could gain from the proposed loan scheme.

I am arguing that the form the dialogue took has had important ramifications for the appraisal as a whole. It seems that the appraisal dialogue had moved on quickly from 'what to do' to 'how to do it', thus becoming the instrument to sanction a decision already made by the implementing agencies. In this case, a primarily agricultural agency was planning to participate in a project for which the importance of agriculture is marginal. Given the circumstances, I feel it is important that certain questions be asked about the capability of the NGOs to serve their village level project partners, as well as vice versa.

Thirdly, when the answers to the above questions are not clear, it is necessary to pursue a different line of investigation. It is here that an understanding of the history of the project could shed much light. I regard it as very likely that those conducting the appraisal did not encourage or were not encouraged to examine the history of the project – by asking how and why the appraisers came to be there. Why did the NGOs want to become involved? For instance, were there political reasons? Could involvement in the Maldive islands help the NGO attract funds for other projects? Such questions might appear cynical, but various discussions I held with expatriates working on existing NGO projects confirmed my suspicion that considerations having nothing to do with the proposed developments had influenced the decision-making process. When this happens, appraisers may find themselves in highly compromising situations. They may have to question the motives of the people who are paying their high salaries; they may come to realize that they are pawns in political wheeling and dealing of little immediate relevance to the design of projects aiming to serve the needs of the community.

Whatever the reality of the appraisal here considered, it is obvious that circumstances influence the position of project appraisers and that, under some circumstances, this position is not as well defined and straightforward as it initially appeared to be. This is not to say that the appraisers in question did a bad job. It is not easy to undertake the task of project appraisal in the Maldive islands, which is a country quite different from others in the region. In conversation, the appraisers certainly seemed to have learnt a great deal, despite the somewhat difficult circumstances they worked in, so I imagine that their final recommendations, which turned out to be quite inappropriate, must have resulted from political pressure. But I do not wish to sound too negative, since my point is that the exploration of particular issues arising from this case study might enable appraisers to produce better reports in the future.

Before looking at the relevance of this example for anthropologists, it is necessary to be realistic about the nature of appraisal work. For instance, the anthropologist can expect

1 to have little or no time to become familiar with the area before being expected to have opinions about it;
2 to be unable to examine in detail the mass of issues which arise during appraisal;
3 to have no opportunity to choose and train a good translator. Hence, with regard to interpersonal communication, it will often be necessary to try and make the best of misleading situations.

Moreover, the anthropologist can expect:

4 to work in a team within which, first, only a proportion of the members are competent, and secondly, many of the disciplines in which skills might be needed are not present;
5 to be asked to make decisions long before it is possible to make a reasonably objective assessment of the situation in hand.

Demands are made by the sponsors for answers, and the anthropologist will have (at least to some extent) to impart opinions based on intuition and previous experience. The task can be particularly frustrating when the anthropologist is also expected to look at issues for which she or he is not trained.

It would be naïve to expect to have the luxury of long-term fieldwork, although two weeks is an unrealistically short time when undertaking project appraisal. Still, in my view, neither time nor money for more detailed work is available now, nor is it ever likely to be in the future, which implies that the anthropologist has to face up to the reality of a situation where there is a strong possibility that mistakes will be made. This can be particularly galling, because most anthropologists are aware of the damage this can do.

Yet it is neither necessary nor advisable to accept this. There are certain actions anthropologists can take to reduce the frequency with which mistakes occur. This is particularly so nowadays, because there is a growing realization (shown in the aforementioned literature) that technological solutions for development problems will not work unless people and social structures are adequately taken into account.

This was not the case in the appraisal to which I have referred. Instead, the appraisers worked on the principle that the loan scheme was needed, so they looked for the best way of implementing it (or imposing it on the community). Epstein's CMR rejects this as a working principle. Culturally adapted market research is not concerned with selling ready-made projects. On the contrary, its aim is to find out (and predict) which projects are and will be needed, so that implementing agencies can build their programmes around the present and future needs of the participants. With regard to the loan scheme, the appraisal would have first looked more closely at the needs of the community and the ways these can be satisfied. Even if this had been done before, it would still have been necessary to reassess the situation since the Maldive islands are changing so quickly. Only then would it have been possible to assess whether or not a loan scheme might have a role in meeting assessed needs and priorities. (If it were then found that a loan scheme was needed, the detailed plan of action would be designed.)

The CMR methodology sets out to find answers to questions and, as with the 'Farmer First' approach, clearly advocates the use of basic anthropological techniques. The need for this kind of approach in the context of appraisal is acknowledged by most of the appraisers I have come in contact with. However, few have any idea as to how to put it into practice. They adhere in principle to the policy that the opinions of the proposed beneficiaries should be the major factor in designing projects, but they ignore the majority simply because they do not automatically make contact with many people in the course of their quick routines. This does not mean that the appraisers are not interested in the social aspects of policy formulation; the problem relates more to the fact that they have no clear guidelines to follow. Because of this, there is reason to believe that the views of anthropologists, who have tried and tested methodologies, will be given more weight than might previously have been the case.

TOWARDS GUIDELINES

There are several areas where meaningful contributions can be made.

First, anthropologists can help develop clear methodologies for the collection of information. For instance, there are bad, good and very good ways of approaching the communities within which appraisals are being conducted (see Bunch 1982, where the discussions concerning project participation are highly pertinent to appraisers). Not only is a very good approach to the communities best for the appraisal, it also eases the work of those responsible for implementation.

This does not mean that appraisers should always follow set procedures. Instead, it is unwise to decide, before entering the field, which methodologies will be most appropriate. Many anthropologists have an intuitive ability to make good snap decisions where, under other circumstances, a detailed preliminary survey would be required. But basic questions must be addressed, wherever one works. For instance, *who* would be the best informants? *How*, *when* and *by whom* should they be interviewed? *How* should the questions be phrased? Are there certain issues which deserve special attention? In group situations, who could and could not be included? Are certain groups likely to be inhibited in the presence of others? Is there something wrong with the answers? Issues such as these require a flexible, intuitive approach. The anthropologist, with a combination of experience and good methodology, is likely to be able to make quick, informed suggestions in such cases.

In the above appraisal the use of semi-structured interviews, in which intuition can be used to good effect, would have been enlightening. If this method is going to be used successfully, it is not enough simply to converse with someone who might appear to be a key informant. The interview has to be planned carefully (see Grandstaff and Grandstaff 1985 for a detailed discussion of this issue) so that the conversation can both flow easily and cover all the areas about which the appraiser needs information. In the appraisal exercise I reviewed, I am sure that even if only two well-designed semi-structured interviews with village-level agriculturalists had been undertaken, the appraisers would have understood that the agriculturalists' needs and constraints were not primarily financial.

The benefits of intuition need not be confined to the anthropologist; on the contrary, intuition often develops through experience *and can be shared*. Thus anthropological guidelines should be drawn up and should include generalized lists of indicators, points to look out for, details concerning recurring problem areas and so on, all of which can assist the appraiser. In this way newcomers to the field will be able to benefit from those who have long experience of social survey work.

It would also have been very simple, in the appraisal reviewed, to collect and analyse data on the supply and purchase of items for which loans might be needed. Simple lists could have been made in such areas as consumer goods marketed through island shops, the items people need and use at present for income-generating activities, and transport facilities. These would have shown how little is available outside of the area close to the capital, and appraises would have been alerted to the serious problems that arise when opportunities, wants and needs change and new resources are required. The collection of such data should have been included at the design stage. Quite clearly, loans are not simply money. A loan scheme can only be successful if the structure within which it operates is complementary to it.

Secondly, the analysis of materials gathered during the appraisal – which should be an ongoing process – will be greatly enhanced by a *systematic* anthropological approach. Many questions have to be asked. For instance, have all sections of the communities been given the chance to air their views? Have the people been saying what the appraisers wanted to hear or were they expressing genuine opinions? Is enough known about possible adverse effects of the action proposed? At this stage, the anthropologist, in conjunction with the other members of the team conducting the appraisal, will have to consider all the evidence to see if it provides sufficient information to allow reasonably informed opinions to emerge.

This process will be facilitated by the ability to refer to anthropological checklists (such as those used by McCracken 1988: appendix IV). In these, information on a whole range of topics could be itemized and checked off during a review of the day's work, so as to reduce the likelihood that important issues are forgotten. Also of practical value is a questionnaire checklist to prepare for interviews (see Epstein 1988: 19). Although they are no guarantee that the information thus gathered will be correct, such checklists will at least ensure that all the right questions have been asked, while also allowing results to be analysed with ease. Finally, lists of the kinds of people who might be asked to participate in semi-structured interviews should be prepared (as used by Conway *et al*. 1987: 27–9). By doing this, the appraisers can make sure that the views of the various sections within a community are adequately taken into account. The use of checklists is particularly valuable where appraisers are working as a team, because the lists make it easy to check the progress each member has made, while they will also reduce the risk of interview replication.

Thirdly, the collection and preparation of supplementary materials could be simplified by having clearer procedures to follow. Prior to the field appraisal, it is normal to investigate secondary sources within the region (government reports, agency documentation) to put together an overview of the area where the field appraisal will take place, and to facilitate the preparation of materials which will increase the effectiveness of fieldwork. With regard to such material there is need for anthropological guidelines in the preparation of culturally relevant visual aids. For instance, it is often useful to take various maps, charts and pictures to the field which can be used both in discussion groups with communities and as an aid to the appraisers. When these are available their value would increase if their forms were more readily understandable by and interesting to the populations with whom they are being used. But what form should these take, and which sort of visual aid is more appropriate for any given situation? Although this issue does not seem to have been widely discussed in the literature, reference to UNICEF (1976) and Bunch (1982: 160–3) gives a clear indication of its importance.

It is primarily in these three areas (data collection, analysis and the preparation of supplementary material), that I am convinced anthropological methodologies and experiences have a clear contribution to make. Although project appraisals can be extremely difficult to carry out, as my case study has shown, it is nevertheless clear that work practices can be improved by making appropriate guidelines more generally available. That this is the case is now widely recognized. What is not certain is whether anthropologists will respond quickly enough to satisfy this need or allow others with anthropological interests to act for them.

REFERENCES

Bunch, R. (1982) *Two Ears of Corn, A Guide to People-Centred Agricultural Improvement*, Oklahoma: World Neighbours.

Cernea, M. (ed.) (1985) *Putting People First, Sociological Variables in Rural Development*, London: Oxford University Press.

Chambers, R. (1986) 'Normal professionalism, new paradigms and development', Sussex: Institute of Development Studies, Discussion Paper No. 227.

Conway, G., McCracken, J. and Pretty, J. (1987) *Training Notes for Agroecosystem Analysis and Rapid Rural Appraisal*, London: International Institute for Environment and Development.

Epstein, T. S. (1988) *A Manual for Culturally-adapted Market Research (CMR) in the Development Process*, East Sussex: RWAL.

Grandstaff, S. W. and Grandstaff, T. B. (1985) 'Semi-structured interviewing', Paper presented at the International Conference on Rapid Rural Appraisal, Khon Kae, Thailand, 2–5 Sept.

International Institute for Environment and Development (1988–89) *RRA Notes*, Nos. 1–4, London: IIED.

McCracken, J. A. (1988) *Participatory Rapid Rural Appraisal in Gujarat: A Trial Model for the Aga Khan Rural Support Programme (India)*, London: International Institute for Environment and Development.

UNICEF/National Development Service (1976) *Communicating with Pictures in Nepal*, Nepal: UNICEF.

7 Anthropology in farming systems research
A participant observer in Zambia

Philip Gatter

The title of this chapter requires some clarification. It concerns both the institutionalization of a social science perspective within a particular mode of agricultural research and the experiences of a social scientist in the institution. Where I think it may be distinctive and useful in this volume is in drawing together anthropological fieldwork in its routinized form of detailed ethnographic description, and the situation of the anthropologist working in a multi-disciplinary applied research team (an Adaptive Research Planning Team – ARPT).

Situated within and outside the team simultaneously, my aim was to reflect on the team as itself a sort of interest group with particular values, assumptions and knowledge concerning development (discourses, if you like) which become enmeshed, in a social sense, in the communities in which research is conducted. Of course there is a problem of reflexivity here, in that my identity became ambiguous both for other members of the research team (I could tell you what I *really* think about ARPT's work; on the other hand, I'm not sure you aren't some kind of spy) and for the villagers with whom I lived (if I was working for the Ministry of Agriculture, why did I want to know about clans or traditional narratives?). For the time being, though, I shall attempt to avoid introspection and concentrate on the practical situation of an anthropologist working in such an institution as ARPT; what problems he or she is likely to face in collecting and representing social information in an environment very different from the university. The task is no easy one, as it involves both developing an anthropological analysis of a particular kind of development initiative and looking at how such a perspective can work in a given institutional framework. Beyond this, questions of the validity of the framework itself arise.

Already I have slipped between talking about social scientists and specifying anthropologists. The debate over what kind of social science is required in Farming Systems Research (FSR) is the source of some contention. It is not so much the *content* of a social scientist's contribution which is debated (though this can never be fully independent of how it is generated) as which kinds of *method* are best suited to working in concert with other disciplines as professions; in this case, natural sciences (represented by agronomists) and economics (agricultural economists). A position that has been strongly argued in ARPT in Zambia (Sutherland 1987) is that it is rural sociologists trained specifically in sociological method who should be incorporated into FSR. Indeed, the institutionalized position within ARPT's regional teams is titled rural sociologist, not anthropologist. There are undoubtedly strong political grounds for favouring sociology over anthropology, at least in terms of professional training, in the context of East and Southern Africa: the ARPTs in Zambia are externally funded in large degree, but in the longer term the aim is to train nationals to fill all professional posts so that projects can be sustained internally. To date, most pairs of regional sociologists consist of a senior expatriate (almost unexceptionally an anthropologist by training) and junior Zambian (usually with a general degree in social sciences which may be followed by postgraduate training abroad in anthropology, sociology of development, or whatever else scholarships allow). It is argued that countries in the region simply do not have training facilities in anthropology, nor are they likely to in future (whereas sociology or social studies departments are more widely available). Further, that anthropology is stigmatized contra sociology as being insufficiently methodological or systematic and a colonial science (or rather practice as the term 'science' is, ironically, denied anthropology by the 'hard-core' disciplines of agricultural research). I think the colonial stigma is more imaginary than real, at least for Zambia. None the less, the question of who is to be the social scientist must be addressed. I will assume for now that expatriate social scientists will continue to be involved in rural development for some time to come,[1] and try through my ethnographic experience to make suggestions about a distinctive role for anthropology in FSR. The politics of professional training would form the subject of another essay. Here I wish to emphasize that a pragmatic opposition of anthropology to sociology is not really what matters: we need critically to appraise the wholesale promotion of 'systematicity'; that, whilst appearing to foster desirable uniformity of method (see also Fairhead's chapter in this volume), it can hide ethnocentric effects: further, that sociology, more easily than anthropology, slots into a 'systems' approach.

FARMING SYSTEMS RESEARCH (FSR) IN ZAMBIA

The emergence of social science in agricultural research in Zambia has to be seen in the context of the new emphasis on a 'systems' perspective which gained ground in the 1970s and has emerged in practice during the course of the 1980s. This new emphasis seems to have stemmed from widespread disillusion over the performance of agricultural development in relation to a particular 'target group': small-scale (largely subsistence) farmers, who constitute a large proportion of rural populations in many African countries, and who became a focus of attention when modernization theory began to lose credibility and be superseded by concerns such as equity and basic needs. Perhaps just as importantly, very large investments in agricultural research along traditional lines (intensive research-station agronomic experimentation, to be conveyed to the clients through extension services), were seen to be benefiting quite small groups of people, usually those who were already relatively prosperous. Though my discussion will concern specifically the origins and current nature of FSR, it should be remembered that FSR continues to be one small element in a very wide debate, inside and outside academia, over the nature of agrarian change in Africa (for example, Berry 1984; Harriss 1982).

The basis for one FSR methodology was laid down in 1976 by CIMMYT (the International Maize and Wheat Improvement Centre) and modified in 1980 to take a more qualitative approach, incorporating social scientists. In the latter form it was taken up as the basis for the work of Zambia's ARPTs, and continues to be used, albeit in a form progressively modified as thought appropriate to local (regional) conditions. It is a methodology intended to operationalize a systems perspective in understanding farmers and provide the basis for developing agricultural technologies which will be appropriate to their needs, aspirations and capabilities, through which *productivity* can be increased.

It is appropriate here to examine more closely what is meant by 'systems', as the insertion of rural sociology into Zambian FSR has in part arisen through problematizing the original assumptions of a systems perspective. The criticisms were made in the context of saying how and why a sociological input to FSR was important, and how then to institutionalize it. I will go further in suggesting a more radical re-evaluation of the status of systems in current agricultural development thought, towards the end of this chapter.

What is a systems perspective?

'A low-cost approach to understanding small farmers': this is the title of a paper concerning the introduction of FSR to Zambia (Collinson 1981). It introduces the two main axes for an interest in systems:

1 That by linking together analysis of the economic, ecological and social production environments of small-scale farmers (conceptualized as a system), a comparatively rich understanding of this large and hitherto neglected sector of the Zambian population should be achieved, on the basis of which appropriate technologies (namely, ones that will be adopted by the farmers) could be developed to improve their productivity.
2 Increased productivity through the small-farmer sector should be a relatively cheap way of achieving national food production targets, simultaneously improving rural standards of living.

The fiscal attractions of a 'systems' approach were perhaps the primary incentive for its development. 'Traditional', field-station-based agricultural research had been producing relatively low returns to investment in the sense of quantity of technologies generated, because intensive attention was going to individual farmers. The opportunity costs of such research were high, with scarce professional resources devoted to covering a very small sample of the population.

The other major incentive was methdological. A point had been reached of general acceptance that Western farm-management models could not be transferred willy-nilly to peasant farmers in developing countries: 'To make recommendations that farmers will use, you must be aware of the human element in farming, as well as the biological element. You must think in terms of farmers' goals and the constraints on attaining those goals' (CIMMYT 1976: 2). Not a very radical statement, perhaps, but an apparent move away from agronomy-led technological 'fixes'. A systems approach would allow exploration of criteria of productivity other than physical yield per unit of land area, and how farmers make 'compromises on the optimum technical management of any one enterprise' (Collinson 1981: 434).[2]

The impetus to include sociology within the new approach came from an established critique of agricultural economics; namely, that sociology could contribute by 'providing a more adequate and informed basis' for its 'simplifying assumptions' (Gasson 1971: 33). Within Zambia the debate was raised over the initial CIMMYT methodology being implicitly based on the theory of the firm

(Behnke and Kerven 1983), so that a notion of 'utility' (an apparent advance over 'profit') lacked the contextual indicators of 'to whom' and 'for whom'. To fill in the context, it was argued, would 'necessarily involve the adoption of more of a community focus taking into account different interests and values within households, and between different groups in the community' (Sutherland 1987: 15). With the need to include sociology within FSR recognized, a national coordinator was appointed with the express role of institutionalizing sociology within agricultural research in Zambia, special attention being paid to developing research methodologies which would work in concert with those of agronomists and economists. To date, the process has gone further than in any other country in the Southern African region; though in the rest of this chapter I will be trying to point up what I see as the limited advantages in the form of sociological input so far achieved.

Describing systems: the CIMMYT sequence

As originally formulated, CIMMYT's methodology for describing farming systems, and providing a background for a long-term programme of field research, consisted of a logical sequence of surveys, to be conducted jointly by biologists (agronomists) and economists. The sequence was designed expressly with economy and 'relevance' of information collection in mind. The form first adopted in Zambia was as follows.

1   Zoning

A broad sweep is made of the geographical area to be covered, interviewing extension staff at the most minute administrative level. With reference to the majority of farmers, questions cover subjects such as types of livestock kept (and for what purposes); the major food crops grown or bought; main (ranked) cash sources; land-use methods, and hire and purchase of resources (including fertilizers and labour). The information so collected is compared to check for bias, and farmers are then grouped geographically (by variables of the natural and economic environment) and hierarchically (differentiated by resource endowment). The grouping is achieved by aggregation of administrative units on the variables found to have fewest categories, these groups being progressively sub-divided in a branching fashion according to the more differentiated variables.

At this stage hypotheses are made about which *sources of variation* are critical in dictating resource allocation in the farming system (or systems) of the study area. These hypotheses are tested in the more detailed surveys which follow. The assumed significance of the kinds of information collected, as a means to understanding the small farmer, is well put thus:

> Accepting the *rationality* of the small farmer and aware of his needs and *priorities*, an evaluation of the local circumstances within which he must operate identifies many of the *management problems* posed by his *production environment*. It establishes a context within which to interpret his choices of *product*, of *management strategy* and of *production techniques*.
>
> (Collinson 1981: 438; emphasis added)

What is meant is, for example, that information on rainfall patterns will be suggestive of how farmers respond to environmental risk, whereas the level and penetration of marketing and other cash-related activities in a sense dictate their economic options. Many of the assumptions involved here are the sorts of things anthropologists delight in attacking, but I think it would be more appropriate for me to raise questions as and when they occurred in my ethnographic experience of FSR, rather than in response to the abstract basis of FSR procedure.

2   Subsequent surveys

On the basis of the findings of the zoning exercise, an exploratory survey is undertaken by economists and biologists, collecting information directly from farmers. This activity is supposed to refine the findings of zoning, the biologists looking at what farmers do within their physical environmental constraints, and the economists explaining why they do what they do in terms of allocation of resources to competing ends (at least, this is the ideal picture of what happens). Possible technical solutions to productivity problems are discussed within the research team, to be reviewed with farmers in the final verification survey, which seeks further testing of hypotheses, and an examination of how farmers who seem to have overcome typical production constraints have managed to do so.

On completion, the sequence of surveys provides the basis for a programme of field trials of possible new technologies. The different zones identified during the surveys are designated as 'recommendation domains', and separate research programmes formulated relevant to each.

At this point I turn to the situation I found in Luapula province, where a trials programme had been in operation for five years. The original sequence for system description was long past, but as we shall see, this in itself threw out questions about the validity of the FSR approach, in the form that has taken root in Zambia.[3]

ARPT IN LUAPULA PROVINCE

I became attached to ARPT Luapula Province, on a voluntary basis, during my doctoral fieldwork. My own understanding of the team's work and my position in relation to it changed during the time in the field, so I shall present my examination in terms of the way in which that relationship developed.

Setting a work programme

There were two broad areas in which ARPT Luapula felt they were lacking 'social' information. First, there was a general dearth of knowledge of the 'traditional' food crops,[4] both in terms of technical aspects of their production, and the kinds of economic relation into which they entered. I too was interested in this kind of information as part of the study of indigenous agroecology and political economy. Secondly, after five years of field trials, pressure was increasing from donors via the central offices of the Ministry of Agriculture and Water Development (MAWD) for ARPT to appraise its achievements to date; namely, to demonstrate that donor money was being well spent. In the context of ARPT's on-farm research being gradualist and iterative, the Luapula team felt it was not yet appropriate to begin a full-scale evaluation of project impact. As a compromise, it was suggested that I look at two of the field trials which had run their course and been passed to the Extension Branch of MAWD for release as crop recommendations. The task might distinctively be a sociological one as the successful adoption of technologies depended on their being socially acceptable as well as technically and economically feasible (an accepted tenet of the FSR approach). The sociological analysis would also view adoption in relation to intended 'target' groupings.

For ARPT, such an 'impact' study would give some idea of the local acceptability of new technologies which, according to experimental criteria, had been a success. For me, the study provided an opportunity to look at modes of dissemination of information in the community, and the relation between the agricultural 'knowledges' of villagers and of the government research team.

With these studies as part of my doctoral fieldwork, I began research in Mabumba chiefdom, Mansa district: one of the three 'recommendation domains' in the province ARPT had chosen to work in. Rather than present all of the study material collected with ARPT, I will restrict myself to examples which highlight what I see as some limitations of FSR in its current (late 1980s) form (see also Gatter 1988a and b).

1   Indigenous agroecology

One purpose in introducing ARPTs in Zambia, in trying to reach the small-scale farmer, was to broaden the base of research away from hybrid and composite maize, which has remained a politically dominant concern in agricultural development since independence (through a continuing need to feed a large and potentially unruly urban population). My focus for this study would be cassava, the starch staple of Luapula Province, grown universally. Additionally, I would pay attention to groundnuts, beans and finger millet, important crops locally which ARPT favoured in terms of their nutritional and remunerative potential (the economist had already collected information on marketing of these crops). Recognizing that maize was becoming a crop of major significance in Mabumba. ARPT was also interested in the possibilities of making its production and use less dependent on state support.

I was to collect information on the production (choice of soils, methods of land preparation, types of labour used and forms of remuneration, and so forth), processing and economic uses (sale, exchange and prestations) of these various crops. The data would, it was hoped, provide some basis for ARPT's future experimentation, and in particular the economists were interested in how it might provide a qualitative frame for the findings of intensive quantitative labour surveys which were in process of analysis.

What emerged from my studies was not so much that the range and quantity of data through which ARPT was working was inadequate, as that relations between data were considered implicitly through the reductionist models of economics and agronomy, so that the explanation for a particular piece of economic behaviour, for example, existed outside of any specified social, cultural and political context. Such a situation would, I argue, have important consequences for the likely appropriateness of new technologies.

To illustrate the point, a broad issue that ARPT wishes to address is how to improve rural incomes without having contingent detrimental effects on, for example, nutrition. There is a growing body of literature on Zambia – Sharpe (1987) gives a recent and thorough account for Northern Province – arguing that increasing the production of cash crops can, under certain circumstances, contribute to poor nutrition, especially of young children. The issue was raised in two areas of my base data studies.

(a)   Village-level maize storage?

Given rapid increases in maize production for institutional sale in Luapula, and the unreliability of supplies of flour from the state milling company,[5] ARPT wondered if it would be worth considering the development of improved village-level storage techniques. Some data already collected by ARPT rural sociologists had suggested that attention to cash-crop maize was diverting resources away from food crops such as groundnuts. Initially, there were thought to be two important considerations, related to the casual empirical observation that very few farmers kept more than two bags they had grown for home consumption, irrespective of production level. First, in an area where maize was not traditionally a dry grain crop, it was felt that indigenous storage technologies were poorly developed. Secondly, there was thought to be a very strong economic motive for selling grain and buying maize flour, stemming from a heavy government subsidy on the latter. Indeed, this second reason was taken for granted as an obvious, overriding motivation.

I proceeded with a qualitative survey, involving respondents with whose circumstances and farming activities I was already familiar. Deliberately, twenty households were chosen over the range of maize production levels typical of Mabumba. With one exception, all households consumed more cassava meal than maize flour (the latter, whether home produced or bought); this might be expected, cassava being the provincial staple.

Older people tended to profess a strong dietary preference for cassava, it being their traditional food. They would only keep some maize in a year when the cassava crop had been badly damaged by mealy bug.[6]

However, some 60 per cent of the households interviewed did consume maize meal regularly, but the uniform small quantity of *home-produced* maize that was consumed obscured important differences between households. Those growing relatively little maize (less than ten bags) experienced a tension between cash needs and the desire to extend spending power in time: if financial conditions allowed, they preferred to keep some of their own maize and take it in small quantities to the local hammer mill, thus avoiding the relatively large investment in 25 kg or 50 kg of state-produced maize flour. Frequently, though, they were constrained to sell all they had grown because of fears of not being able to pay back input loans or not having cash for commodities such as soap, salt and school uniforms. When the latter conditions applied, households would go without maize meal for some time, or buy by the plateful at the village market.[7] Households at higher production levels (up to forty bags) expressed quite different reasons for not keeping more of their own maize. In general, these households were at a later stage of the development cycle, with children already married off or at least at an age where they were making major contributions to farming. Under these circumstances, there was more free capital for spending on commodities such as maize flour. Respondents in this group opined that they would rather buy meal, as the hammer mill was unreliable and frequently out of action, and because stored maize was prone to pest attack. Their concerns, then, were primarily technical, and approximated to what ARPT had expected. But they constituted less than one-third of the cash maize croppers.

Interestingly, none of the respondents mentioned any economic comparison of retention of maize for consumption as against buying maize flour. The assumption by ARPT of this comparison as a primary motivation seemed not so much wrong as irrelevant; an easily adopted economistic piece of reasoning, and one which tended to homogenize diverse motivations for not retaining more of one's own maize crop. The relatively simple qualitative study suggested that the development of village-level storage technologies would not be much of a *cause célèbre* in Mabumba, for any group in the community, with the possible exception of some of the bigger producers (the very group whose interests it is no longer fashionable to promote).

(b)   The use of cassava

Questions over the nature of economic motivation emerged also for cassava. Unlike hybrid and composite maize, the crop requires no artificial fertilizer, it is perennial, and yield is much less sensitive to environmental variation. Over the past two years the state producer price has increased beyond that for maize. ARPT was interested to know, then, why so little of the crop came onto the official market. It was thought likely, prior to my study, that labour was a constraining factor: the economists' quantitative labour survey indicated cassava culture and processing as the most labour-consuming agricultural activities for women. To some extent this idea was vindicated in my study, though labour appeared as only one factor among several.

Marketing arrangements, I found, did exist for cassava, but they were informal ones whereby women took relatively small quantities of tubers and flour to the swamp fishermen around Lake Bangweulu, to sell and to exchange for fish. With few exceptions, cassava was grown to meet subsistence and reciprocal exchange needs, and surpluses for sale were considered a bonus. 'We fear starvation', was the reply of most women when questioned as to why they did not wish to sell more.[8] They also felt that growing more would involve too much work. Married women feared that if they started making much money out of cassava, their economic autonomy would be increasingly eroded by their husbands (in principle, women have control over the income from any food crops in excess of household requirements; but men generally appropriate cash-orientated activities, especially maize production).

The exceptions to the general rule were women in large households with many active farming members, or where income from maize was allowing easy access to piece-work labour through cash. An example was the wife of a village headman: both she and her husband had their own maize farms, he ran a village store, and they had eight children with them working on the fields. Such women, from time to time (though not every year), would have a cassava field surplus to needs. In these circumstances the entire field contents would be sold, by area, to other women, who would then sell on at the higher prices commanded at the swamps. Occasionally others would sell in this way, if forced to meet sudden cash needs.

In many cases women were unaware even that the state would buy cassava. Those who did know expressed a lack of confidence in the system, the services of the Cooperative Union being notoriously inefficient, and past prices for cassava extremely low. Even at 1988 prices, the unofficial market offered some fivefold advantage, on quantities as small as a plateful.

So far, what I have said about the economic use of cassava could be seen as various kinds of economic exigency; just a filling in of detail which anyone might get by a little patient questioning in the community, given some degree of familiarity with the area: the sort of thing a sociologist in an ARPT would be expected to do more than other team members. But the description is not very rich in terms of a sociological/anthropological analysis. Having identified commitment of female labour as a constraint to expanded cassava production, ARPT still asked, given that perhaps the majority of households are entering and expanding cash maize production, why not extend cassava production *instead*? An adequate response to this question, *ex post facto*, involves a complex set of issues arising out of fieldwork, which, as we shall see, cannot necessarily be accommodated by methodological improvements in FSR.

How cassava was used in Mabumba is a reflection of its identity as the people's primary food – much like the centrality of maize and millet to Bemba culture as recorded by Audrey Richards (1939) – which only in a minor way would appropriately enter the cash economy.

The senses in which crops have identities (and how these relate to personal identities) is one of the major themes I have treated in my thesis (Gatter 1990). Comparison of the economic uses of maize and cassava in Mabumba seems to be one point at which such an anthropological approach to looking at crops becomes indispensable. To ask why one crop cannot be substituted for another (labour constraints allowed for) rests on the assumption that one crop is much like another, an element ('enterprise' in the language of farm management) replaceable by other elements in the pursuit of economic gain. That assumption would appear not to fit the situation I encountered. In terms of producing a crop in relatively large surplus, for sale through state mechanisms, a near universal preference was shown for maize. And it would seem that this preference did not reflect a technical and economic imperative so much as a set of values and attitudes – an ideology, in a sense – which identified maize with the state and aspirations towards personal and national development (see also Hedlund 1984, on North-Western Province; Pottier 1988, on Northern Province). I will not go into details here, but simply make the point that if my analysis is correct it has a crucial bearing on understanding the meanings people attach to their farming activities, and on reflecting on the assumptions underlying the current practice of FSR.

These two examples, of the economic use of maize and cassava, engaged the particular interests of the ARPT economists, and were in a sense prospective, generating information as the basis for future technological developments. In contrast, my study of the impact of two field trials was retrospective, and more closely involved the agronomists.

2 Impact of trials

The first of the two trials I was to consider concerned planting methodologies for different varieties of beans. ARPT had decided to work with beans as they were known to command a high unit price on local markets, and are much favoured by nutritionists (concern had been expressed over child nutrition in rural Zambia for some time past, and cassava is generally viewed as nutritionally inferior to grain crop staples). In the field, the agronomists had observed that villagers tended to plant beans at very high population densities. A trial was designed to compare 'traditional' planting methods with line planting at different seed rates – seed dressings (a new exogenous variety), weeding and fertilizers being included as extra treatments.

The second trial was a standard comparision of several maize varieties grown under different fertilizer regimes: it was an attempt to make national maize-growing recommendations better tailored to suit local conditions.

Observations

I discovered, for the beans trial, that although most trial farmers remembered fairly well how they had planted the trial, their notions of why the trial had been conducted were quite vague, and their perceptions of the trial results were considerably at variance with those of ARPT. Whereas the team had concluded in an annual report that there was a clear case for line planting at low seed rates, the reactions of farmers were preponderantly negative.

What, then, constituted this negativity? In part, the reasons were those suggested by ARPT, both in advance of my study and in response to my report. It had been conceded that the trial was designed with inadequate attention to technical detail. The supposed 'traditional' method of planting was an artefact, the farmers having been asked to plant as they normally would, but on narrow ridges. On their own farms they would have planted on wide beds or intercropped with cassava, sweet potatoes or local maize. The apparent advantage of low seed rates were also misleading: some dressed seed was used in the trial, giving far higher germination rates than farmers might normally expect.

Rather more contentious was the issue of communication of trial objectives to the farmers. Whilst most of them maintained that they had learnt nothing of these from the ARPT Trials Assistant, he claimed to have briefed all of them, though, he said, they could not all understand well what the trials were about. My wider observation of the social situation of government staff resident in the village suggested that social relations played an important role in the channelling of communication. Those farmers who did have some idea of the purposes of trials were usually those with some status, political and financial, who were part of the social circle of government staff, the 'progressive', 'civilized' elite who wanted 'development'.

Where results of the trial were concerned, the farmers' appreciation of these rested on assessment of yield, the factor most often considered in *extension* demonstrations.[9] In contrast, ARPT was interested in cost minimization through lower seed rates. So, if two treatments gave the same yield farmers regarded them as equal, regardless of seed rate, suggesting that bean seed was not thought of as a cost.[10] It was labour input, rather than seed, which tended to govern farmers' preference when they perceived yields to be equal: line planting was seen as an unnecessary imposition. But these particular details of responses to the trial have to be seen in a wider context. At the time of interviewing, more than half the trial farmers were growing no beans at all. They stated there was a general shortage of seed, and that they only ever devoted a small area to growing the crop (perhaps this was why seed rate was not considered). Some had given up growing beans altogether because there was no time for planting after the maize had been attended to. They would still desire beans but saw maize culture as a higher priority.

The priority accorded to maize was clear also in the much more positive response to the other trial. Indeed, for this trial some two-thirds of trial farmers had adopted new agronomic practices as a result of participation, and to a limited extent their friends and relatives had copied from them.

Nevertheless, when considered from ARPT's view of what the trial was about, similar problems existed as with the beans trial. The practices adopted, such as wider plant spacing and weeding at a specific growth stage, were not themselves among the trial variables. In fact, these particular practices had been described in the Extension Branch's Lima Crop Memo for the province, published nine years before. ARPT had introduced some farmers to practices which, according to another branch of the same government department, were already well established.[11] When I discussed this observation with other team members a potential source of methodological rigidity became apparent. One response was that it did not really matter how trial farmers reacted to their trials, so long as they were representative of the selected 'target' groups. The benefits of the new technology were *designed* to be felt through extension recommendations. Of course, to take this position is to ignore that ARPT is having effects whilst work is still at an 'experimental' stage. Given their interest in the farming 'system' and the ways it changes, it is not logically correct for ARPT to make such omissions, a tendency encouraged by overenthusiasm for methodology as against careful observation.

Another problem lay with the actual target–group categories and how they were defined. The terms 'subsistence' and 'lima' were applied to differentiate two groups of small-scale farmers who were to participate in the trial. This had been done, as the economist felt that existing cropping recommendations did not pay sufficient attention to the variety of economic conditions and capabilities existing in the village.

The term 'subsistence' has been used generally by the Zambian Department of Agriculture to mean farmers having little or no involvement in the formal sector cash economy. Whereas 'lima' farmers have received some training, from whatever source, in cash-crop (most often maize) production, and produce and sell to state organs on a small scale. ARPT, for the purposes of the trial, interpreted the terms as referring to levels of management, and selected farmers according to observations of their field practices: the 'lima' trial farmers were people with relatively good soils, who were seen to manage their maize crops well according to Department of Agriculture recommendations, and who practised some form of crop rotation. Subsistence farmers were defined as the reverse.

In the presentation of results, ARPT showed strikingly different fertilizer response curves for the two groups of farmers. My own observations suggested that the difference was misleading. Among the 'subsistence' farmers, all had received input loans from the cooperative union for growing maize, and most had learnt some cultural practices from regular contact with the ARPT Trials Assistant. The senses of 'lima' and 'subsistence', as applied in the trial, were not congruent with their use by the Extension Branch. The apparent confidence with which ARPT might pass on the results to extension for release as a recommendation was misplaced. Later I will discuss how it is not just the consistency in use of categories which is a problem, but their relevance in the first place, and that a tendency to work with categories can be a tendency towards analytical rigidity.

THOUGHTS ON AN ANTHROPOLOGICAL CONTRIBUTION

At this point I shall try to draw together some ideas about avenues for making an anthropological contribution to the process of FSR which have arisen from my ARPT studies.

In response to these studies there was broad agreement within the team that trial objectives had tended to be set on the basis of insufficient or inappropriate information, the beans trial being the chief exemplar. Early trials had been based on rather scant data collected in the original systems description sequence, supplemented later by a sample frame census in which production levels of different crops had been recorded, and a number of intensive quantitative surveys (cropping patterns, labour, nutrition and so on) conducted by the economists. To an extent the new information was allowing for better trial selection: observations on cropping patterns had suggested intercropping as a practice worthy of research; both an established practice (with a variety of crop combinations) and one which could combine production of a cash crop with a nutritious minor crop. One such combination, of maize and beans, has been both generating interest among trial farmers, and advantageous according to ARPT's productivity criteria. It was the sort of trial which might have been conceived earlier (rather than the solo beans trial) if existing practices and relative priorities accorded different crops were better understood.

There are several points to be made here about improvement in the selection of objectives for field trials, a matter which has been a focus for those involved in institutionalizing sociology in FSR (for example, Sutherland 1987). These I will deal with first, as they relate to ARPT Luapula, but inevitably they lead into a wider anthropological questioning of the validity of the FSR approach, which entails suggesting changes which lie outside the methodological scope of a regional research team.

Choosing trials objectives

By the time of my involvement with ARPT, a considerable body of information existed on the Mabumba farming system (though not on all crops). What seems, on reflection, more important is not the quantity of information, but what sorts of information are deemed relevant to the identification of a problem and the proposing of a technical solution. There has been a tendency to construct problems out of broad themes which buzz around developmental agencies:

malnutrition, labour bottlenecks, soil degradation and so forth. All these, to a greater or lesser degree, have been identified in Mabumba. In themselves, they may be problems worthy of attention, but the procedure from there on tends to be deductive, drawing on well-established Western modes of agricultural experimentation.

A hypothetical example might run like this. Malnutrition, considered agronomically, could be responded to by selecting one or more pulse crops for trial (maybe two already in the farming system, and an exotic, such as soya beans, which the national government is promoting). If there is a labour bottleneck associated with a starch staple crop (that is, a bottleneck as identified by quantitative comparison of labour inputs to crops), then intercropping the pulses could be tried. It has been observed that repeated monocropping of the starch crop has followed the decline of a swidden system devolving from increased population and lack of virgin forest. So, rotation could be included in the trial as an attempt at sustaining soil fertility.

A trial designed along these lines would be analysed in agronomic and economic terms. Yield would always be considered, and where intercropping is concerned, a Land Equivalent Ratio or similar measure of performance would be computed.[12] In economic terms, the treatments might be compared according to net benefit, returns to labour, returns to cash and, given the nutritional interest, energy (as opposed to financial) returns to these two factors.

The example is slightly facetious, as in practice no trial would be attempted with so many factors at once. However, to take a real example, after one year of an ARPT intercropping trial, broad recommendations were stated in the following terms:

1   When the farmer is only considering what to do with one piece of land, whether he is concerned with earning the most cash, producing the most food, or maximizing returns to his time, a plot of maize alone is the best alternative.

2   If the farmer is planning in any case to plant two plots, he would be financially better off by interplanting both with maize and beans. It would also take up relatively less of his work time. On the other hand, it would sap more of his energy and give less in return than one plot each of maize and groundnuts.

(ARPT Luapula, *Annual Report* 1986–87, vol. 1, p. 14)

Banal it is, but still worth saying, that a trial of this sort could have been proposed in virtually any tropical country, and the results interpreted to make identical recommendations. I suggested earlier that trials concerning intercropping would be a move forward from the earlier beans trial. Here I am going further to consider how a contextual understanding of intercropping matters. An attempt to make sense of these recommendations by reading back to my ethnography is one way in which to consider how an anthropological approach within FSR might make it more truly adaptive.

The recommendations implicitly address a farmer who is an individual decision maker, choosing freely between a limited array of options. In actuality, most people in Mabumba live in social units in which more than one person makes decisions about farming activities, in spheres that may be more or less exclusive – the most obvious division, though a negotiable one, being between male and female. For nearly all crops men prepare the land, whilst women plant and perform all subsequent operations.[13] The major exception is maize as a cash crop, which has been largely monopolized by men.[14] In conjugal households, if there is one maize farm it is the husband's business, and he will manage the crop in the field to a greater extent than the food crops, though expecting assistance from his wife when required. There are cases, usually where the children of the household are adult, of the wife having her own maize farm as well, and managing it independently of her husband, but I did not find any cases where only the wife grew maize. In these kinds of household men gain access to pulse crops through their wives; intercropping with the cash-crop maize is not really an issue for them. Nor is it for their wives, who do not make decisions about how to grow the maize.

Empirically, ARPT had observed that where maize *is* intercropped with pulses, it is local maize, grown in small quantities as a vegetable crop. Cash-crop maize is always, so it appeared, grown alone. This brings me back to the importance of the identity of crops. In Mabumba, cash-crop maize is not perceived as food so much as the pre-eminent means of access to cash. It is logically separate from other crops.[15] Yet its ability to generate cash provides extra channels of access to food crops, including the pulses. Households generating relatively much cash begin to use some of it to purchase food crops, locally or from markets in the provincial town, Mansa. Alternatively, or in addition, lineage and other relatives outside the household who are not involved in cash-crop production may make gifts of food as reciprocation for gifts of money in continuing exchanges through which social relations are maintained. In relation to this, it is important that the values of beans and groundnuts, both in exchange and marketing senses, are related to their scarcity (using the word in a loose sense, not necessarily as the wellspring of the tendency to accumulate surplus in capitalist production, with profit as the motive). The possible uses of the crops would change dramatically if produced in considerable excess to subsistence requirements. So, if one is to have a reasoned basis on which to think about experimentation with intercropping, one must learn about a whole constellation of factors connected with means of access to the crops which are to be produced; and this cannot be seen in isolation from how these crops will be used once grown.

One further observation to continue the argument: I did come across one example of someone growing beans intercropped with *cash* maize. She was a woman in her late thirties, with no husband, and no children old enough to help with fieldwork. She depended for outside labour on selling beer. This year she had not recruited labour for growing food crops as she had to devote resources towards building a new house. Her small maize farm (one-eighth of a hectare) she was managing alone. Under these circumstances, and given that she had been a trial farmer for ARPT's beans trial and had some seed left over, she had decided to plant them with the maize. From experience of growing maize in mixture with beans in slash-and-burn shifting cultivation, she felt that growing some climbing beans would not be detrimental to the maize crop.

I have implied in these observations on intercropping and intra-household relations that a trial involving the intercropping of beans and maize in Mabumba chiefdom might most appropriately have been addressed to female-headed households involved to some degree in maize cash cropping.[16] In contrast, the people ARPT had chosen to participate in the intercropping trial were of both sexes and were all defined as 'subsistence' farmers, except for one man, a 'lima' farmer. However, a categorical statement that they were not the most appropriate 'target' group is not possible: as in the case of the maize trial, the terms were applied too ambiguously to be useful. One of the women, for example, was growing cash-crop maize with loans from the local primary cooperative society, as was her husband (I assume she was denoted as 'subsistence' because of her poor soils and field management).

Defining groups of people was a recurrent problematic in ARPT's work; or, more to the point, the understanding of crops in relation to groups of people, as a prerequisite to arriving at suitable objectives for on-farm trials, was poorly developed. It is the relational understanding of crops and people which I see as one distinctive contribution for an anthropologist to make, accepting the current institutional setting of ARPT. Initially, a crop might be considered according to some abstracted characteristic such as biological value. Thereafter, it must be understood as it is produced and used in the geographical area of on-farm research: how it is grown, consumed, sold and exchanged, in relation to other crops. In other words, its social identity must be established. Secondly, it must be known who is involved in the growth, consumption, sale and exchange: which kinds of household or household members take part in which activities, and under what circumstances. I have argued that in Mabumba the reasons why female-headed households might be targeted for a maize–bean intercrop (or other maize-food crop combination) are to do with gender-specific attachment to crops, and access to complementary labour to obtain the range of crops that most individuals require for subsistence. In a striking related case in Zaïre (Fairhead, personal communication) a particular intercrop (coffee and beans) is found to be the outcome of shifts in gender relations within the household. Together, the examples point to the need to understand agricultural practices as being as much the result of historical and political imperatives as they are expressions of 'indigenous technical knowledge'. To date, intercropping (to take but one example) has been seen by agricultural researchers as a rational technical and economic use of natural resources: this is fair enough, but casts the interpretative net into too narrow a channel.

Some problems: fluidity and rigidity

What I am suggesting is that a properly social understanding of crops in relation to interacting social groups (units of production) would be an improvement over the economistic way of understanding 'peasant' agriculture which has so far tended to influence ARPT's thinking. For example, it would be appropriate to get away from classifying households according to number of bags of crops produced each year (the primary line of economic differentiation drawn by ARPT Luapula) towards considering the complementarity of men's and women's productive activities and the sorts of exchange net-works into which products are inserted. This elaboration could be incorporated within the existing set-up of ARPT, though it would necessitate a more complex set of criteria for defining households.

The possibility for incorporating this kind of approach with the work of ARPT economists did emerge during fieldwork. The economists were concerned that their quantitative surveys led to predictions and deductions which might approximate the situation 'on the ground', but which did not assess the subjective relationships between different activities. For example, it was accepted that the labour surveys, while providing great detail about the way people divided their time, did not allow for statements about how new technologies could appropriately reorganize that time. Perhaps as much to the point, there was pressure from other team members and administrators in the ministry to restrict these kinds of surveys on the grounds that they were very expensive and time-consuming in comparison to the amount of usable information generated (for example, local crop rotation systems were being described by complete mapping of land use in a sample area over several years). There was agreement that anthropological data could provide a better focus for economic analysis, and discussion of what kinds of recommendation emerging from a trial could be relevant to the farming system.[17]

Unfortunately, these conventional modifications in the way ARPT works I see as producing space only for slight improvements in their understanding of rural peoples, and this is because of a misalliance of fluidity and rigidity, both in what ARPT are trying to observe and the approach taken to that observation.

1 Category versus process

So far I have used words like 'household' as if they were not problematic. Guyer (1986) has warned against the uncritical use of 'household' as a unit of analysis, since there has been a tendency in development thought to conflate the relatively corporate unit of many Asian societies with the more fluid arrangements typifying much of rural Africa.

For planning purposes, MAWD has produced a definition of 'household' which is supposedly applicable throughout Zambia:

a household includes all those individuals who live in close proximity to each other and who form one work-team under the guidance or direction of the leader, the head of the household. Most members of the household would be related to each other by either blood or affinal ties; others would be members of the extended family. The household may include young married couples and their children if for their subsistence and other economic activities these young couples depend on the larger unit headed by the household leader who decides where to direct resources such as oxen, implements, tools and time and labour of household members for that particular day or week.

(RDSB and MAWD 1986)

There are a host of problems with this definition, and its cumbrousness speaks of the difficulties.[18] In Mabumba's chiefdom, it emerged from fieldwork that if one tried to define 'household' as some kind of residential unit, the associations between members (generally matrilineal and affinal relatives) were confusingly variable; and, furthermore, that the composition of any one of these units could vary considerably over quite short periods. Given the still identifiable matrilineal paradox (to use Mary Douglas's term (1969), productive individualism being in tension with requirements for distributive communalism within matrilineages, and long-term, primary loyalties going to matri-kin), marriage tends to be a fairly unstable union, and most people will go through several marriages during their adult lives. Thus, the empirically common 'unit' of a married couple with their biological children living in a single house is not the structured and fairly permanent entity which it is in the West.

Other such units in Mabumba could consist of an adult, unmarried woman and some of her younger siblings; a woman and her children and grandchildren; or a group of elderly siblings relying on one another and junior relatives living nearby. One can interpret membership in units glossable as 'household' as to do with strategies to meet personal economic needs and the needs of dependants, making use of the array of possible social attachments deemed appropriate in Mabumba society. Minimally, association requires the presence of one man and one woman (however connected) because their productive activities are complementary, at least in the sphere of food production.

The crux of the problem is that if one insists on having a *unit*, such as household, at the centre of analysis, one finds that the composition of units is so variable (at an instant in time and across agricultural seasons) as to make the unit of little analytical value; worse, that having defined one kind of boundary, one obscures certain important similarities and differences. For example, apart from production level, ARPT has tended to discriminate households on the basis of whether they are male-headed or female-headed. The reasoning behind this is that female-headed households are empirically common in Luapula (a legacy of male labour migration to the mines of the Copperbelt) and (because of supposed shortage of male labour) have been identified as one of the most disadvantaged groups in

Luapulan societies. If one looks closely, though, one finds that women employ similar strategies in garnering resources whichever type of 'household' they may be in. For example, I knew one older, divorced woman in Mabumba who was living with several of her children, including an adult son not yet married. He had his own maize farm on land given him by his mother adjacent to her fields and, as would be expected (the tie between a mother and her children being strongly emphasized in this matrilineal society), he gave her some of the income from it, as well as assisting her by cultivating her food-crop fields. Her household was better placed economically than many based on a married couple in which the wife supposedly benefited from the income of her husband's maize farm. That is not to say that many women in Luapula are not in dire economic straits; merely that one cannot make a straightforward woman–household category association.

One possible way out of the problem is to think in terms of processes, rather than units, and to see 'households' as the outcome of people making strategic use of legitimate claims to the resources of others. As Crehan has suggested (1987: 140), the analytical basis of such an approach should be the individual male producer and individual female producer, as they underpin all the other observable processes.[19] I do not think that this change of approach would be easy to foster, because agricultural research is so much centred on easily identifiable and comparable units: a fluid approach is difficult in research where the agronomic side is heavily quantitative and there are expectations that the other disciplines (which have, historically, been appended to agronomy) should lean that way. Even the form in which rural sociology is being institutionalized in ARPT is biased towards the development of replicable, uniform methodologies. A more intuitive, anthropological approach is not being strongly encouraged, precisely (if not explicitly) because it tends to subvert methodological uniformism. If I can suggest any compromise, it is that an anthropological analysis might help indicate which sorts of unit might least inappropriately be chosen as the basis of field research on technologies relating to specific crops/activities. But that is not a very good compromise.

2   Are systems systematic?

The second problem which needs examining is one concerning 'technical' aspects of production (as opposed to its social organization), and at a higher level of abstraction. It exists in the very nature of a 'systems approach'. To see agricultural activities as being related in a system orientated towards a number of goals is, perhaps, fair enough, and an improvement over the solidly Western technicist approach to agricultural research which has operated in the past. The problem is that the systematic analysis gets read into what is being observed; that is, farmers' activities are seen as being systematically related *by them* in a *body* of local agricultural knowledge.

Agriculture is in a considerable state of flux in Mabumba, with a great expansion of maize cash cropping since 1980, a cropping 'enterprise' quite separate from other, established agricultural practices, and decline of certain crops (especially finger millet), once grown in swidden fields. Under these conditions, people are experimenting with new techniques as seen in my earlier example of the woman who intercropped climbing beans with cash maize. She was trying this practice for the first time, and deemed it a success. At the same time, some individuals who found themselves short of finger millet after giving up shifting fields were trying new ways of growing the crop on semi-permanent fields. Some were incorporating vegetation into the soil on cultivation; or burning areas where there was much grass so as to approximate the effects of tree burning; or even testing the effects of different inorganic fertilizer applications.

One person's way of doing things may change considerably from year to year, and be different from anyone else's. Agricultural 'knowledge' is hypothetical, not fixed in an encyclopaedic fashion (a point made strongly by Fairhead; this volume). To return to my earlier example of the beans trial, the problem there was not just that villagers had been asked to plant beans in the traditional way but on the wrong kind of beds. To ask for 'the traditional village way' is to pose a non-question, because it assumes a uniformity and certainty which simply does not exist: it is an artefact of a systems approach (and again reflects a tendency to deal in fixed categories and be poorly equipped, practically and analytically, to cope with fluidity). Ignoring for now the political relations between villager and ARPT (see below), it is perhaps not surprising that the trial farmers did not object to ARPT's 'wrong' way of planting beans: they were interested to see what would happen. Appreciation of the provisional nature of much 'local agricultural knowledge' requires deep familiarity with an area, developed over time. This way of researching is well established in anthropology, but it is the approach, rather than the discipline, which is important.

As a concluding comment to this section, I would suggest that an unnoticed problem of rigidity exists also within the interdisciplinary nature of ARPT, engendered in the mode of identifying problems and proposing solutions. One claim for FSR is that it is a participatory research scheme which, given the systems perspective, allows true identification of farmers' problems. In practice, some broad problem is identified, and a trial arrived at in the deductive way I described earlier, each discipline suggesting one or more variable to be addressed by the trial. Each researchable problem is treated as a discrete entity, not something that exists in dynamic relation to other problems. The result is that trials are synthetic products originating within the research team: they do not grow out of the farming 'system' as lived in and understood by the farmer, the sort of position an anthropologist might strive towards.

To this point I have restricted my discussion to possible improvements in the process of FSR which an anthropologist might make, more or less accepting the *status quo*. Specifically, I have suggested refining the process of identifying objectives for the sorts of trials in which a particular research team was engaged.[20]

As an anthropologist who studied both in and outside an FSR team, though, I have the luxury of being able to adopt a partially independent viewpoint in which the wider context of the team's work becomes part of the analysis. Switching now to bring in this wider view, I have to suggest that the relationship of anthropology and anthropologists with FSR is likely to remain an uneasy one, in both theoretical and practical senses. Some of the problems here lie in the nature of interdisciplinarity. Others are in the scope of a systems approach in its current institutional setting.

Anthropologist on the outside?

It is quite common to see anthropology advertised as a holistic discipline, contrasted with the particularity of, for example, economics or political science. To express the difference in this way is to suggest a complementarity which does not always exist. Though anthropologists working in multi-disciplinary research teams will assert, at a practical level, the need to learn the languages of other specialists, there is a tendency for anthropologists to take apart languages and look at what kinds of premise they are based on, thereby appearing to subvert the work of others. This does not make for easy professional relationships. An ethnographic example of a related kind occurred in the neighbouring province, where collaborative work was started on soil taxonomy, involving both social and soil scientists. The project was to develop an indigenous soil classification to provide an informed basis for adaptive research on long-term soil fertility, indigenous soil terms becoming a resource for use in extension.

Problems arose over what would constitute an indigenous classi-fication. The social scientists wished to discuss soils with villagers in an open-ended way to discover the criteria by which they identified and used them. The soil scientists were planning to map soils and identify them according to their usual criteria, such as colour and texture. Samples of the different soils so identified would then be taken to villagers for them to supply the indigenous terms. The situation became one in which the soil scientists accused the social scientists of encroaching on their territory, soils not being social variables, after all (Sikana, personal communication).

The problem, I suppose, is that anthropologists are not just interested in 'social variables', whatever they may be, and that anthropological fieldwork is about becoming a jack-of-all-trades, learning new things in all spheres of a society's life. Anthropology is always already interdisciplinary. Anthropologists appear both to encroach on others' professional territory, and not to have some field which is distinctively their own. (I think the problem is less acute for sociology, for reasons alluded to earlier.)

These kinds of tensions continue in settings where rural sociologists arrive late on the scene and are put in the position of having to legitimize their presence: at one regional meeting I attended, the presentation by a rural sociologist was geared entirely to demon-strating the usefulness of sociology. That a particular profession should concentrate much of its time on self-legitimation is clearly not a healthy sign. Anthropology/sociology will not be able to make the best possible contribution to FSR as long as it remains marginalized. Yet there is a tendency to self-marginalization, because of the (I think defensible) lack of methodological rigor or clearly delineated professional boundary.

In concluding this chapter, I wish to turn to a much broader set of issues which question the possibility of much improvement in the way FSR understands and works with rural populations. They are prob-lems which anthropologists have tended to be good at pointing up, but which by their nature are intractable.

ANTHROPOLOGY: IN OR OF FARMING SYSTEMS RESEARCH?

My experience in looking at the impact of the two ARPT trials was that farmers' perceptions of them were very different from those of

ARPT. The ARPT team leader saw this as a problem of communication, and wondered if the level of technical complexity of trials was inappropriate. Other problems existed on the ground, such as difficulties in recruiting 'subsistence' farmers to take part in trials, and a high drop-out rate among those who did become involved. At field days, where trials were discussed with groups of farmers at the field sites, a particular kind of impasse was often reached. ARPT saw these as occasions to gather more information about farmers' problems, but after some time the question would arise, 'Why are you asking us these things when you are here to teach us?'

These kinds of difficulty are not really about inappropriate communication, at least not in any unmediated sense. They are to do with the historical and political context of government institutions working in rural Zambia, out of which the insubstantial form of farmer participation in agricultural research has grown. In other words, they relate not so much to the theoretical and methodological preoccupations of FSR as to real 'on-the-ground' political relations between government and villager.

The need to understand the relationship of ARPT with the community as growing out of the history of involvement of government institutions is, in my own analysis, most clearly to be seen in the relationship between cash maize and all the other crops produced. As discussed earlier, this element of the farming system arrived through government extension,[21] with much rhetorical fanfare about national development depending on the farming population being able to feed the nation.[22] A problem for ARPT is that government involvement has become associated exclusively with maize, so in spite of having a mandate to work regionally on food crops, it is very difficult to find a way in.

In part because institutions have not previously shown interest in traditional cropping systems (indeed, the shifting *citemene* system has been denigrated by government, both pre- and post-independence), interest is not expected of them now. Furthermore, the growing of food crops is perceived by the villagers primarily in terms of satisfying dietary needs and fulfilling social obligations through exchange. This last observation is a key theme in anthropological literature on Zambia, and indeed in the Southern African region. An important argument is that indigenous economies are strongly 'distributionist' in nature, with people acquiring and maintaining access to resources through networks which usually have kinship as their organizing principle (for example, Crehan 1987; Poewe 1981). Given that production of resources is fairly individualistic, production analytically becomes a subservient category of behaviour; indeed, it can be argued that many productive processes are geared towards distribution of resources, not production as an end in itself (for instance, Gould 1988). This is in complete contrast to ARPT's work, which is strongly 'productionist' in nature, with increasing productivity, in a measurable way, the prime motivation of its work. Under real-life conditions, then, addressing the productivity constraints of an individual farmer becomes a rather pointless task when access to that particular resource may be gained by a number of means, depending on the context. Often it is more socially appropriate to obtain food from someone else than to produce it (the gendered division of labour being the most obvious referent).

Looking from a different perspective, the distributionist emphasis in the local political economy of Mabumba can also be seen in the way the community has responded to government interventions in agriculture. There is a sense in which the package that the government has offered for maize production has come to be seen as a resource which villagers may legitimately claim, as some kind of return for allegiance to the state. It is there to be taken, and is. It is not really seen to be about encouraging self-sufficiency through sustainable increases in productivity. I think this goes part way to explaining why maize production seems to be mentally 'parked off' from all other agricultural activities, and why the failure of ARPT field trials does not mean rejection of their efforts or ridicule: villagers will write off failed trials and just wait until 'Agriculture' (the collective term used in Mabumba for governmental agencies involved in agriculture) does bring something useful (Sikana, personal communication).

Once received from the government, these 'prestations' are quite frequently entered into the networks of exchange established within the village, and not put to the ends which extension officers expect. Several times when I toured Mabumba agricultural camp with the Agricultural Assistant (extension officer) we came across large fields demarcated for maize production, with a small area planted in one corner. I learned from various informants that this often happened because seed and fertilizer could provide quick access to much-needed cash; or that some would be given to a relative to allow him to produce beyond his government-specified credit limit, in return for some future patronage. Whilst doing these things, villagers realized they were breaking conditions imposed by government agencies. With posters of loan defaulters behind bars liberally displayed in the provincial town, this made for a tendency to be secretive about agricultural production, to avoid too close surveillance by government representatives. The multifariousness of networks of exchange can allow for the paying back of input loans from sources other than the income from maize, but villagers know that financial institutions tend to take a narrower view.

Instances of cleared land being left unplanted do not in all cases indicate a reallocation of resources. In one or two cases I heard of men who had paid to get large areas of land stumped and cleared (the machinery can be hired from the district council) but who did not have the resources to continue with planting. It seems that their interest in clearing land was to demonstrate their ability to obtain resources, and produce clear indications of being progressive, commercial farmers who would lead the community, as powerful individuals, towards the nation's agricultural goals. In a sense they were using agricultural activities to make social statements about themselves. This is an important point, which I cannot dwell on here. Agricultural research organizations look at agricultural production, and increasingly consider its social context. What they cannot do is think in terms of agriculture as an idiom for social expression, since the products then become subordinate to the statements – and agricultural research, as I have argued, is all about production of physical resources. This is one area in which anthropologists are making a unique contribution to understanding agriculture in developing countries; but it is not one that can be fitted within Farming Systems Research.[23]

What I have been saying here is that an ambivalent relationship between government and village has grown out of a history in which government has played a paternalistic role, mediated through the promotion of one crop. The historical context has defined a situation in which ARPT has relatively little room for manoeuvre. Any field trial including maize is readily, even enthusiastically, received, because it implicitly contains the promise of further resources from government. For research on other crops the reception is much more lukewarm, because there is no apparent government 'prestation' on offer, and a disinclination (though not universal) to satisfy the curiosity of a government institution over issues such as how much of a particular crop is grown, how much income is gained from it, and how that income is used.

The differential reception of proposed technologies for experimentation has social correlates as well. I earlier mentioned how communication between ARPT and farmers is related to the degree

and types of identification between the Trials Assistants and individual community members. This identification with certain groups
gets reinforced by the educational background of Trials Assistants,
who are usually seconded from Extension. My wider experience of
extension staff shows they tend to think of 'subsistence' farmers as
laggards, loafers (a favourite term in Zambia), ignorant and risk-
averse. Inevitably, placed at the 'interface' between institution and
village, Trials Assistants can have a large influence over how the
research programme operates. The tendency is for those people
whom ARPT most want to help to become alienated, an alienation
adding to the difficulties of working with 'traditional' food crops (the
'peasant' farmers also grow these crops, but do not see them as
relevant to their relationships with government).

To break out of this impasse would require, in my opinion, quite
radical shifts in the way government institutions work, and relate to
rural communities. As things stand, a role could be argued for
anthropologists/sociologists working as brokers between institution
and villager, as they tend to spend more time in the villages, and
develop closer relationships with the subject communities than
do other research-team members. This has been a theme in
anthropological literature for some time (for example, Bailey 1969).

However, an individual cannot overturn the barriers which exist
by virtue of the institutional *status quo*. The relationship between
rural people and government institutions in Zambia has to be seen
as a political arena, and one in which the people have become the
domesticated and muted objects of institutional research (though in
some senses, as in the use of credit inputs, resisting and manipulating
this objectification). The agenda is one that has existed since before
independence, and while the state has patronized, many rural people
have come to internalize their supposed intellectual and practical
dependence on external agencies.

What is necessary is for these people to be able to move from an
object to a subject position; for farmers to be empowered to play a
role in determining the research agenda in agriculture. FSR may be
an improvement on 'traditional' research in some senses, but it is still
top-down, in spite of the claims of some of its promoters. A much
closer look needs to be taken at what is meant by 'participatory
research' (a subject much debated now in relation to FSR; for
example, Sagar and Farrington 1988), with the realization that the
term has no genuine currency in the absence of a decentralization of
power on a scale which remains a remote possibility in many states,
Zambia included.

Some writers (such as Brush 1986) would distinguish the earlier and later parts of this chapter as referring to applied and basic (or pure) research, respectively. I do not think the distinction a helpful one as there tends to be little dialogue between the practitioners of each. Ideally, it should be possible for an anthropologist working in FSR or other forms of agricultural research to do both, though time is always constraining. The promotion of a specifically sociological perspective does fit relatively well with the current institutional set-up of agricultural research in Zambia. What I have done in this chapter is to illustrate how a more intuitive, qualitative approach can bring out certain issues which a routine sociological one might not, and, importantly, continually press questions on the wisdom of maintaining the institutions as they stand. The agenda needs to be made more public, inside and outside academia, for an anthropologist who argues alone against the 'establishment' (in both senses) of FSR is likely to be disenfranchised.

NOTES

1 A comparison would need to be drawn between consultancy work and contract appointments. Consultancies are almost by definition external, whereas FSR teams such as ARPT are integral to the local ministry of agriculture and have localization of posts as a key concern.
2 In a sense these new concerns in the 1980s can be seen as part of the continuing debate over the nature of peasant economies, especially the 'rational peasant' literature set against the 'moral economy of the peasant' sort.
3 An important issue which I cannot cover in this chapter relates to the nature of the initial systems description process. This process is one manifestation of Rapid Rural Appraisal (RRA), a controversial subject raising much debate contra 'traditional' survey methods in development projects and, importantly, the long-term fieldwork practices of anthropologists.
4 As opposed to hitherto state-supported cash crops, especially maize.
5 Increasingly, maize flour is being consumed in rural Luapula as a supplement or alternative to cassava flour.
6 There were senior village members who liked to eat maize as well as cassava, these usually being people who had spent some time away working in the mining towns.
7 Maize flour was occasionally sold at Mabumba market, usually by resource-poor women. A bag of meal would be bought specifically as a commodity for sale, none of it to be eaten in the household.
8 A fear exacerbated by the depredations of mealy bug during the 1980s.
9 I should emphasize that the various institutions involved in promoting agricultural development are not generally distinguished by villagers; they are all part of government (*buteko* in CiBemba). Where distinctions

are made, these are between the activities of the particular *individuals* who are representing government departments.

10 The agronomists had an alternative suggestion: that local farmers did not have a concept of plant population. This is perhaps unlikely, as they did express strong opinions on how closely cassava cuttings should be planted in relation to a cassava planting density trial.

11 A certain remoteness from field realities, and from one another, is not untypical of government departments in Zambia.

12 Assuming a two-crop intercrop, the Land Equivalent Ratio is the comparison of yield from a given area of intercrop with the yields from the two crops grown singly on half that area each.

13 This is a simplification. Details of the gender division of labour and its variability are covered in my thesis (Gatter 1990).

14 This monopoly seems to have grown out of the post-independence preoccupation with national food security through maize, which was purveyed through an almost exclusively male-staffed extension service to male villagers. In crude terms, men have greater authority in the realm of the political than do women.

15 This logical separation, its origins and consequences, are matters I treat in detail in my thesis (Gatter 1990).

16 This idea, arrived at inductively through participant observation, echoes some findings of more quantitative studies of cropping patterns and nutrition in northern Zambia (for example, Sharpe 1987): that nutritional problems may follow from increased involvement in cash cropping in households with little ability to redeploy or acquire labour (that is, a vulnerable group is identified for whom some form of intervention might be appropriate).

17 Here it is worth stressing that the approach was intended to be anthropological as opposed to sociological. In the ways the two disciplines are usually applied in the field, sociologists, like economists, tend to conduct extensive surveys and employ quantitative techniques for analysis, producing a reductionist view of people's behaviour. Where writers have argued for a specifically sociological contribution on political grounds (for example, Sutherland 1987, for Southern Africa), they usually suggest that training courses for sociologists be modified to include qualitative techniques.

18 Also, the role of the household head has been overplayed in exactly the way that Guyer (1986) has criticized.

19 The same could be applied to most of the matrilineal peoples of Zambia.

20 All of ARPT's work in chief Mabumba's had been agronomic to 1988. ARPT may also work on questions of crop processing and storage, but did not have the necessary professional expertise within the team yet to work on these issues.

21 The main institutions involved in Mabumba have been agricultural extension, the Department of Social Development (through its 'Grow more maize' functional literacy courses) and the Roman Catholic church (through the Family Farming Scheme and *Misapela* Youth Club).

22 In the early years after independence the government played a paternalistic (labelled 'humanist') role which encouraged dependency on government. Provision of agricultural credit went along with universal free

primary education and free medicines. In a declining economy the government has been forced to introduce various austerity programmes, an element of which is a change in rhetoric towards encouraging self-sufficiency at village level. The consequences of this shift should be interesting to follow.
23 I am indebted to Melissa Leach for making this point for me in relation to upland rice farmers in Sierra Leone.

REFERENCES

ARPT Luapula (1987) *Annual Report, 1986–87*, ARPT, PO Box 710129, Mansa, Zambia.

Bailey, F. G. (1969) *Stratagems and Spoils: A Social Anthropology of Politics*, Oxford: Blackwell.

Behnke, R. and Kerven, C. (1983) 'FSR and the attempt to understand the goals and motivations of farmers', *Culture and Agriculture*, Newsletter of the Anthropological Study Group on Agrarian Systems, no. 19.

Berry, S. (1984) 'The food crisis and agrarian change in Africa: a review essay', *African Studies Review* 27(2): 59–112.

Brush, S. B. (1986) 'Basic and applied research in farming systems: an anthropologist's appraisal', *Human Organization* 45(3): 220–8.

Centro Internacional de Mejoramiento de Maiz y Trigo (CIMMYT) (1976) *From Agronomic Data to Farmer Recommendations: An Economics Training Manual*, R. K. Perrin, D. L. Winkelmann, E. R. Moscardi and J. R. Anderson (eds), Mexico City: CIMMYT, *Information Bulletin* 27.

Collinson, M. (1981) 'A low cost approach to understanding small farmers', *Agricultural Administration* 8(6): 434–50.

Crehan, K. A. F. (1987) *Production, Reproduction and Gender in North-western Zambia: A Case Study*, Unpublished Ph.D. thesis, University of Manchester.

Douglas, M. (1969) 'Is matriliny doomed in Africa?' in M. Douglas and P. M. Kaberry (eds) *Man in Africa*, London: Tavistock, pp. 123–37.

Douglas, M. and Kaberry, P. M. (eds) (1969) *Man in Africa*, London: Tavistock.

Gasson, R. (1971) 'Use of sociology in agricultural economics', *Journal of Agricultural Economics* 22(1): 29–38.

Gatter, P. N. (1988a) *Indigenous Farming Systems Information in Mabumba*, Mimeo: ARPT Luapula.

—— (1988b) *Beans and Maize in Mabumba*, Mimeo: ARPT Luapula.

—— (1990) *Indigenous and institutional thought in the practice of rural development: a study of an Ushi chiefdom in Luapula, Zambia*, Unpublished thesis, SOAS, University of London.

Gould, J. (1988) 'Toward a conceptualization of economic strategy: distributive entitlements and households in Southern Africa', Paper presented to the Society for Economic Anthropology meeting on The Informal Economy, Knoxville, Tenn., April 1988.

Guyer, J. I. (1986) 'Intra-household processes and farming systems research: perspectives from anthropology', in J. L. Moock (ed.) *Understanding*

Africa's Rural Households and Farming Systems, London: Westview Press, pp. 92–104.

Harriss, J. (ed.) (1982) *Rural Development: Theories of Peasant Economy and Agrarian Change*, London: Hutchinson.

Hedlund, H. (1984) 'Development in action: the experience of the Zambian extension worker', *Ethnos* 49(3–4): 226–50.

MAWD (Extension Branch) (1979) *Lima Crop Memo: Luapula Province*, Lusaka: MAWD.

Moock, J. L. (ed.) (1986) *Understanding Africa's Rural Households and Farming Systems*, Westview Special Studies on Africa, London: Westview Press.

Poewe, K. O. (1981) *Matrilineal Ideology: Male–Female Dynamics in Luapula, Zambia*, London: Academic Press.

Pottier, J. (1988) *Migrants No More: Settlement and Survival in Mambwe Villages, Zambia*, Manchester: Manchester University Press.

RDSB and MAWD (1986) *Rural Household Survey*, Lusaka: Rural Development Studies Bureau and Ministry of Agriculture and Water Development (Planning Division).

Richards, A. I. (1939) *Land, Labour and Diet in Northern Rhodesia: An Economic Study of the Bemba Tribe*, Oxford: Oxford University Press.

Sagar, D. and Farrington, J. (1988) *Participatory Approaches to Technology Generation: From the Development of Methodology to Wider-scale Implementation*, London: ODI Agricultural Administration (Research and Extension) Network, Network Paper 2.

Sharpe, B. (1987) *Report of the Nutritional Anthropology Investigation*, Zambia: IRDP (SMCD/NFNC).

Sutherland, A. (1987) *Sociology in Farming Systems Research*, London: ODI Agricultural Administration Unit, Occasional Paper 6.

Personal communications

Leach, M. A., IDS, Brighton, Sussex.

Sikana, P. M., Rural Sociologist, ARPT Northern Province, PO Box 410055, Kasama, Zambia.

8 Representing knowledge

The 'new farmer' in research fashions

James Fairhead

This chapter explores Indigenous Technical Knowledge (ITK) in local agriculture, and its representation and use by agricultural research organizations. The issues raised stem from my own difficulties with representing local knowledge about crop health. I was a cultural 'broker', positioned at the interface between researchers in the CIAT bean improvement programme of the Great Lakes region of Central Africa, and local farmers there; specifically those in one village in the Zone of Rutshuru, Kivu, Zaïre, where I lived for twenty months between 1986 and 1988.[1] In Box's (1989) terms I was charged with the job of reducing the 'social distance' between CIAT and 'the farmer'.

This farmer is very much the *'new* farmer', that rational, experimenting, 'enknowledged' farmer who is to be 'put first' by state-of-the-art agricultural research organizations such as CIAT, which at last openly acknowledge such farmers as research partners. CIAT-Rwanda can rightfully claim to be among the pioneers of this research orientation.

In keeping with the recurrent concern over the 'power in definitions', which runs through several other contributions (especially Hutson and Liddiard, in this volume), this chapter explores the imagery of *'new* farmer' within the 'Farmer First' movement (see Chambers *et al.* 1989) of agricultural research and development. Specifically, it explores this image within my own reports to CIAT.

In the Great Lakes region, CIAT has been using two closely related, complementary and often overlapping research approaches better to ally the farmer with the researcher. The first incorporates farmers into the research programme from as early on in the technology development phase as can be achieved (for example, Sperling 1988). The second, to which I was a party, incorporates researchers into farming so that they may better appreciate the skills, complexities and difficulties of current local agriculture. As a Ph.D. student in Social Anthropology embarking on fieldwork in the region and as a graduate in Agricultural Sciences, I was well suited to what can best be described as the 'semi-formal *ad hoc* cooperation' which CIAT and I arranged. Towards the end of my stay, this took the form of a liaison with the team's plant pathologist who wanted to improve his knowledge of the way farmers understand crop failure.

An abridged version of my findings is reproduced here. I then go on to discuss problems with my representational style.

CROP FAILURE

Bwisha farmers control their bean crop's architecture to regulate its humidity. Fertility, soil type, field slope, field aspect, crop associations, weed types, sowing density, sowing dates and staking density/ length, which all interact to influence the crops' microclimate, are either altered or accounted for by farmers in managing the crop. So, for example, in field conditions where there is a tendency for the microclimate to be too moist (for instance, high fertility, soft soil, flat field, bottom of a valley, in a banana grove and so on) farmers can sow less densely (*kutanya*), sow a less vigorous variety (*ubwoko butafura*) which resists the rain (*butapfaga cane*), reduce the foliage on the climbing beans (*kusoroma*), space longer stakes wider apart (*kutanya*), weed the climbing beans more frequently to let the sun and the air in (*kubagara kuingiza izuba n'umuyaga*), sow later in the season (*kuter'inyuma*), and sow on mounds (*kuhig'imitabo*).

The effects of rainfall (*imvura*) and dew (*ikime*) are considered to be closely related, and to have positive and negative characteristics. In areas, places or seasons known to be drier than others, dew is used as the crop's defence against drought, and farming practices encourage its collection and retention. For example, farmers refrain from weeding in drought-susceptible areas so as to leave a greater surface area for dew to form on. Weeds also restrict air movement through the crop (*kutingiza umuyaga*), and prevent it drying. For the same reasons, farmers sow densely or in banana groves to create closed (*kufunga*), cool (*harakonje*), windless (and therefore relatively humid) crop conditions.

But dew, rain and ground-water are also recognized to damage plants in several ways. Farmers note that dew forms on the insides of flowers, where rain does not normally reach, making the flowers limp and shrink. This makes leaves much more likely to fall off (*kugwa hasi*) too early, or just to suffer irreparable damage (*kuzambya*) from the rain. For this reason, farmers dislike rain at night or in the early morning before the dew is gone. Also for this reason, in high-altitude regions where rain and dew are more prevalent, farmers sow later and rely upon dew alone as a water source at the end of the cropping season; the dry season sets in once the crops have reached their flowering stage. Furthermore, as dew also loosens the flowers from the stem, the crop is more fragile and flowers fall more easily if they are disturbed mechanically, either by the wind, rain or people. Farmers try not to weed a crop at the flowering stage when dew is still on the plant, or during or just after rain. Some farmers say that a reason for weeding, and for creating empty space between bean plants, is to stop the plants bumping into one another when there is a wind, as the constant movement knocks off the flowers. Villagers have different hypotheses over the cause of plant death. Some recognize that when stagnant surface water persists in a bean field for an hour or more, the crop rapidly dies off, indicating that it is water which kills beans. By deduction, 'When plants are sown too close together, the leaves meet one another so the water rests on the leaves without falling to the ground. When the dew rests on the leaves for a long time, the plants will begin to rot.'

One generally held principle which derives from the farmers' understanding of plant death is that bush-bean plants should not touch one another (except those which are sown in the same pocket, in which case beans from different pockets should not touch). Similarly, for climbing beans, plants climbing on one stake should not touch others on other stakes. In normal times there ought to be a gap between plants. In conditions where plants are likely to do well, and grow larger, farmers therefore sow plants further apart, or alter other conditions, such as by sowing the crop later.

Plant density is altered in this way not only to regulate the microclimate. Farmers sow more densely in response to reduced fertility, because each plant will take up less space. Farmers sow more densely the greater the estimated weed pressure mainly because a dense crop early in the growing period will stifle the potentially competitive weeds. Sowing densities are also increased if the seed's viability is poor. Seed which contains many *ibipfu* (literally, 'dead ones'; identified as those which have brown patches covering the 'eye' of the seed) will be sown at higher densities, as will seeds which are damaged, either where there are brown patches over areas of the seed other than the 'eye', or where there has been infestation by bruchid insects. In the same vein, if the field where the seeds are to be sown has been badly prepared, or is likely to provide a hostile environment to the growing plants, more seed is sown. To take poor field preparation as an example, there must be a delay of about two weeks to a month between the incorporation of plant debris into the soil during the first cultivation, and sowing, or else the 'heat' caused by the decaying debris will 'kill' (*kwica*) many of the growing plants.

Although these influences alter the sowing densities, the micro-climatic influence is, nevertheless, always taken into account. The importance which farmers attach to decisions concerning sowing density and conformation is revealed in the fact that sowing was often a specialist's task allocated to the few people regarded as particularly good judges of the relationship between fields, varieties and climate.

To understand further local ideas concerning the death of crops, and the choice of varieties, it is important to bear in mind that generally held local attitudes towards health (of people or crops) are slightly different from popular Western perceptions. Simply put, one's 'state of health' seems to be considered as logically prior to illness, and villagers have ways of evaluating their 'state of health'. If it is bad, then a natural result may be to become ill. 'Health' is therefore not directly contrasted with 'illness.' In the body, one of the indicators of this 'state of health' is the amount of blood one has. A person who has 'too little' (*amaraso make*), is weak, down, needs to take it easy. A person with 'too much' (*amaraso menshi*) can become tense, get headaches and is likely to be taken ill. The same idiom is used for plants. If the plant has too little 'plant water' (sap) then it will not grow strongly, and will be uncompetitive with weeds and yield poorly, whereas if the plant (crop) has too much sap, then it becomes 'over-extended', and is prone to sudden death.

These idioms used for understanding the health of people and crops are linked by the use of the term *ivitamin*. *Ivitamin* is the current term used for both soil and body nutrients, and the more of it there is, the more sap or blood there will be. When people feel that they are low on blood, they often go to the local para-medic for an injection of vitamin B12, or alternatively eat certain plants known to give one more blood. Headaches are treated by blood letting. For plants, too little *ivitamin* in the soil restricts the sap and leaves the plant uncompetitive. Too much *ivitamin* leads to too much sap and to overextension (*gufura*; *gufura* is a state of overlushness or overextension caused by too much sap). In this condition, a plant almost seems to forget what it is for; that is, to produce flowers and not leaves.

The state of *gufura* in bean plants is considered to be damaging for several reasons. First, for reasons stated above, leaves of different plants should not touch one another. Secondly, plants in this state are more susceptible to damage. To quote one farmer: 'Plants which *gufura* will mature later, as it takes longer for the extra sap to go to the seed. There is too much sap, and not enough plant, so the leaves and the pods die as if one had poured boiling water over them.' Thirdly, in an overly vigorous crop, the plants on one stake grow over into other stakes and close the canopy, which increases humidity lower down and reduces the viability of flowers in the lower areas of the crops.

The tendency to *gufura* is linked to variety. Varieties which are more likely to *gufura* are more sensitive to high fertility and rain. As a result, farmers with varieties prone to *gufura* prefer to sow them in drier and less fertile conditions (for example, they are sown later, or on 'hard' clay soils). Less vigorous varieties grow better in fertile conditions. None the less, if vigorous varieties are grown in fertile conditions, other measures are available to mitigate the potential damage, giving the farmer extra flexibility. These measures include sowing at reduced densities, partially defoliating the plants (*gusoroma*) or altering the staking density and height.

Farmers understand the relocation of nutrients similarly to Western plant scientists. If, during *gusoroma* (defoliation), many leaves are left on a plant in a state of *gufura*, the quantity of flowers lower down the plant will be reduced not only because there is less sun, but also because the leaves take the 'vitamins' that flowering needs. Equally, if there are too many leaves (*gufura*), then farmers consider that there will be a reduction in the number of pods.

Gufura is an important principle in the local assessment and choice of bean varieties. Through experience, farmers identify the characteristics peculiar to each variety, and, once these are known, farmers can adapt field conditions to the variety or the variety to the conditions. Such flexibility is increased by leaf removal (*gusoroma*). Mature leaves can be picked from the middle level of the plant when the plant is at the flowering stage; this is normally done simultaneously with weeding. Farmers choose to remove leaves which do not cover and protect flowers from the rain, which are mature, which touch neighbouring plants and which are still lushly green. The stated purposes of leaf removal are, first, to reduce the shade at the middle level of the crop's architecture, so that when the flowers grow, they will grow all the way down the plant and not just at the top, so increasing yield. Secondly, as the pods fill out and mature, they will get some shade and some sun, rather than too much shade, and are less likely to rot. Thirdly, picking off leaves reduces competition for nutrients at flowering time between flower and leaf growth. Fourthly, it prevents the leaves of the plants climbing up one stake touching those of plants climbing up neighbouring stakes.

Leaves are not taken from the bottom of the plant as these 'protect the ground' (*kulind'ubutaka*) – positive connotation – and if one takes them off, the plant's roots may dry out (*kuma*). Equally, leaves are not taken off the top of the growing plant (except when these more tender leaves are used as food), because it is believed that this would take away the plant's ability to set more flowers (*kuyanga*).

This understanding of microclimatic control should enable researchers to correct certain errors derived from a more narrow disease- and variety-focused approach to the understanding of plant disease and its control. Earlier investigations, which had been based on the European disease-focused paradigm for understanding plant protection, failed to reveal the above control measures. Their approach presupposed that if farmers did not know about disease, then they did not know about plant protection. Researchers looked for (and failed to find) direct translations for plant diseases, and when farmers were shown examples (real or photographic) of the diseases, and asked for the causal conditions of the phenomenon, their responses were vague and usually hard to interpret. Farmers were, in fact, relatively uninterested and unconcerned to hear that plant death is due to 'disease'. Not that farmers do not understand diseases: farmers in the study village have a name for a disease of millet, and use a fumigation method for its control; rather, their perspective bypasses disease as a causal agent, and focuses on the factors which we would regard as conditions in which diseases develop. This difference reflects the different techniques which the holder of each perspective has available for controlling crop failure. Just as we know the conditions in which disease attacks, so farmers know the conditions in which rain attacks. It is not surprising that farmers call new fungicide 'medicine of the rain' (*umuti w'imvura*).

PROBLEMS IN THE REPRESENTATION OF ITK

On reflection, this presentation worries me for several reasons. It hides creativity, it extracts farming knowledge from its social and political context, assisting the belief that farming is somehow a-social and a-political, and it tempts researchers to see knowledge behind every practice they observe.

1 'The uncreative farmer'

The first reason for worry is that the above presentation seems to construct, simultaneously and mutually interdependently, 'the Banyawisha' and 'their system' of thinking about crop failure. Such a flat presentation of a knowledge system at best renders invisible, and at worst denies, creativity. The shift in focus from 'farming systems' to 'farming knowledge systems' retains this inherent problem of 'systematization'. Systems can be misrepresented as – or easily misinterpreted as – 'traditional' and 'inherited', which thus marginalizes farmers' creativity and innovation.

Such systematization is inherent in the methodologies promoted by Werner and Begishe, and other 'ethnoscientists'. They write: 'Although we start with informants (consultants) and their individual knowledge, we end up with the total knowledge of an idealized member of the culture' (1980: 152). Whilst this methodological and descriptive strategy enables generalizations to be made about farmers' knowledge, it does not permit discussion of the extent to which there is a shared 'system' of knowledge. Many other questions are also excluded from consideration. How confident are people in what they know? Whence is the knowledge derived? Who talks to whom about it? How has the knowledge changed?

Farmers' knowledge is more empirical and dynamic than often imagined. In Bwisha, the dramatic and ceaseless changes in local agriculture and social organization over the last seventy years mean that each new generation of farmers faces new agricultural problems. Local knowledge is better envisaged as empirical and hypothetical. Nobody locally is in a position to say what is 'right' or what is 'wrong' and to turn a farmer's hypothesis into truth. Perhaps those who document ITK have taken up this role, and have become 'arbitrators of truth' for this knowledge. But they (we) should recognize that local knowledge lies as much in its methods, in its lack of overbearing authority, and in its fluidity as in 'what is known'. It is living and dynamic, so in describing it one ought to be very careful not to see it as – or worse, turn it into – stone.

These worries create problems and challenges for those involved in working with farmers to find avenues for improving on local techniques. First, getting to know the knowledge which informs farmers' practices is difficult. Like all strangers, researchers inevitably plug into the polite social idioms when discussing agriculture with local farmers. Although there is much that can be derived from discussions in these socially easy terms, one misses out on a tremendous amount of farming 'wisdom'. The catch is that local knowledge is good precisely because it is hypothetical and relatively unformulated, and yet precisely for this reason it is almost impossible to access. This is not only a problem for the researcher, but also for the farmer. Currently in Bwisha there is no forum for open discussion by farmers of their ethnoscience; no institutionalization that could lead to the pooling, exchange and local assessment of their knowledge. This has the positive effect of forcing all farmers to be inquisitive and innovative, but the negative aspect is that advantageous ideas used by one farmer are often not replicated on other farms. Improving farming does not just involve offering farmers new information, but can also involve giving farmers more confidence to follow their own initiative.

2 'The a-political, a-social farmer'

A second sleight of hand in my representation is that other ways in which people explained plant death and fertility changes to me have been omitted. The different contexts in which different types of explanation are appropriate have not been discussed.

Detailed explanatory agricultural discussions among villagers are rare outside the close family or groups of friends. As farmers' practical knowledge is empirical, hypothetical and continually reviewed, people are not confident enough to express it easily, and would not want to be held responsible for the mistakes of those they advise. Most farming discussions fall into easy and acceptable 'safe idioms'. Explanations are couched in terms of 'tradition' or 'routine'. For example, farmers often explain their practices in terms of the inherited systematicity of crop sequences. They give the impression of 'talking shop' without saying anything new or important. Farmers do not lay themselves on the line. 'Live' hypothetical exploratory agricultural ideas, perhaps couched in metaphor, can actually be socially dangerous to voice in many contexts. It is easier not to voice ideas of which one is uncertain at best, and which potentially invite sorcery accusations at worst.

So apart from my presentation above, there are several different ways in which farmers explained crop failure or abundance to me. These root the cause in the realms of taboos, sorcery, ancestors, God and 'the way of the Bwisha'. Examples are given below. Some are taken from the literature, as certain idioms are no longer used.

In the realm of taboos, Bonte notes that from puberty onwards

it is strictly forbidden for the young girl [during menstruation] to cross a field of squash (pumpkins), as these will putrefy; she cannot pass through a field of sweet potatoes, as they will perish of *agahuzu*; she cannot cross a field of sorghum, as the ears will be reduced to the syrupy state, *ibigombyi*; she cannot go near a field of beans, as these will contract *ibeja*, when plants shrivel dry and die. She cannot cross a field of peanuts, tobacco or ignames, as these plants will be attacked by the rust and wither away.

(Bonte 1973: 12)

In the realm of sorcery, one woman told me that to control beanfly one can 'collect some larvae and place them on a tin lid, put the lid over a tiny three stone fire, and fry the larvae'. Correctly done, the beanfly infestation will come to nothing. A farmer who participated in a bean trial had yields of one variety five times higher than anyone else. His neighbour told me privately that the stunning yield was because of 'something' (implicitly wrong and evil) the farmer had put in his field. Another reminiscing farmer said: 'In the past we considered yields to be in the hands of the ancestors, rather than because of vegetative decay [which leads to fertility].'

Similar explanations enabled the team's plant pathologist to write: 'The justification [for disease control in farming systems] is ingrained in folklore and taboos which have a mystical quality, in which farmers' beliefs are not dissimilar to that of their religion' (Trutmann, personal communication). But why did my report mention nothing of this?

Researchers on ITK, myself included, fail to deal satisfactorily with the coexistence of these explanatory forms alongside those we judge to be efficacious.

Although farmers talk about crop failure in many ways, each fits particular social contexts. I would not argue that these explanations are now (or were) instrumental in influencing farming practice. But they are absolutely important in understanding how farming and farming knowledge is embedded in social and political life. By not coming to terms with these different explanations (for example, in my reports) and in presenting only what might be termed the optimistic front, researchers construct an almost 'antiseptic' image of the new farmer, in which farming, and talking about farming, take place out of any social, political or cultural context. My point is not that these explanations are directly important in local farming but that, by ignoring them, one creates the image of an 'unembedded' agriculture, carried out by 'unembedded' farmers. That farming practices must not be understood in isolation from their social context can be exemplified with reference to perceptions of fertility management, land tenure and erosion.

Perceiving farmers' actions specifically in terms of farmers' knowledge is particularly dangerous to researchers who are not fully aware of the socio-political context in which farmers practise. During several Toyota Land Cruiser-based journeys around Kivu, I found that other members of the CIAT team – and myself – were deducing farmers' knowledge (and ignorance) merely from our observations. For example, we once interpreted ignorance and stupidity merely from observing farming practices on steep slopes which led to soil erosion. Cultivating vertically rather than horizontally, and cultivating cassava on very steep slopes, were taken to be sufficient indicators of this.

Generally, farmers are well aware of the problems of erosion (*isuli*) and declining fertility on steep slopes, and they have several techniques to reduce these effects. They can reduce the time and extent that the soil is directly exposed, or may create contoured ridges of various descriptions. However, throughout Kivu, most farmers, especially poorer ones, have land under various tenure arrangements. Tree crops can only be grown on land with secure tenure, and by men. Women are usually not permitted (or do not try) to plant trees. As these trees belong to the planter, planting trees is a statement of tenure to the land on which the trees stand. Landlords do not allow their tenants the right to plant trees, as it would call the owner-tenant relationship into question. Conversely, tenants do not often wish to invest in trees and tree crops on land which they know can be reclaimed by the landlord.

As the most secure land must be devoted to tree crops, the more seasonal food crops tend to be marginalized to fields where tenure is less secure. A historical legacy of land possession is that ecologically marginal and highly erodible land has come to be owned by large landowners who now let it to land-poor farmers. The latter can only cultivate seasonal food crops there, and these crops render the land most susceptible to erosion. Erosion control is not a priority for tenants who have little incentive to invest in long-term care for a field that they will shortly lose. Letting land be eroded can, in fact, be seen as a form of 'protest'.

This relationship between land tenure and agricultural practices which promote or reduce erosion should be the central issue in any debate on erosion and its control, as it affects a large proportion of Kivu's population. Yet just as we had overlooked this, other distanced observers, who either do not understand the socio-political context of farming or who do not consider it relevant, continue to focus on demographic factors in their analysis of erosion, malnutrition and agricultural non-sustainability. For example, in 1979 an important and influential policy report argued that overpopulation and erosion underlie increasing malnutrition in Kivu. It concluded that 'without deep structural modification, the interaction of demographic, nutritional and soil degradation components will lead to a rapid aggravation of the situation' (Carael *et al.* 1979: 28; my translation). The report advocated urgent intervention via the implementation of anti-erosion measures, and the stimulation of massive emigration to less densely populated areas. Those in favour of such policy measures were unaware of how they could aggravate the socio-political difficulties of farmers in Kivu. Whilst erosion, population pressure and malnutrition are obviously related pressing concerns, Carael's analysis completely ignored the social, political and economic realities of the Zaïre in which farmers (and aid agencies) operate.

Such reports can be held partially responsible for the continuation, if not the aggravation, of the problem which they purport to try to solve. They perpetuate idealistic and rationalistic development perspectives, which distance the analysis and findings from local, national and international politico-economic structures, and they ignore their own historical and current position within these structures.

3   Farmers' knowledge in the eye of the beholder

A third cause for concern is that current representations of local knowledge fail to distinguish between practices that are directly informed by 'knowledge', and practices in the eyes of the observer, judged good or bad, which are not seen as practices at all by their practitioner. The latter ought perhaps to be considered as 'fortuitous side consequences'. But an overemphasis on looking for knowledge (reason) behind the practices can lead researchers to deal with such fortuitous side consequences by assuming that nothing observed is truly fortuitous. New types of 'knowledge' can be created in which agency for the action is located subliminally either in the practitioner, or in the culture to which they belong.

It is easy to impute more subliminal and unconscious 'forms' of knowledge on farmers, which explain farmers' actions as perceived by the observer in terms of a knowledge 'unrealized' by its bearers, perhaps incorporated into 'their traditions' by a kind of 'natural selection' if the evolutionary paradigm is followed. I remember my own temptation to impute subliminal (cultural) evolutionary adaptation to farmers when explaining a weeding practice which mulches a field, and which, unbeknownst to them, prevents rain splashing pathogen inoculants up onto the plants, thus reducing crop infection by several diseases. Farmers had other reasons for this, but I wanted to give them one more! The practice of highlighting the agronomically explicable when depicting ITK exaggerates the tendency to explain in terms of 'knowledge' what may be nothing more than fortuitous side consequences.

Given these problems in understanding ITK, it would nevertheless be quite wrong to dismiss the importance of what farmers do know. In a polemical piece, Richards (1989) has argued that, for example, it is wrong for researchers to assume that crop layouts in crop associations result from the implementation of an indigenous 'general theory of inter-species ecological complementarity', as such a crop layout may only be a fortuitous side consequence of the social and ecological conditions which the farmer faced during sowing. Although one cannot explain farming patternings in the field in terms of agriculturally rational knowledge (for example, the general theory above), or in terms of indigenous technical ignorance, knowledge can nevertheless inform, if only underdetermine, such activities. One cannot understand the practices without understanding the knowledge which informs it, even though there is not a one-to-one relationship between them. One cannot interpret local people's knowledge (or ignorance) from what they do, nor vice versa.

The ecological understanding shared by Bwisha farmers enables them successfully to cultivate beans, a crop particularly sensitive to the environment, in diverse circumstances. It does not determine what they do. To quote one farmer:

> Often to reduce the bad effects of the rain we alter the sowing density, but that is not general as there may be a time when you think that there will be a lot of rain, and it does not come. This is why many people sow at a uniform density each season, and if there is too much rain, we pick off the leaves of the beans to allow light and wind in between the plants.

If there is no choice over the field, association, bean varieties, or sowing date, then the farmer may still alter the sowing density. If the density is found to be wrong, one can thin the crop, stake it differently or reduce the foliage.

Knowledge which gives this type of flexibility must be considered a key element in Bwisha (and African) agriculture (Richards 1987). And although the social and ecological circumstances of African agriculture defy systematic crop planning, as Richards (1989) has highlighted, and systematicity is not found on the ground at the level of crop patterns, some systematicity can nevertheless be found in these sources of flexibility; namely, in farming knowledge. However, as argued earlier, shifting the site of the quest for systematicity from visible agricultural patternings to the knowledge which informs such practices leaves us with the problem of systematization; that of extracting knowledge from the social context of its expression.

IMAGES OF FARMERS AND SELF-IMAGES OF RESEARCH INSTITUTES

The image of the '*new* farmer' I portrayed shares with the image of the old 'ignorant farmer' the same basic error. The reductionism which conflates good farming practices with ITK is the same reductionism which conflates bad farming practices with 'Indigenous Technical Ignorance'. Arguably, all that has changed is the optimism or pessimism through which farmers' practices are observed.

What has not changed in the switch from ignorance to knowledge seems to be the 'social distance' between the farmer and the agricultural development researcher. The focus on 'technical knowledge' helps isolate agriculture from the social context, or put another way, the farmer from the person. Researchers who are permitted to examine agriculture in terms of agricultural knowledge can maintain themselves in ignorance of the multitude of non-agricultural influences which inform farming practices. ITK helps farming researchers, who are poorly placed to engage with these influences anyway, by providing the easy option of conflating practice directly with knowledge or ignorance.

The reproduction of social distance and 'myths' of difference

The maintenance of social distance between researchers and farmers through the focus on knowledge (through the object 'ITK', the methods of elucidating, observing, formulating and presenting it, and the institutions involved in hawking and harnessing it) led me to look at the way that difference and distinction between researchers and farmers is mythically constructed according to their different types of knowledge. My source here is limited to a review article called 'Farmer participatory research: a review of concepts and practices' (Farrington and Martin 1987), which is a discussion paper put out by the Overseas Development Institute (ODI), a front-runner in these new methodologies. Nevertheless, one might expect to hear these quotations reproduced in ITK discussions around the world.

1   ITK as complementary but inferior

Howes and Chambers (1979) – summarized in Farrington and Martin (1987) – argue that 'ITK and science can be contrasted and evaluated according to three criteria: as systems of classification, as systems of explanation and prediction and in terms of speed of accumulation'. They also claim that 'ITK and science are comparable on the first criterion, but science is generally superior on the second and markedly superior on the third' (Farrington and Martin 1987: 16).

> ITK contrasts with institutionally organized science in its much more limited capacity to break down data presented to the senses, and to interpret and reassemble them in different ways: the mode of ITK is concrete, not abstract; it relies almost exclusively on intuition and on directly perceivable evidence.
>
> (1987: 16)

> ITK is limited because it is 'error prone' as it is passed on orally and held in the heads of practitioners.
>
> (1987: 17; ITK is only implicitly contrasted with science here)

> The dominant 'science' sees its roles in the 'broadening of technology options', whereas the subordinate ITK is seen to be 'an important complement to formal scientific knowledge, principally in its capacity for location specific classification, though it may supplement science in the functions of explanation and prediction.
>
> (1987: 22)

2   The creation, perpetuation and destruction of ITK

There is an unresolvable ambiguity (contradiction) between the 'fall' of ITK (ITK as something which can 'fall') and ITK's ever-continuing creation.

On the 'fall' side, we are informed that only vestiges of ITK may survive after social organizational rupture (Farrington and Martin 1987: 18), and that 'there are strong *a priori* grounds for supposing that indigenous knowledge can develop and be passed on only under stable conditions'. Moreover, the evolutionary processes (of its formation) can be interrupted, and its lessons disregarded; it may break down, and so there may only be 'fragmentary remains of ITK' (1987: 22).

On the creation side, we hear that ITK 'relies on intuition and directly perceivable evidence', and is a 'dynamic process of experimentation and knowledge formation', or of 'enquiry' (1987: 23).

These depictions are elaborated by people who are 'in science'. They parallel strongly the old myths of origin of 'women's ways' in Bwisha and Rwanda. On the one hand, there are myths of loss of completeness and fall; and on the other hand, women are seen to be creative and impulsive, and to have different sources of creativity. The point is that the distinction is drawn, and that it is drawn in relation to knowledge. In both cases, the creation of difference between groups of people is reproduced in the construction and depiction of their different types of knowledge, and in the location of agency for action in that knowledge.

In Rwanda and Bwisha, differences are created and social distances maintained between men and women, and between ethnicities (for example, Batwa, Bahutu and Batutsi or Banande and Banyabwisha) through the ideological production of such 'myths of difference' and through related depictions of 'different knowledges'. These define what people can and should know, what they can, or should, or should not do, or have done. Although there is a concomitant ideology of complementarity between the groups, it is a complementarity within a hierarchy; complementarity within domination. I consider the representations of difference between researcher (science) and farmer (ITK) according to their knowledge as a similar mythology of difference in which complementarity (science-researcher and ITK-farmer) is created between the ideologically created entities, but in a hierarchical way (science/researcher > ITK-farmer). It leads us to think that the farmer complements the scientist, and not vice versa.

In Bwisha's past, male farming knowledge was broadly related to the issue of ancestral involvement. Knowledge of forests, fallows and fertility in ancestral terms seems to have been considerd by men as complementary to, but nevertheless more important than, the more location-specific women's agroecological knowledge, of the kind that I presented earlier. Similarly, as shown in the first quotations, science gains ascendancy for the researcher in the complementary arrangement by claiming to be broader and more universal than location-specific ITK.

3   The breakdown of difference

Certain changes in the basis on which difference is constructed can be discerned. Recently, researchers have had to alter their position, somewhat, *vis-à-vis* farmers. In some quarters there is a change in the way in which researchers are rewarded (pay and promotion and prizes) towards increased reliance on farmers' acceptance as the acid test of research success, rather than quality and quantity of research publications of the necessary statistical significance. Expediency is forcing farmers to be incorporated into research as early as possible. And as farmers become researchers (on station and on farm), qualitative differences between farmers and researchers – between ITK and science – are harder to maintain. This is evidenced in the work of Rhoades (1987), who argues that the farmers he knew, at least, used 'scientific methods' and were scientists.

REDUCING SOCIAL DISTANCE

These ramblings have examined the imagery of the '*new* farmer' and the self-imagery of agricultural research organizations. Although ITK was coined and constructed to help convince researchers that there are benefits to be had from working with farmers who, it has been 'found', were intelligent and not ignorant about farming, I have tried to show that its elaboration can also be continually used to distinguish and distance researchers from farmers.

My exploration of the relationship between (farming) knowledge and practice has tried to show that neither can be elucidated, understood, or represented outside the social political and economic dynamics of any community. As a result, methodologies designed to reveal either ITK or farming practices outside these contexts are extremely suspect. They are not only founded on, and subliminally assume, social difference and distance; they also reproduce such distance, and lead subsequent research to be inadequate at best, and damaging at worst.

An auto-critique of my own reports to CIAT is that, in the act of reducing social distance, paradoxically, I have also created and reproduced it.

NOTE

1 Fieldwork was carried out between October 1986 and June 1988, and was funded by the Economic and Social Research Council of Great Britain (A00428524351), and in cooperation with the Centro Internacional de Agricultura Tropical (CIAT) and their Programme Régional pour l'Amélioration du Haricot dans la Région des Grands Lacs, and the Centre de Développement Rural (CEDERU). A return visit was made during a consultancy of Oxfam in November 1989. I would especially like to thank Peter Trutmann and Joachim Voss for their combined help in the research for this chapter, and Niyitegeka Rwiyereka, who helped collect the data. Grateful acknowledgement is made to these people and institutions, but none of them is in any way responsible for errors of fact or interpretation.

REFERENCES

Bonte, M. (1973) *Aspects traditionnels et coutumiers de la sexualité au Rwanda*, New Haven, CT: Human Relations Area Files.

Box, L. (1989) 'Virgilo's theorem: a method for adaptive agricultural research', in R. Chambers, A. Pacey and L. A. Thrupp (eds) *Farmer First: Farmer Innovation and Agricultural Research*, London: Intermediate Technology Publications, pp. 61–7.

Carael, M., Tondeur, G. and Wils, W. (1979) 'Le Kivu Montagneux: surpopulation, sous-nutrition, érosion du sol', *Les Cahiers du CEDAF*, nos 2–3.

Chambers, R., Pacey, A. and Thrupp, L. A. (eds) (1989) *Farmer First: Farmer Innovation and Agricultural Research*, London: Intermediate Technology Publications.

Farrington, J. and Martin, A. (1987) 'Farmer participatory research: a review of concepts and practices', London: Overseas Development Institute, Agricultural Administration (Research and Extension) Network, Discussion Paper 19.

Howes, M. and Chambers, R. (1979) 'Indigenous technical knowledge: analysis, implications and issues', *IDS Bulletin* 10(2): 5–11.

Rhoades, R. (1987) 'Farmers and experimentation', London: Overseas Development Institute: Agricultural Administration (Research and Extension) Network, Discussion Paper 21.

Richards, P. (1985) *Indigenous Agricultural Revolution: Ecology and Food Production in West Africa*, London: Hutchinson.

—— (1987) 'The politics of famine – some recent literature', *African Affairs* 86(342): 111–16.

—— (1989) 'Agriculture as a performance', in R. Chambers, A. Pacey and L. A. Thrupp (eds) *Farmer First: Farmer Innovation and Agricultural Research*, London: Intermediate Technology Publications, pp. 39–43.

Sperling, L. (1988) 'Farmer participation in research: the case of bean trials in Rwanda', Paper prepared for the Rockefeller Foundation/International Potato Centre Workshop on 'Farmers and Food Systems', held in Lima, Peru, 26–30 Sept. 1988.

Werner, O. and Begishe, K. (1980) 'Ethnoscience and applied anthropology', in D. Brokensha, D. Warren and O. Werner (eds) *Indigenous Knowledge Systems and Development*, Washington, DC: University Press of America.

9 *'Eze-vu'* – success through evaluation

Lessons from a primary health-care project in North Yemen

Tim Morris

A decade ago no country seemed better suited than North Yemen to be a testing ground for the gospel of primary health care proclaimed by the World Health Organization in the Alma-Ata Declaration.

North Yemen, the Yemen Arab Republic (YAR), now part of the re-united Republic of Yemen, was an impoverished country without natural resources, where life expectancy is less than 50 and up to 280 children per thousand die in the first year of life. Diseases easily prevented by vaccination – diphtheria, whooping cough, measles, polio, tetanus and tuberculosis – and equally preventable water-borne and water-washed illnesses, often prove fatal. The population of 10 million is widely scattered in a mountainous country the size of England and Wales. Less than 15 per cent of the population live in the three major cities, the majority living in isolated settlements, the average size of which is less than 150 people. The rugged terrain, lack of sealed roads and near complete absence of educated health practitioners, together with the willingness of a newly victorious republican government to open the Yemen Arab Republic to the world and exploit its strategic position guarding the southern entrance to the Red Sea, led to an influx of foreign aid. What better venue could there be to train barefoot doctors who, with their knowledge, enthusiasm and basic drugs could make serious inroads into the horrendous mortality figures and achieve, in this small corner of south-western Arabia, the goal, proclaimed for the whole world, of 'Health for All by 2000'?

By the time I arrived in North Yemen in 1981 to commence my ethnographic fieldwork, the YAR was receiving more aid per capita than any other country in the Middle East apart from Israel. Sana'a, the capital, was awash with *khubaraa* (experts) from the United States, Europe, the Eastern bloc and China. Aid was being directed to health, water and sanitation projects in an urgent effort to improve the health of rural Yemenis. Half the YAR's income was being provided by the aid community, the remainder by the labour of an uprooted, ill-educated peasantry working in Saudi Arabia. In order to maximize aid inputs the YAR was sedulously guarding its position among the twenty-eight Least Developed Countries (LDCs), despite the evidence that the Saudi currency, gold and commodities brought back by its male migrants were bringing considerable wealth to those communities whose members had had the foresight to go to Saudi Arabia before cheaper Asian labour threatened the earning power of Yemenis. The controlled media lavished nothing but praise upon the *khubaraa* and the governments which had sent them. The president, a young officer steadily increasing his grasp on power since his coup a few years earlier, was forever shown meeting competing foreign delegations come to Sana'a to proffer more assistance.

Much as I tried to avoid the experts, the high profile given the *khubaraa* dogged me throughout my fieldwork. Though few people in my remote community atop an inaccessible mountain had yet seen any, they all knew of their wealth, did not believe me when I told them the size of my grant and suspected me of duplicity and meanness. A mentality of dependence was taking root. Rural Yemenis were anxiously awaiting the foreigners and the electricity, road and water networks they were sure to bring. My presence gave rise to great expectations. A brief period of employment with a West German company, which at the time had the development mandate for the province in which I researched, proved disastrous. My anthropological perceptions were ignored by my employers, my carefully fostered identity – as a researcher rather than an 'expert' – was fatally compromised in the eyes of my informants.

In 1985, having completed my thesis, I returned to Yemen to work for a British aid agency of Christian persuasion (which I shall call the British Social Development Agency). BSDA had been among the first NGOs to get involved in Primary Health Care (PHC) schemes in the YAR, and ran three projects, two in highland regions, the other in the Tihama, the torrid coastal plain along the Red Sea littoral which is mostly populated by non-ethnic Arabs who have missed out on the benefits of both the aid influx and the consumerist boom sparked by labour migration. BSDA appointed me not to the position of social researcher for which my ethnographic career had prepared me, but to an incongruous position on their team in the Tihama project. I was to be the PHC/TF (Primary Health Care Training Facilitator), the first of many acronyms, the in-house jargon of BSDA developmentalism I was to become accustomed to during the twenty months I remained a volunteer.

The Tihama project had begun four years previously at a time when BSDA, like other NGOs, was agonizing over the realization that the original recipients of its aid were not as poor as they had imagined. In an urgent desire to identify the neediest of the needy, and in search of an indigent community not already being 'developed' by other aid agencies, the BSDA coordinator had settled upon a town adjacent to the Saudi border. An abrupt ethnic divide clove the town in two: on the fringes the grass huts of the despised ex-slaves and *akhdaam* ('those who serve'), in the centre the concrete dwellings of the *qabaai'l* (tribesmen). Foremost of the *qabaai'l* were those, with appreciably lighter skins, whose origins lay in the mountains and who monopolized posts in the bureaucracy and security forces.

A complex evaluatory procedure, known as *Eze-Vu*, had been created for this and the other two BSDA projects in the YAR. *Eze-Vu* had identified fourteen major, and numerous subsidiary, objectives to be realized over the projected ten-year span of the project ending in 1991. The presence of BSDA was to transform the services provided by the modest health centre to which the enthusiastic British team attached themselves. The goals were heady: the expatriates would bring about a greater preventive orientation, all the children under 5 years old would be vaccinated and their growth monitored on road-to-health cards to be distributed to all families. Hundreds of thousands of sachets of oral rehydration solution would be distributed and women told how their use could save their children from death from diarrhoea. Women would be given greater authority and autonomy and family planning made available. Health services would be less mystified, traditional medicines would be encouraged and there would be a greater degree of community control and funding. Health education would become more widely available, modest health posts would be built throughout the hinterland, traditional practitioners and health-link persons would be trained to work in them and existing health workers in the hospital re-educated to a greater sympathy towards PHC. The young British team would monitor the deleterious consequences of the dumping of food aid and unsafe pharmaceuticals, involve locals in national and international health campaigns and aid the political development and personal satisfaction both of project workers and their Yemeni counterparts.

By their example, the BSDA team would motivate their counterparts, do away with corrupt practices in the health centre and transform it into a centre of tertiary excellence which would also serve as focal point of a PHC network serving the quarter million people of the north Tihama. Yemenis would become self-reliant, inspired by the catalyst of the foreign presence not only to mould their own relevant health service but also to scorn the inappropriate and unnecessary food aid being provided by the West and to engage with renewed enthusiasm in agriculture. In short, BSDA's heady objectives were the crest of the wave of proselytizing enthusiasm for PHC which characterized so many NGOs in the late 1970s.

On my arrival, it was soon apparent that none of the other players in our aid game – the bureaucrats in the multifarious ministries and quangos in Sana'a, the functionaries in the provincial health office, the civilian prefect and his military counterpart who ran our town, the elected officials of the local development association, the local hospital administrator and his staff, nor the ordinary Tihamis in whose name we acted – shared our vision. None had been consulted when project goals were set. They welcomed the arrival of someone who seemed to show some ability to speak their language. To a man they demanded to know when we would bring more foreign doctors, equipment and a wider range of drugs. When would we start building rural hospitals? Would we employ them as the contractors? What kind of vehicles would we provide? What kind of top-up would we pay our Yemenis to boost their meagre pay from the state? When would we send them abroad to learn English? Only a handful of the more astute, those who had mixed with *khubaraa* in other parts of Yemen, knew the terminology of PHC. One or two sought to ingratiate by using it.

Four years into the project little forward movement was to be seen: no rural health posts had been built and nobody had been trained in primary health apart from two men whom the Ministry of Health ignored, barred from working and refused to pay. Grassroots initiatives to raise money and build health posts had been discouraged by officials in the provincial capital and in Sana'a. A health unit built with joint funding from villagers and the British Embassy was closed by force. The YAR had ample supplies of donated vaccine but the hospital often ran out; it was forbidden for vaccinators to go out into the countryside, and less than 5 per cent of children were vaccinated. Local officials showed no interest in bringing down from the capital the copious stores of oral rehydration solution given the YAR. We had ample supplies of various contraceptives in our office but were barred from distributing them or educating health workers in their use. Our enthusiasm for growth monitoring and promotion of road-to-health cards was regarded as eccentric and amusing. Untrained injectionists masqueraded as doctors, ran pharmacies and held key positions in the hospital. The hospital pharmacy was empty while nearby private pharmacies were full of inappropriate drugs smuggled across the nearby Saudi border with the connivance of local officials. UNICEF drugs, donated to the YAR for free distribution, were openly sold for profit. Traditional medicine and practitioners were ignored or maligned. The provincial health director and his staff on their rare visits down to the torrid Tihama treated their dark-skinned compatriots with contempt. Food aid continued to arrive and to be distributed by the avaricious hospital doctor.

My colleagues were not a happy lot. None could speak Arabic with any fluency; they did not know the Arabic for 'primary health care', 'preventative health', 'mother and child health', 'traditional birth attendant' or other seminal terms of the ideology they were espousing. They had come to teach and motivate, not to lay on hands, but no teaching was taking place and no local officials showed any interest in starting courses. One of my colleagues, a paediatrician, actually worked and was totally overwhelmed by the hundreds of parents who daily fought to reach the desk of the one person in the hospital who did not see patients as a resource. She returned drained from her work, while the rest of us had virtually nothing to do. We were well provided for, officially described as 'volunteers . . . paid at local rates', though in fact earning five times the salaries of those we dubbed 'counterparts'. However, the savings we were accumulating brought no satisfaction. For young doctors and nurses socialized to rigorous work schedules, enforced idleness was a crippling burden. I realized why more than half of my predecessors had left before the expiry of their two-year contracts.

A destructive cycle became apparent. New recruits had not been put in touch with predecessors critical of the agency, discordant reports had been 'lost' from the files in London. Imbued with hope prior to departure, told little of conflicts or the controversial nature of the changes they were to bring about, untrained in the language or dialect they were supposed to use, volunteers had been ill equipped to cope with the discrepancy between image and reality. For those whose technical training had not accustomed them to controversy the fact that our goals were actively opposed by vested interests was traumatic and hard to accept. Many blocked out this knowledge until they had finally left Yemen. Others, failing to achieve the goals set them, became consumed by guilt, attempted to disguise their enforced idleness by a charade of hard work, immersed themselves manically in diversionary activities, projected their guilt at non-success onto others, shouted at the Yemenis (and were then crippled with remorse for having done so), complained about their colleagues or became cynical or racist about the 'natives' they were working with.

Over time I came to realize that others shared my misgivings about the sincerity of the YAR Ministry of Health's commitment to establishing a PHC system. One by one the NGOs which had invested heavily in PHC began to withdraw from Yemen. In the case of our project, the agency which provided BSDA with funding, a much larger and better-known British NGO, decided first to halve their support then to pull out completely. Relations between the two agencies, their field staff and desk persons in Britain became charged with suspicion and animosity which, as I was preparing to leave Yemen, exploded into an angry confrontation. My agency did not forgive me for taking the side of our funding agency and advocating either withdrawal or a firmer stance against the foes of primary health.

Since we parted ways, my former employers have continued to project an impression of the success of their three projects in Yemen. From BSDA's glossy Annual Reports one gains the impression that Yemen is committed to establishing a relevant health-care system, that male and female primary health-care workers and midwives are being trained and supported by their government, that volunteers, proficiently trained in Arabic, readily socialize with their Yemeni counterparts, receive only minimal recompense while doing so and return to Britain spiritually enriched. Sadly, none of this is true.

How, I have wondered in the intervening four years, can such a discrepancy arise between the conviction of failure and disillusionment reached by myself and others and the image presented by BSDA? If BSDA were a commercial development organization, of which there are many in Yemen, a cynic might suggest a deliberate suppression of negative reports and negative persons, an agency not wishing to bite the hand that feeds it. Indeed, such had been my experience years before with the German company loath to lose the franchise to develop a master plan for the province it had acquired. But BSDA cannot be so categorized, for it is a Christian, non-profit-making charity priding itself on its frankness.

The answer to the conundrum lies, I am now convinced, in the peculiar mix of Christianity with a mystifying and ramified system of evaluation. A teleological insistence, peculiar to Christianity, on the ultimate triumph of altruism has no parallel in Islam. The belief that persistent do-gooding and moral example will, eventually, dispel corruption and selfishness I saw as a non-transferable cultural construct. *Eze-Vu* came to seem an Orwellian evaluation process essential to mystifying the interaction of the aid agency and clients, to boosting optimism, to creating a conviction of the inevitability of our success; to giving rise to a symptom of malaise fatal to any development agency – projectismo. I wondered at a surprising disjunction: the conviction that the foreign developer could lead by moral example and bring about profound changes in another country seemed at odds with my agency's modest realization that they could bring little influence on the wielders of political power in Britain.

An *Eze-Vu* pack was given to all new recruits on arrival in Yemen. This 'systematic evaluation procedure' was so central to our mission that new volunteers were initiated into its arcane mysteries on their very first, still jeg-lagged, day in the country. The papers presented us formally and lengthily described how to define a 'project problem', set a 'project objective', establish a 'criterion criteria' for success in achieving the objective, 'evaluate the fit, adequacy and side-effects' of each objective against the international ideals of BSDA, the BSDA programme in Yemen and each particular project. We were told how to define an activity to reach the strategy, to produce a timetable sheet for each activity, to 'timetable a strategy review' and how to 'identify an indicator', 'to compartmentalize tasks', and to quantify the extent to which each project worker was to be involved in a particular objective and strategy.

Eze-Vu generated a mountain of paperwork. There were *Eze-Vu* sheets of many kinds to be filled in on a regular basis: summary sheets, activity review sheets, project objective review sheets, project strategy review sheets, checklists of constraints, checklists of resources, six-monthly reports detailing how individuals had been involved in particular objectives, strategies and activities.

For my chronically underemployed colleagues, *Eze-Vu* had obvious therapeutic properties. The sheer amount of cerebral energy it demanded accorded an impression of forward movement. Shortly before my arrival in the project, two whole weeks had been given over to 'Eze-Vuing' objectives and strategies, to measuring degrees of fit, to quantifying the human and material resources required for achieving each objective, to measuring the negative and positive side-effects, to assessing cost-effectiveness and prioritizing activities. A considerable amount of paperwork had been generated by this deep introspection. As I waded through the mass of files, all in English open only to ourselves and restricted viewing to our 'counterparts', I was particularly interested in the role of 'health-link persons'. For these were the people I had been sent to inspire and motivate. I searched through the carefully chronicled minutes of the day devoted to 'Eze-Vuing' for these collaborators in development. I found that the degree of fit, averaged over the three scales of quantification, was 8.2 over ten, an impressive degree of correspondence. I asked my colleagues to introduce me to some of these people, but was rudely disappointed. No such persons actually existed.

Eze-Vu, being such a time-consuming activity, gave rise to meetingitis, a holding of meetings for meetings' sake, a syndrome of those seeking to disguise their chronic inactivity. It encouraged a proliferation of administrators such that we had no less than three project coordinators, one programme coordinator and a full-time and part-time Yemeni administering the work of another six actually involved out in the countryside implementing our vision. Job descriptions (JDs) were constantly being tinkered with by the coordinators to bring them into closer alignment with the prescriptions of *Eze-Vu*.

Eze-Vu enshrined our fourteen project objectives with talismanic force. They became an immutable and unquestionable credo passed on from one volunteer to another. When word-processors arrived, my project coordinator created a template from the objectives which was ritually pasted onto each report we were obliged to send on to Sana' and London. Each act of creating a hard copy of our idealistic objectives somehow brought their realization closer, and gave the impression to those at home in Britain that we were still true to the radical global agenda set by BSDA.

Eze-Vu led some of the most chronically underoccupied up bizarre diversionary paths. The previous project coordinator, never admitting the setback of our hopes in PHC, prepared memos on a catholic list of displacement activities. He imported, and cleared through customs with much difficulty, a ciné camera and a slide projector, now lying broken, with which to entertain the natives with health-related entertainment. His slides of the bilharzia schistosome and falciparum malaria could not compete with the pleasures brought into people's lives by the televisions and videos found in almost every household. He wrote round the world investigating the possibility of introducing solar power, improved seeds, fruit trees, more benign – albeit expensive – pesticides, better irrigation techniques, new kinds of vegetables and more appropriate building materials. A flood of obscure journals and newsletters – all in English – arrived and were filed away unread. He also 'Eze-Vued' the possibility of training local people to construct latrines, though most already had well-dug pits. He had even assessed the possibility of introducing from his native Australia the infamous outback dunny seat, a wooden contraption quite unsuited to Arabs accustomed from earliest childhood to squatting. Even more optimistic, given the strict sexual segregation of this traditional Muslim society, were his plans to involve himself in women's income-generating activities. Nothing had come of his plans, yet his successor had inherited much of the neo-colonial burden the Australian had taken upon himself. He continued to state on his JD that he was active in monitoring the effects of drought, measuring precipitation and the cost of grains in local markets. He did no such thing.

Eze-Vu legitimized and extolled a penchant for quantification, a mistrust of anything non-quantifiable. Its scientific precisions appealed to those of my colleagues who had had a strictly technical or medical education. Some of these true believers seemed nagged by a sense of their own unworthiness, their inability to make the most of the tool of *Eze-Vu*. We sat round during our conferences in Sana'a or our endless project meetings castigating ourselves: if only we had more expertise in the science of evaluation, could fully garner the data *Eze-Vu* wanted, all would be well. We earnestly debated whether to admit our own inadequacy and ask the London office to fly us in an expert in evaluation. Never did we address the question of the relevance and feasibility of our objectives.

Bars to the fulfilment of the national PHC plan were always seen in terms of technical imperatives. A blind eye was turned to deliberate expropriation of resources (drugs, medical equipment, 4WD vehicles) by those well-connected, to dereliction of duty, to the sale of positions on the state payroll to the unqualified, to the failure to pay those who had real health qualifications. It was constantly suggested that such practices were the product of a lack of education, an ignorance of the principles of management and finance, an inefficency which – by implication – was ingrained in all non-Western cultures, an inability to prioritize tasks. It was regularly proposed that those most obstructive of our aims should be sent abroad for management training and courses in the English language.

Eze-Vu also mystified power relations. We had dealings with many loci of power – in Sana'a with the planning ministry, health ministry, health manpower institute, headquarters of the local development association, the interior ministry and security police; in the provincial capital with the military governor, health ministry officials, army and police; in our town with the centrally appointed prefect, his military counterpart, the hospital officials, officials of the centrally funded local development association and a bewildering array of sheikhs and other traditional leaders. Spheres of authority were always overlapping. We were forever being told either that we should go elsewhere for a decision, to have a paper stamped or a signature obtained, or that individuals who had made such executive decisions had had no right to do so. We were frequently told that we were breaching security regulations by being where we were, even when on the direct road between our place of work and the capital. Often we would come across state employees whose humble official positions belied the immense influence they wielded. At times we saw that nominal superiors were obviously in awe of their subordinates. Chains of command were chaotically cross-cut by alliances of tribe, natal status, sect of Islam, military regiment, regional affiliation and kinship. Week after week was lost as we trudged backwards and forwards from project to province to capital, from office to office, from diwan to diwan, in search of those unequivocally equipped to help us.

We all sensed the administrative disorder, yet the agency seemed blind to its consequences. The BSDA programme coordinator wrote to London that with the help of the World Bank and USAID 'institution-building programs' a real and precise demarcation of authority between ministries, quangos and individuals would be established. Courses were organized, powerful men went off to the United States and came back with IBMs which no one in their offices could use, yet the disorder remained. In response, BSDA sought to dispel anarchy by preparing flow charts of authority and circulating them to new recruits. They invested the daily disorder of power relations with a comforting illusion of stability. I saw parallels with earlier colonial endeavours in the Middle East. Foreign administrators, faced with the constant flux of authority and allegiance inherent in tribal society, also tried to ossify boundaries and relations of power in this fashion.

Yemen has a highly centralized military government centred upon a personality cult round a personable, and quite popular, young colonel. His regime, like those of the short-lived officers who briefly held sway before him, legitimizes itself by constant reference to the tyranny of the ruling dynasty finally toppled in September 1962. This 'revolution' – in effect a military *putsch* which triggered eight years of civil war between royalists and republicans – has given rise to a rhetoric of egalitarianism which fits oddly with the reality of a centralized autocracy. Official discourse and exchanges between the citizenry and bureaucrats are littered with redolent terms such as 'democracy', 'cadre', 'brother', 'citizen', 'cooperation', 'self-reliance' and 'development'.

It is easy for those who know little of Yemen to take the rhetoric of equality and justice espoused by its leaders as a signifier of social reality. Visitor after visitor flew out to Yemen from London and seemed enthralled by the charming Sana'ani bureaucrats adept in presenting the progressive credentials of their country. Impressions gained from such meetings obviously meant more than any number of reports sent back from volunteers pointing to continued racial discrimination and suppression of any form of local initiative.

As my own Arabic improved and I became more attuned to rhetorical performance, I wished to fight back against the provincial officials, to use the language of the Yemeni revolution, to join with Yemenis in discussions on the political dimensions of health care, not to hide the fact that primary health care, wherever it has been established, is against the material interests of certain officials in positions of power.

I received no encouragement to do so. I pointed out that our agency had a radical global agenda, that in Central America and Southern Africa we hardly had any official dealings with the state, that we explicitly took the side of 'grassroots' organizations and communities fighting the kind of prejudice and discrimination we were facing in Yemen. I argued we had a duty to do so in Yemen in order to protect those of our Yemeni colleagues fighting for a just health service. I met with rebuke after rebuke. The programme coordinator told me he was sick of anthropologists and anthropologizing. I had to stop trying to emulate Yemeni behaviour; it was my duty to remain British.

I returned to Britain convinced the Yemeni people deserved both a better government and more forthright foreign supporters, yet buoyed up by the knowledge that my observations and arguments had met with the approval of our funding agency. This agency scaled down its operations in the YAR, and subsequently engaged in earnest and prolonged debate about whether to continue working in a country where the kind of grassroots conspirators for change it works with in other countries are regarded with such relentless suspicion. Sadly, BSDA, tied to its procedures, has engaged in no such evaluatory soul-searching.

NOTE

A full account of Tim Morris's experience with development work in North Yemen can be found in his 1991 book *The Despairing Developer*, London: I. B. Tauris.

Index